Problem Behaviour
AND PEOPLE WITH SEVERE LEARNING DISABILITIES

Problem
BEHAVIOUR
AND PEOPLE WITH SEVERE LEARNING DISABILITIES

THE S·T·A·R APPROACH

Second edition

EWA ZARKOWSKA AND JOHN CLEMENTS

CHAPMAN & HALL

London · Glasgow · Weinheim · New York · Tokyo · Melbourne · Madras

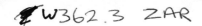

Published by Chapman & Hall,
2–6 Boundary Row, London SE1 8HN, UK

Chapman & Hall, 2–6 Boundary Row, London SE1 8HN, UK

Blackie Academic & Professional, Wester Cleddens Road, Bishopbriggs, Glasgow G64 2NZ, UK

Chapman & Hall GmbH, Pappelallee 3, 69469 Weinheim, Germany

Chapman & Hall Inc., One Penn Plaza, 41st Floor, New York NY 10119, USA

Chapman & Hall Japan, Thomson Publishing Japan, Hirakawacho Nemoto Building, 6F, 1-7-11 Hirakawa-cho, Chiyoda-ku, Tokyo 102, Japan

Chapman & Hall Australia, Thomas Nelson Australia, 102 Dodds Street, South Melbourne, Victoria 3205, Australia

Chapman & Hall India, R. Seshadri, 32 Second Main Road, CIT East, Madras 600 035, India

Distributed in the USA and Canada by Singular Publishing Group Inc., 4284 41st Street, San Diego, California 92105

First published as *Problem Behaviour in People with Severe Learning Disabilities: A practical guide to a constructional approach* by Croom Helm Ltd., 1988

Reprinted 1992 by Chapman & Hall

Second edition 1994 by Chapman & Hall

Typeset in 10/12 Palatino by Best-set Typesetters Ltd., Hong Kong
Printed in Great Britain by TJ Press (Padstow) Ltd., Cornwall

ISBN 0 412 47690 8   1 56593 122 X (USA)

A catalogue record for this book is available from the British Library

Library of Congress Catalog Card Number: 94-70258

∞ Printed on permanent acid-free text paper, manufactured in accordance with ANSI/NISO Z39.48-1992 and ANSI/NISO Z39.48-1984 (Permanence of Paper).

Contents

Introduction

This book is concerned with helping adults and children who have learning disabilities and who, in addition, suffer a behavioural or emotional disturbance. It is a practical guide for those involved in their daily care, education and development, intended to help them analyse and deal effectively with the behavioural challenges posed by their clients and students. More specifically, the aims of this book are to:

- provide a structured framework within which behavioural and emotional disturbances can be understood;
- describe a systematic method of assessing behaviour which is considered to be problematic;
- present a step-by-step guide to planning high-quality therapeutic interventions;
- describe methods for implementing high-quality programmes aimed at reducing behavioural disturbance;
- describe methods of ensuring that people with learning disabilities are protected against misuse or abuse of behavioural change strategies;
- describe methods of supporting professional caregivers in their endeavours to implement and sustain therapeutic intervention programmes.

The approach described here is derived from the authors' extensive experience of working in a variety of day and residential settings with learning disabled people who present their carers with a range of behavioural challenges. It is based upon their wide practical experience of training staff from various professional disciplines in the principles and strategies for helping those people with learning disabilities who suffer behavioural and emotional disturbances. It is a multi-dimensional approach in which the analysis of behavioural problems takes place at several levels. The analysis leads to a number of possible intervention strategies. These are determined by the nature of the problem, the individual characteristics of the person, the environment in which the problem occurs and the resources available for dealing with the problem. The result is a comprehensive therapeutic package aimed at producing long-term solutions to what are, frequently, longstanding adjustment difficulties.

Each aspect of the therapeutic package is described in a separate chapter of the book. We have tried to ensure that each chapter is relatively self-contained in order that the reader can more easily use the text as a reference when devising and implementing different aspects of therapeutic packages. However, there is some cross-referencing between chapters to avoid unnecessary repetition of details.

Chapter 1 presents an overview of the approach that is taken, discussing its theoretical, philosophical and practical perspectives. Chapter 2 deals with the broad issue of assessment and how this leads to a comprehensive and multi-level intervention plan. Chapter 3 describes how to translate the management plan into specific goals for intervention, while Chapter 4 is concerned with environmental interventions and with interventions aimed at helping the individual overcome or cope with related emotional difficulties. Chapter 5 considers the various ways of reducing the incidence of behavioural disturbance by addressing the factors which directly trigger the behaviour. In Chapter 6, procedures for teaching alternative skills relevant to the long-term resolution of the problem behaviour are described. In Chapter 7 techniques for encouraging the use of important alternative skills in place of inappropriate responses are presented. Chapter 8 is concerned with techniques for discouraging unhelpful behaviour by directly reinforcing its absence and Chapter 9 considers strategies and skills which can be taught and encouraged, which help the individual to manage his own behaviour. In Chapter 10, appropriate methods of directly responding to inappropriate and unhelpful behaviours are discussed. Chapter 11 describes procedures for monitoring and evaluating progress. In contrast to the client-oriented focus of earlier chapters, Chapter 12 discusses the broader issues involved in the management of severe behavioural disturbances: these are issues of organization, staff support and client protection.

The approach described here is a complex one, reflecting the complex nature of the behavioural problems of people who have severe learning disabilities and the challenge which these problems present to those charged with their care. It is unlikely that the individual reader acting alone will be able to carry out all aspects of the work that may be necessary for the long-term reduction or resolution of a problematic behaviour. For this, a more concerted team effort may be required and the reader should bear this in mind when using this text.

Each aspect of the work described requires a thorough understanding of the principles behind it. For this reason each chapter of the book has been divided into two parts: the first describes the general principles involved in interventions at that level; the second part is a more practical step-by-step guide to constructing appropriate interventions.

Throughout the text we refer to people with learning difficulties in the masculine gender. This has been done for practical reasons and not in any way out of prejudice or discrimination.

Understanding and managing behavioural and emotional difficulties

IDENTIFYING BEHAVIOURAL PROBLEMS

A question frequently asked by caregivers is how to decide whether or not a behaviour should be defined as difficult or challenging. This apparently simple question reflects the complexity of the phenomenon which is the subject of this book.

Recognizing the presence of a behavioural problem is not always as clear-cut as it might seem. A person may have been acting in a particular way for a considerable time before anyone decides to call that action 'a problem'. Alternatively, there may be several people showing similar sorts of difficulties, but only one is identified as having a problem. There may be several people working with an individual, some of whom find the individual's behaviour to be problematic, others who do not. Thus, the apparently simple decision about whether or not a person has a problem is in fact a complex judgement determined by the behaviour of the person, the behaviour of those around him and the beliefs, attitudes and feelings of the person making the judgment.

This state of affairs is compounded by a tendency to group together people with learning difficulties in day and residential facilities and to separate them from others of a similar age. As a result, both the people with these difficulties and those who work with them can become isolated from the mainstream of society. In such circumstances it becomes easy to develop routines, expectations and standards which may be inappropriate for the age and developmental level of the individual, or standards which are designed to assist in the smooth running of an agency but which are quite at variance with the needs of the individual (for example, setting an 8.00 p.m. bedtime for adult users of a residential service simply because night staff arrive on duty at 8.30 p.m. and there are insufficient night staff to help all service users with bathing and bedtime routines). Such problems are by no means confined to large institutions. They can occur in small-group care settings and even in natural family settings.

Inappropriate standards and expectations are particularly evident in care practices around adolescents and young adults. Like others of their age, adolescents with learning difficulties may become moody, defiant and resentful of authority. They may become better able to articulate their opinions, thoughts and feelings. They may start to stand up for themselves in a way that they did not do as children. In the course of normal development, caregivers (parents and teachers) learn to accommodate to these developments. They may reduce the number of direct demands and learn to qualify requests with explanations of why these are being made. They may reduce external boundaries and begin to negotiate more over important issues. They start to give the adolescent more privacy, more space, decision-making responsibility and financial independence. In this way adulthood and the independence and responsibilities that go with it become a natural progression.

Such adaptations often do not take place in the development of the person with learning disabilities, partly because such people, and those who work with them, may be isolated from the mainstream of society, so that caregivers may be unaware of what the 'norm' should be; and partly also because of the conflicting cues presented by people with severe learning difficulties. Physically a person may look his age. Sexually, he may be developing interests and needs appropriate for his age. Emotionally, however, he may be functioning at an immature level. His understanding of language and ability to articulate his thoughts and feelings may be limited. This is an important issue to face, as many behavioural problems which develop in adolescence and young adulthood arise when carers respond to the person in a way in which adults might approach young children. This may be reflected in the style in which demands are made upon the individual or in the way in which the individual's expression of a wish or preference is denied. Other problems, too, may arise for the person in the quality of his life. Frustrations may develop as life seems to proceed aimlessly, with no prospect of work or useful activity, no sense of purpose.

It is perhaps such issues which give rise to conflicting views about whether or not a person's behaviour should be identified as challenging or problematic. Clearly the answer to the question 'Whose problem, the individual's or the service's?' will have major implications for what is done to alleviate the problem. Nevertheless, regardless of the perceived cause of a disturbed or inappropriate behaviour a problem can be acknowledged to exist if it satisfies at least some of the following criteria.

1. The behaviour itself or its severity is inappropriate given a person's age and level of development.
2. The behaviour is dangerous either to the person or to others.
3. The behaviour constitutes a significant additional handicap for the person by interfering with the learning of new skills or by excluding the person from important learning opportunities.
4. The behaviour causes significant stress to the lives of those who live and work with the person and impairs the quality of their lives to an unreasonable degree.
5. The behaviour is contrary to social norms.

If it is clear, using the above criteria, that a behaviour is indeed a problem then the reasons for the problem need to be assessed and steps need to be taken to alleviate or reduce the presenting difficulties.

UNDERSTANDING THE CAUSES OF BEHAVIOURAL DIFFICULTIES

Behavioural difficulties present a serious and continuing challenge to those who live and work with people who have learning difficulties. The incidence of significant behavioural disturbance among this group is considerably higher than in the general population. Whilst many of the problem behaviours are similar to those which may be found in the general population (for example, tantrums, aggression, absconding), there are also other kinds of behaviours less commonly found in the general population (repetitive and stimulatory behaviours, such as rocking or finger flicking; socially inappropriate behaviours, such as masturbating, stripping in public or smearing faeces; and, occasionally, more distressing self-injurious behaviours, such as self-hitting, self-biting or eye poking).

Historically there has been a tendency to use rather simple models to understand people with severe learning difficulties. They have been seen as 'sick' (passive, ignorant, in need of expert care), 'dangerous' (irrational, untrustworthy, violent, in need of control and supervision), 'perpetual children' (not developing, needing to be indulged at times but directed on all important matters). Their inappropriate or disturbed behaviours have often been interpreted as simply attention-seeking behaviour which has been learned and which needs to be stopped. Such simplistic models reflected (and still reflect) a lack of understanding of the special problems and needs of this group.

It is unusual to find a simple or single cause for behavioural disturbance in people who have severe learning difficulties. There are a number of factors which are likely to contribute to the presence of behavioural difficulties and which may explain their high incidence in this group. None of these factors is exclusive to people with learning difficulties and, when present in people of normal intellectual ability, they are also associated with a greater likelihood of a person showing behavioural disturbance.

In the first place there are a number of **biological factors** that can increase the likelihood of a person developing a behavioural problem. Such factors include organic brain dysfunction, epilepsy, hearing and visual difficulties, and certain temperamental characteristics, such as a high intensity of emotional responding and poor adaptability to new situations.

Social factors too have an important influence on behaviour. For example, people who receive poor quality care, or who are rejected by society and by their caregivers or by their peers, are more likely to develop behavioural and emotional problems than are their con-temporaries who are not subjected to such influences. Environments in which there is a high level of tension and interpersonal conflict are more likely to engender behavioural problems in those who live within them than ones where there is harmony and cohesion. Individual learning histories, such as consistency in child discipline and manage-ment or childhood abuse, are also very important influences.

People with learning difficulties are likely to have experienced a lot of failure in many areas of their lives. In addition, they frequently remain highly dependent on others for their needs throughout their adult lives. Their self-concept may therefore be poor and their self-esteem quite low. Such **emotional factors** can themselves be important determinants of behavioural or emotional disturbance.

Finally, there are a number of important **cognitive factors** which have been associated with the occurrence of behavioural disturbance and which are frequently encountered in people with learning dif-ficulties. These include poor problem-solving skills, poor communica-tion skills and poor social skills.

Any of the influences described above – biological, social, emotional and cognitive – can affect a person's emotional adjustment and con-sequent behaviour, whatever that person's intellectual status. The more of these factors that occur together, the greater the likelihood of behavioural and/or emotional problems developing. Many people with learning disabilities are exposed to a large number of these influences, which are likely to interact with each other. Thus the determinants of behavioural and emotional difficulties in this group are likely to be many and they are likely also to be complex. Helping an individual to overcome behavioural and emotional difficulties will therefore require identification of the specific factors which may be contribu-ting to his difficulties and understanding how these factors may be interacting.

APPROACHES TO THE MANAGEMENT OF PROBLEMATIC BEHAVIOUR

Approaches to the management of the behavioural disturbances of people with learning difficulties have, just like the models for understanding the people themselves, been simplistic and quite narrowly focused, often influenced by the carer's own professional background.

BIOLOGICAL APPROACHES

Biological approaches to the management of behavioural difficulties have focused on pharmacological interventions, for example, to reduce anxiety or suppress aggressive behaviour, or to reduce obsessional and ritualistic behaviour.

SOCIAL APPROACHES

Social approaches have emphasized the importance of high-quality 'normal' living environments, stressing the need to treat people with learning disabilities with respect and dignity, and to give them greater autonomy over their own lives. The underlying assumption is that if people are treated well they are likely to behave in more adaptive and appropriate ways.

EDUCATIONAL APPROACHES

Educational approaches have emphasized the importance of increasing people's skills and experiences on the assumption that, in the absence of things to do and in the absence of more appropriate responses, people will use whatever skills they have available to meet their various living needs.

PSYCHOLOGICAL APPROACHES

Psychological approaches, too, have tended to be simplistic and quite narrowly focused.

The behavioural perspective

Until very recently the major psychological approach to helping people with behavioural difficulties was based on learning theory – the behavioural approach. This approach focuses exclusively on observed behaviours rather than on people's thoughts or emotions. It emphasizes the role of learning, stressing the importance of environmental factors in the genesis and maintenance of disturbed or problematic behaviour. The environmental outcomes which behaviours achieve during learning are considered to be of critical importance. When people achieve positive outcomes for their behaviours, these behaviours are likely to be strengthened. If people consistently receive negative or unpleasant outcomes for their behaviours, those behaviours are likely to reduce or disappear. Observing other people achieve positive or negative outcomes for their behaviour is also a powerful learning experience and will influence the observer's own future behaviour.

Stimuli which are present in the environment when positive or negative outcomes are achieved for behaviours come, over time, to act as cues for the individual to inform him when specific behaviours are likely to succeed in achieving particular results. Thus, a child may become aggressive because he frequently achieves positive outcomes for his aggressive behaviours (other children let him have his way, they share their games and sweets with him). He will also learn to discriminate which children to target for his aggression, for example, experience of retaliation by bigger and stronger children will have taught him not to show this behaviour towards bigger and stronger individuals.

Within the traditional behavioural framework all problematic or disturbed behaviours are analysed by looking at environmental factors (rewards, punishers and triggers), and interventions aimed at changing these behaviours are largely based upon the manipulation of triggers and consequences for inappropriate and appropriate behaviours – contingent reinforcement/reward for the use of appropriate skills and contingent punishment/withholding of reinforcement for the use of behaviours deemed to be inappropriate.

The psychodynamic perspective

The psychodynamic perspective takes as its basic assumption the view that much of human behaviour is driven by unconscious processes. During development basic drives and instincts, such as aggression and sex drive, may be punished and forbidden and this serves to force such drives and instincts into the unconscious from where they may manifest themselves subsequently as emotional problems. Helping prople overcome these problems requires understanding the unconscious basis of the difficulties and bringing repressed emotions and drives into awareness so that they can be dealt with in more rational ways. The psychodynamic framework was considered for a long time to have no potential for helping people with learning difficulties, because of their limited intellectual capacity and because of their limited expressive language skills.

The cognitive perspective

A relatively recent approach to helping people overcome behavioural and emotional difficulties is one which focuses on people's interpretations of events. According to the cognitive perspective, people's thoughts and interpretations will influence their mood: negative thoughts will lower mood, while positive thoughts will raise a person's mood and consequent motivations. Thoughts can become distorted with adverse consequences for both mood and motivation. By accessing a person's unhelpful thoughts and interpretations of events he can be helped to develop more useful ways of thinking and to develop better analytical and problem-solving strategies.

The humanistic perspective

Another recent approach to helping people overcome behavioural and emotional difficulties is one which focuses on the 'inner life' or subjective experience of the individual. According to 'humanistic' perspectives, people are viewed as motivated by a desire for personal growth and self-fulfilment. When difficulties arise, these desires are temporarily halted. At such times people may need help to get them back on the road to self-fulfilment. This can be facilitated by relationships with significant other people, who show warmth, respect and unconditional regard for the person.

A 'coming together' of approaches and perspectives

The psychological perspectives outlined above have until recent years been thought to be incompatible and mutually exclusive. Now within mainstream psychology it is increasingly acknowledged that human behaviour is too complex to be viewed from any single perspective. Each perspective – the conscious mind, subjective experience, unconscious processes, environmental influence and the quality of relationships – has something to offer in relation to our understanding of people who experience coping difficulties. Each has something to offer in relation to the kinds of help that can be given. Biological, social and educational perspectives are equally important in terms of the help which can be given.

Within the field of learning difficulties, this 'coming together' of approaches and perspectives has been a somewhat slower process. The most influential model for understanding disturbed or inappropriate behaviour has traditionally been the behavioural model. The most frequently used therapeutic interventions have historically been pharmacological and behavioural. Social, educational, cognitive, psychodynamic and humanistic models have had a more limited and more recent influence. However, just as within mainstream psychology, their relevance to personal well-being is now increasingly acknowledged.

Recent years have seen new debates about the use of behavioural interventions – particularly with regard to the use of punishment as part of the strategy for behavioural change. Such debates are driven by new, more humane attitudes towards people with learning disabilities and by a determination to use only such therapeutic approaches as are morally acceptable.

THE S.T.A.R. MODEL

The approach described in this book reflects recent approaches to understanding and alleviating emotional and behavioural problems in people who have learning difficulties. It takes from the traditional behavioural approach its emphasis on a scientific hypothesis-led strategy, and emphasis on monitoring and evaluation. It stresses the importance of environmental factors and learning in the understanding and treatment of behavioural difficulties. It acknowledges the importance of key skills in maintaining personal well-being and mental health, and it stresses the importance of focusing on the teaching of critical alternative skills and new ways of coping when difficulties arise. It acknowledges the influence of the physical and emotional environment on a person's well-being and also the importance of cognitive factors – how a person thinks, interprets situations and solves problems. It emphasizes the importance of positive relationships as the context in which human growth can occur. It acknowledges the influences of biological factors in human emotion and behaviour, and the influence of early childhood experience and life events on a person's emotions and behaviour. It is thus a multi-component approach which encompasses the many factors – social, cognitive, emotional, biological and learning – which may be influencing a person's behaviour.

The complexity of the analytical and therapeutic process involved in achieving lasting behavioural change in troubled people cannot be understimated. However, it is a fact that much of the assessment and change must be undertaken by caregivers, the people who have the greatest influence over the lives and well-being of the individual. Yet caregivers are often the people with no appropriate professional training or background knowledge to assist them in this endeavour.

The aim, therefore, is to offer a structured and logical framework within which behavioural and emotional difficulties can be understood and systematically assessed; a framework from which appropriate therapeutic interventions can be systematically planned and implemented, so that those living and working day-to-day with the person

Figure 1.1 The STAR model for helping people with behavioural and emotional difficulties.

who poses such difficulties can develop effective programmes of change. It is a broad problem-solving approach rather than a cook-book of ready-made treatment packages.

The problem-solving framework that we have developed for assessing and helping people who present with behavioural and other coping difficulties is called the S.T.A.R. model (Figure 1.1). Within the problem-solving framework, we have separated the various factors which may be involved in the development and maintenance of behavioural disorders into four broad categories: (S) settings, (T) triggers, (A) actions and (R) results. Analysis of behavioural problems and interventions take place within these four levels. The four critical elements of the S.T.A.R. framework are described below.

SETTINGS

Settings are those factors which influence motivation. They influence both the general motivations of an individual and the strength and prominence of specific motivations at any moment in time. They operate over varying time-spans. Thus settings are the context in which actions occur. They determine what results a person seeks or strives to avoid and the triggers that the person will respond to. Thus, if a behaviour is understood as a means of escaping from a situation (the result), the settings are those factors which make escape so important. If a behaviour is understood as a means of getting someone's undivided attention (the result), then the settings are those factors that make the need for undivided attention so strong at that time.

The factors which influence motivations are numerous and varied. They can broadly be divided into environmental setting conditions (factors related to the environment) and personal setting conditions (factors related to the individual). Environmental setting conditions will clearly have a knock-on effect on the individual and thereby influence personal setting conditions.

Among the most important environmental setting conditions are the following.

1. The physical climate. Physical aspects of the environment (noise, temperature, lighting, crowding, smell, smoke) can have an important influence on a person's immediate motivations. The influences may be direct (creating a strong desire to escape from the unpleasant situation) or indirect (increasing the general level of tension or anxiety experienced).
2. The social climate. This includes the quality and style of social interactions and relationships within the environments where a person lives or spends his day. These will have important influences on the needs and motivations of the individual. Hostile, authoritarian, controlling interactions may increase anxiety, frustration, anger and a need to exert counter-control. Harmonious, friendly interactions based upon equality and respect will enhance the motivation for cooperation and will enhance self-esteem.
3. The occupational climate. The quality, structure and appropriateness of the activities in which a person engages is another important source of influence on motivation. Appropriate, high-quality occupation will strengthen the motivation to participate and is likely to enhance self-esteem. Inappropriate, poor-quality occupation will strengthen the motivation to escape and may decrease self-esteem.

Amongst the most important personal setting conditions are the following.

1. Physical state. A person's physical well-being will clearly influence the things that he seeks to achieve, the pressures he is prepared to tolerate and the activities in which he feels able to engage.
2. Psychological state. Mood states such as anxiety, sadness or fearfulness will influence a person's motivation in ways which are quite different from the influences exerted by mood states such as happiness, joy or excitement. Mood states may be influenced by recent life events or unresolved personal traumas from early years. They may also be influenced by biological factors.

3. Cognitions. The things people think and how they interpret events will inevitably interact with a person's mood and are likely to influence it. Negative interpretations are likely to lower a person's mood. Positive interpretations are likely to raise a person's mood and increase his sense of well-being.

TRIGGERS

Triggers are the signals or stimuli that are present in a situation which 'set off' specific actions. They occur **immediately** before the behaviour of concern. There are various reasons why triggers can 'set off' behaviour.

1. They may signal the availability of the thing a person may want. (For example, the smell of dinner cooking may signal to the hungry person that the food he wants is potentially available.)
2. They may signal the imminence of the thing a person does not want. (For example, the sight of a spider approaching may signal to the fearful person that action needs to be taken immediately if contact with the spider is to be avoided.)
3. They may trigger habitual behaviour – a behaviour which always follows a stimulus because it has always done so. (For example, the light being turned off in the bedroom may be the trigger for a child to close his eyes, pull up the blankets, turn on his side and go to sleep.)
4. They may directly elicit a behaviour – an automatic reaction in a situation. (For example, a person may scream as he experiences a sudden, sharp pain.)
5. They may create emotional overload. (For example, a relatively insignificant occurrence may serve as 'a last straw'.)
6. They may cause a sharp and rapid increase in arousal or emotion. (For example, when a person is insulted or hurt.)

ACTIONS

Actions are observable behaviours. The definition of and agreement upon the action which is of concern is the starting point within the S.T.A.R. model. Subsequently, actions refer to any relevant behaviours – new skills which need to be learned or existing low frequency skills which need to be encouraged and strengthened. Actions are influenced by many variables both directly and indirectly. They are to some extent determined by the environmental settings in which a person finds himself, they are to some extent influenced by personal setting factors, they are 'set off' by specific triggers and they are likely to achieve a positive result for the individual on at least some occasions.

RESULTS

Results are the events that follow an action. They provide information about the appropriateness of that action in a given situation. They can also influence the likelihood of a person performing that action in similar situations on subsequent occasions. There are three classes of results which can follow an action: reinforcers, punishers and neutral results.

Reinforcers

Reinforcers increase the likelihood that an action will be performed again under similar circumstances: in other words, they strengthen or encourage behaviour. **Positive reinforcement** occurs when an individual's action is followed by something which the person desires (a gain). Such positive results may include social attention, occupation, sensory stimulation or material gain. **Negative reinforcement** occurs when an action is followed by the cessation of something unwanted: in other words, escape. People frequently seek to escape from situations which they find difficult, unpleasant, frightening, confusing or boring.

Punishers

Punishers decrease the likelihood that an action will be performed under similar circumstances in the future: in other words, punishers serve to weaken or discourage behaviour. Being admonished, being deprived of privileges, being ignored or ostracized can all act as punishers.

Neutral results

Neutral results following an action are likely eventually to weaken the future use of such action under similar circumstances. Neutral results are neither positive nor negative. The behaviour simply achieves little, if anything, for the individual.

In attempting to understand a person's behavioural difficulties, each of the four S.T.A.R. factors described above needs to be taken into consideration – the specific actions which are of concern, the immediate circumstances which give rise to the behaviours (triggers), the outcomes the person achieves by performing these actions (results), the environmental conditions which make the behaviours more likely (environmental settings) and the 'personal' conditions which influence the person's motivations (personal settings). Behaviour in any given situation is thus the accumulation of past experience and present states and environments. At the same time, each occurrence of the behaviour is itself a learning experience and this learning in turn influences the likelihood of subsequent occurrence of the behaviour.

A THERAPEUTIC RELATIONSHIP

This book is concerned with the development of therapeutic interventions directed at meeting the needs of people with learning and behavioural difficulties. The aim is to effect change in, for and with the troubled individual. The context of this work is a therapeutic relationship which must be developed between caregivers and the individual concerned.

The relationship between professional caregivers and people with learning difficulties is a complex one. Caregivers see the task as comprising many roles, such as parent, friend, teacher, nurse, protector, advocate. Those who care for people who present with severe disturbances of behaviour or emotions sometimes see themselves as fulfilling a further role, which is a custodial one involving the containing and controlling of difficult and sometimes dangerous behaviour.

People learn about various social roles largely through personal experience. From personal experience people develop their own views of the nature of the role and how to act within it. For example, many people believe that a parent–child relationship is essentially an unequal one, the parent's role being to socialize the child using various forms of discipline and control. If a child misbehaves, the natural response may be to punish the child. Similarly, many people believe that a teacher–pupil relationship is an unequal one – the teacher holding a position of authority and demanding respect from the pupil. If the student does not conform to the authority of the teacher, the student may be expelled or rejected from the class. Even within a friendship, certain rules may apply so that if a friend punches one in the face, the natural response may be to terminate the friendship.

Transferring personal views of social roles out of the context of people's everyday experience into the professional role of caregiver, particularly one which requires a therapeutic alliance between the carer and the troubled individual, holds many dangers. Social roles of the type described above, which are based upon inequality, upon power or upon control, have no place within a therapeutic relationship. The starting point for the caregiver entering a therapeutic alliance is that the relationship is based upon equality and mutual respect. The helper gains respect and effects influence within the relationship only in so far as credibility is achieved – influence is based upon credibility not formal authority or physical power.

Within the relationship the helper must offer **respect** (respect for the individual and the individual's opinions and preferences), **warmth** (a genuine interest in the person's feelings and thoughts) and **unconditional positive regard** (acceptance of the individual whatever the person may do or think or feel). The relationship develops as the helper struggles for empathy with the person in difficulty or in distress. Empathy does not mean liking or sympathizing with the other. Empathy means trying to see the world from the other's point of view and respecting that point of view and the decisions that the other makes.

The purpose of the therapeutic relationship is to facilitate change for the troubled or distressed individual. Change may occur in the person's feelings, thoughts or actions. Such change may be effected through a variety of skills which the caregiver may bring into use: listening, empathizing, problem solving, information giving, skill teaching, helping or even containing. The role can have both directive and non-directive elements. Helping is not always comfortable. For one thing the distressed individual may need to be supported to confront issues which create great personal distress, as part of the change process. For another thing, the person being helped may become increasingly difficult and challenging towards the helper as first he tests the relationship and second, as he starts to feel safe within the relationship.

It is important to recognize that within a therapeutic relationship both parties have rights and there are limits to what is tolerable. Thus the helper is entitled to set limits on behaviour which infringes these rights. For example, verbal or physical abuse may not be tolerated. Similarly the person being helped has the right to expect certain standards of behaviour from the helper. For example, it is not consonant with the role of professional helper to engage in a sexual relationship with the person whom he is paid to help nor to inflict physical pain upon that person, except under exceptional circumstances of self-defence.

In sum, then, helpers achieve credibility by consistently showing respect, warmth and regard for the person. They achieve this through a calm, non-judgmental approach; through an assertive manner; through the constant acknowledgement and acceptance of the person's feelings and thoughts, whilst at the same time setting clear limits or boundaries upon behaviour which is unacceptable.

The professional helping relationship is thus distinctive from other kinds of social relationships and it is the context for the work described in this book. The skilled helper requires many skills. The precise nature of those skills remains open-ended. Advances occur all the time in understanding how better to help people. The basic characteristics of the relationship remain, however, the same. They are equality, respect and unconditional positive regard for the individual concerned.

THERAPEUTIC INTERVENTIONS – AN OVERVIEW

The S.T.A.R. framework provides a multi-level view of behavioural difficulties. It follows, therefore, that the approach to helping individuals with such difficulties will similarly occur at many levels. Thus, a single intervention strategy is unlikely to follow. Rather, for any individual experiencing difficulties a highly individualized therapeutic package needs to be developed. The components of such a package should include a whole range of interventions – some very focused and specific, some more general and diffuse; some requiring considerable staff-intensive input, others requiring far less input. The various components of the therapeutic package are outlined below.

A COMPREHENSIVE ASSESSMENT OF THE INDIVIDUAL AND THE BEHAVIOUR OF CONCERN

Appropriate long-term help cannot be provided without a thorough understanding of the specific factors – settings, triggers and results – which are involved in the disturbance or difficulties presented by any individual. For each person and for each behavioural problem which the person displays the specific factors involved are likely to be different. A thorough assessment is therefore the essential first step in helping the individual. The assessment leads to a formulation of the problem – a theory about the factors which are involved and their relative contribution. The formulation becomes the basis of the intervention package.

MODIFYING SETTINGS IN WHICH PROBLEMATIC BEHAVIOURS OCCUR

The emotional and physical environments in which problem behaviours occur are important not just for the understanding of behavioural disturbances. They form the critical first area of intervention. Changes may need to be made within the physical or social environment (increasing stimulation, providing greater autonomy for the individual, addressing staff/teamwork problems, providing more personal space). Help may be needed to reduce emotional difficulties (for example, reducing generalized anxiety or stress, treating depression or fears). Help may also be needed to develop more appropriate ways of thinking about events (for example, helping the person come to terms with a loss or bereavement). Physical and general health problems may also need to be addressed at this early stage.

MODIFYING TRIGGERS THAT SET OFF PROBLEMATIC BEHAVIOURS

If clear and circumscribed triggers can be identified as reliably 'setting off' problematic behaviours, then interventions may usefully be carried out at this level. It may sometimes be possible to remove triggers completely and permanently, or it may be possible to work on triggers so that they no longer elicit inappropriate responses. For example, it may be possible to remove triggers and gradually reintroduce them in a way that avoids the problem behaviour occurring. Thus, if the appearance of a dog (trigger) consistently 'sets off' a behavioural (screaming) and emotional (fear) response, then dogs may be very gradually and systematically introduced to the person in a way which minimizes the likelihood of the emotional and behavioural response occurring.

REPLACING PROBLEMATIC BEHAVIOURS WITH APPROPRIATE ALTERNATIVE SKILLS

Problematic behaviours should be regarded as purposeful actions which are generally directed at achieving specific results. As such, they can serve important functions for the individual: they may be a means of communicating that the individual wants comfort or help or that a situation is unacceptable; they may be a means of protesting against an imposed unpleasant event; they may be a means of occupation or stimulation. For this reason, simply trying to discourage actions considered to be inappropriate is unlikely to provide a lasting solution if the individual is left with no appropriate alternative skill by which to achieve the same goals.

Lasting solutions to resolving behavioural difficulties are more likely to be achieved if appropriate skills can be taught and encouraged in their place. Such skills are likely to be ones that can serve the same function for the individual as the behaviour considered to be inappropriate (for example, a more appropriate means of protesting or communicating the unacceptability of a situation or of obtaining stimulation). Alternatively, they may be skills that are physically incompatible with that behaviour. It may be useful to teach or encourage physically incompatible skills because, while performing these, an individual cannot simultaneously be performing the unacceptable action (for example, holding a comforter rather than sucking one's hand). They may be skills which are functionally incompatible with the behaviour (for example, teaching a person to take turns in a game will reduce his anxiety in this situation and the consequent need to escape from the situation by disrupting the game).

ENCOURAGING THE ABSENCE OF THE INAPPROPRIATE BEHAVIOUR

In addition to teaching and encouraging the use of specific skills, more general help may be provided by directly encouraging the individual to desist from trying to meet his needs using inappropriate behaviours. Such help can be provided in the form of direct rewards for the non-performance of the behaviour.

ENCOURAGING SELF-MANAGEMENT

At all levels of the therapeutic package, consideration needs to be given to ways of involving the person in the management and control of his own behaviour. The person can be taught and encouraged to set goals and targets for himself, to monitor his own actions, to provide positive reinforcement for his own appropriate behaviours. He can be helped to take control over triggers that 'set off' his inappropriate actions and to use appropriate strategies to reduce his own high arousal. Such involvement increases the individual's control over his environment and his actions and may enhance his commitment to change.

REMOVING OR ALTERING RESULTS ACHIEVED BY BEHAVIOURS CONSIDERED TO BE INAPPROPRIATE

When a behaviour which is considered to be inappropriate is assessed as achieving positive results for the individual then it may be necessary to find a way to directly discourage use of the behaviour. This may require finding ways of ensuring that looked-for results no longer occur as a consequence of the behaviour or by communicating more directly the unacceptability of the behaviour to the individual.

IMPLEMENTING INTERVENTIONS – THE CORE METHODS OF THE S.T.A.R. APPROACH

USE OF CONTRIVED S.T.A.R. FACTORS

In the early stages of implementing the various therapeutic interventions, contrived S.T.A.R. factors may need to be introduced in order to accelerate learning and change. Contrived settings, triggers and results are ones which would not naturally be present when a given action is performed but which have been added deliberately to make learning easier and to make the incentive to learn greater. Thus artificial environments may be used in the early stages of skill teaching to create the optimal conditions for learning (for example, individual sessions in a special teaching area). Contrived triggers, in the form of prompts and reminders, may be used to accelerate learning. Arbitrary results, in the form of special reinforcers, may serve to increase motivation for behavioural change.

A GRADED APPROACH

In order to increase the opportunity for the person to learn new skills and new ways of responding to personal challenges, it is helpful to adopt a graded approach to change. A graded approach increases the likelihood of progress occurring and of progress being seen both by the individual and by his caregivers. The experience of progress is an important motivator both for helpers and those being helped. It makes it easier for people to persist with their long-term efforts at behavioural change. Thus longer-term goals may be broken down into small achievable steps and practised one step at a time. Programmes for responding to appropriate and inappropriate behaviours may be introduced gradually – first in one setting during specific sessions, then systematically extended across settings and time. New skills may be taught in stages – first one part of the skill, then another. Inappropriate behaviours may be discouraged using a gradual approach – the person being reinforced for performing the behaviour increasingly less often and in increasingly fewer situations. Arbitrary S.T.A.R. factors will be gradually and systematically phased out. A graded approach makes learning for the individual easier and it eases the workload for caregivers. It therefore has many advantages.

AN EFFICIENT APPROACH

The development of new, more adaptive ways of coping with one's world and the learning of new skills to facilitate coping may be a slow and lengthy process for the person with learning difficulties. For this reason, great emphasis is placed upon efficiency on the part of caregivers in order that change may occur as quickly as possible. This requires attention to important details which ensure that all aspects of the work are meticulously planned, consistently delivered and constantly monitored and evaluated. To facilitate such a high level of efficiency and professionalism importance is attached to the following.

1. A precise definition of the behaviour which is problematic and which is to be the focus of change – this before any assessment or intervention is begun. This ensures that all those involved have a common starting point and a shared focus for their work.
2. A precise statement about the aims of intervention. This ensures clarity about what is being done and it allows people to judge when goals have been achieved.

3. Written plans which detail the methods of intervention. This increases the likelihood of consistency across time and across people.
4. An objective system for monitoring progress. Such a system provides objective information about a person's progress. From this decisions can be made about the need to adapt or change any programmes of work.

SUPPORT STRUCTURES NECESSARY FOR THE S.T.A.R. APPROACH

Attention to the practical aspects of working therapeutically with people who have behavioural difficulties is frequently overlooked. Working with people who have longstanding behavioural difficulties requires more than an understanding of principles and techniques, it also requires careful attention to organizational factors and support systems which facilitate the long-term and, often, stressful work involved. Key factors include the following.

1. Organizational support to facilitate the time-consuming and detailed work which is required in order to effect change. This means providing time for planning, for writing programmes and for monitoring change, and a forum for decision-making and for reviewing progress.
2. Emphasis on team work to facilitate a consistency of approach. Consistency is more likely when there is a unity of purpose among those working to effect change, when there is clear and effective communication between carers.
3. Emotional support for carers to help them cope with the stress of working, often day after day, with disturbed individuals.
4. Ensuring that the rights of the disturbed individual are protected – the right to refuse to participate in a change intervention, the right to disagree with the goals and methods of change which others may select on his behalf.

SUMMARY

Helping people who have learning disabilities and who show disturbed or inappropriate behaviour is not a straightforward matter. There are no ready-made solutions. Rather, each person's difficulties and inappropriate behaviours must be assessed individually, within the context of his own skills and within the context of the environments in which the problem occurs, so that strategies can be developed which are best suited to that individual and which are feasible to carry out within the organizational set-up in which the problem occurs. There is unlikely to be just one 'correct' strategy. A number of alternative procedures may be equally effective.

In this book a framework is presented which enables carers to develop, implement and evaluate comprehensive therapeutic packages for troubled individuals. The approach is multi-dimensional and it is one that may in some cases require considerable time and human resources, particularly when problems are of a severe nature. It may additionally require careful attention to organizational issues, especially where interventions are carried out within residential or day-care settings, rather than in natural home environments.

It is acknowledged that it may not always be possible to develop an ideal therapeutic package, particularly where staffing levels are low and available resources are poor. Nevertheless there are many levels at which change can take place and there are many ways of tackling problems at each level. Doing a little is always better than doing nothing at all. Doing the best one can under existing circumstances is all that can be expected of any individual or team. Settings can often be improved or altered within existing structural frameworks. New skills can be taught by a single individual without the need for a full back-up organizational system. Use of appropriate skills and behaviours can sometimes be encouraged informally without too much demand on resources. The problem-solving approach presented in this book should thus provide the reader with a framework for analysing and tackling the behavioural challenges of troubled and disturbed individuals in a way which is adapted both to the needs of the individual and to the settings in which programmes of change need to be carried out.

Assessing the problem

2

When a person has been identified as needing help in overcoming a behavioural difficulty, the situation has often been present for some considerable time but a sudden escalation in its frequency or a dramatic increase in its severity means that the situation is now perceived as a crisis. Such a sense of crisis and urgency may encourage those working with the individual concerned to adopt measures which are not necessarily in the individual's best interests. For example, they may adopt punitive measures in order to discourage the behaviour or look to control it through the use of medication. Such measures, even if effective in containing the immediate problem, may be ethically and socially inappropriate and, in any case, are unlikely to be helpful in the longer term.

Effective help for people with longstanding behavioural problems and severe learning disabilities must be based upon a comprehensive understanding of the relevance of the behaviour for the individual. In addition to its relevance for the individual in the context of the person's immediate situation and environment, the behaviour needs to be understood within the broader context of the entire person (past history, physical state, emotional state, personality, coping skills and other personal skills) and the world in which he lives (the physical, social and occupational environments). A comprehensive assessment is thus the first step towards developing a therapeutic intervention package.

ASSESSING THE MEANING OF BEHAVIOURAL DIFFICULTIES – GENERAL PRINCIPLES

Assessment starts with a precise objective description of the behaviour (or behaviours) which is the focus of interest and which will be the subject of the assessment. Once the behaviour has been clearly de-

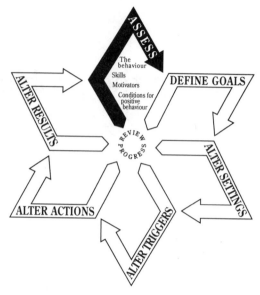

Figure 2.1 Assessing the problem.

scribed, a comprehensive assessment can be undertaken. The assessment will cover a number of areas.

1. Assessment of the function of the behaviour for the individual and the things which set it off (results and triggers).
2. Assessment of the environments/environmental conditions in which the behaviour occurs and also those environments in which the behaviour is less likely to occur (environmental settings).
3. Assessment of the physical or psychological states of the person which are relevant to the problem and also to the person's well-being (personal settings).
4. Assessment of background factors which may be relevant to the problem (early history, recent life events).
5. Assessment of the person's skills, particularly as they relate to the occurrence of the behaviour (actions).
6. Assessment of the individual's likes and dislikes (preferred results).

DEFINING THE BEHAVIOUR

Defining the behaviour of interest may not be quite as straightforward as it may seem. In everyday language there is a tendency to describe the behaviour of others in terms of inner states and processes, such as feelings or attitudes, which are not visible to the outside observer.

Thus, if a person looks serious, talks sharply to others, sighs loudly and slams doors, he may be described as being frustrated or angry. If a person talks in a derogatory way about another, he may be described as being 'jealous'.

Another way in which people describe the behaviours of others is in terms of personality traits. For example, a person who frequently shouts at others may be described as bad-tempered, a person who spends long periods of time alone may be described as unsociable, a person who spends hours watching the television might be described as lazy.

These ways of talking about people are problematic when it comes to trying to help an individual to change. Inferences about inner states or intentions can be very much influenced by the caregiver's own feelings. For example, if the carer is feeling sad, he may only notice the negative things that other people do and is more likely to see in their behaviour feelings of hostility or rejection towards himself. Inferences are also influenced by the individual's own interpretations of events. Thus different people may make different judgements on the basis of seeing the same thing. For example, if two people observe a child snatching back a toy which has been snatched from him, one may see this as a sign of underlying insecurity, the other as indicating assertiveness.

Assessment requires that an objective approach be adopted – free from subjective interpretations and personal feelings. For this reason it is essential to start by defining the problematic behaviour precisely in terms of observable actions.

ASSESSING THE RESULTS WHICH THE BEHAVIOUR ACHIEVES

The behaviours which carers perceive as inappropriate or problematic may serve important functions for the individual by achieving a range of important and desired results; results may be positive gains; results may be the successful escape from or avoidance of a potentially aversive situation.

Social results

For many people, the achieving of social outcomes is an important factor in maintaining behaviour. The social outcome may be positive gains – for example, being noticed, being talked to, having someone's undivided attention for a period of time, being comforted. The social outcome may, alternatively, be escape or avoidance of social situations – for example, being removed from a group of people, being separated from someone one dislikes, having time to oneself, people moving away and giving one a greater area of personal space, being allowed to spend time away from people.

Sensory results

Sensory stimulation – sight, smell, hearing, touch, taste, the sensation of movement – can be a source of pleasure or discomfort. For the person with severe learning difficulties sensory pleasure may be derived, for example, from the sound of a noisy hollow surface reverberating as it is banged with the fist or head, the sight of the flicker of light on saliva as it is spread over a surface, the sensation of the body rocking to and fro, the texture of earth as it is chewed and ingested. Escape from unpleasant sensory experience may occur when, for example, a person is removed from a noisy, hot or foul-smelling environment, when wet or soiled clothes are changed to dry ones.

Material results

Gains in this area are easy to identify – a tantrum that results in a fizzy drink or cup of tea for the person concerned, the scream that results in access to the thing that the person seeks. Escape and avoidance are also to be observed – the act of aggression which causes the unwanted food to be removed, the destructive outburst which results in unwanted objects being removed from one's bedroom.

Occupational results

This is an important area where there is much to be gained from acting in ways which others find difficult or challenging. Occupational gains may take many forms: being given an errand to run as a result of picking fights with other residents, having the TV switched on as a result of pinching and scratching a carer, being taken out for a walk as a result of an outburst of temper.

Occupational escape or avoidance may occur when, for example, a puzzle is taken away as a result of head banging, a demand to complete a task or activity is withdrawn as a result of throwing a cup across the floor, a trip to the shops is cancelled because the person has stripped off his clothes.

Physiological results

Some behaviours are aimed at achieving physiological arousal. Masturbation and other sexual behaviours are the most obvious examples of this. Other behaviours, such as prolonged outbursts of screaming or aggression or self-abuse, appear to relieve or simply to express intolerably high levels of arousal and emotion, as experienced in anger, distress or even excitement.

The assessment process aims to identify the functions which a behaviour serves for the person. It is worth remembering that a person will continue to use a specific behaviour to obtain particular outcomes, even if those outcomes are not successfully achieved on each occasion. Thus the assessment is likely to show inconsistent achievement of positive outcomes for the individual's behaviour.

ASSESSING THE TRIGGERS FOR PROBLEMATIC BEHAVIOURS

Identifying the things which trigger behavioural outbursts or other problematic behaviour not only helps to better understand the possible function of the behaviour but it enables those working with the individual to predict when the behaviour is likely to occur. It goes without saying that, if the occurrence of a behaviour can be predicted through a knowledge of its triggers, then this opens up an important area upon which interventions can focus.

The triggers for problematic behaviours are likely to fall into one of the categories discussed below.

Reward/punishment signal

A stimulus may signal to the person that the thing he wants is potentially available or the thing that he does not want or wishes to avoid is imminent. Provided that the individual actually desires the outcome (gain or escape) at the time the stimulus occurs, the stimulus will serve to trigger a behaviour directed at achieving that result. Selection of the most appropriate behaviour for any particular situation will have been learned over time. Thus specific trigger–action–result sequences are likely to be observed.

Triggers for gains

Triggers can be any of a multitude of stimuli. For example, if one carer always reacts to a person's screaming by stroking and cuddling the person, and this is something that the person enjoys or find comforting, then the appearance of that particular carer may trigger screaming (action) because of his association with 'cuddles' (results). If an individual loves the sight and sounds of scattering materials, then the presence of glass, crockery or cutlery may trigger throwing and tipping. If an individual enjoys the sparkle of a light on liquid then the sun coming out can trigger spitting and playing with saliva.

Triggers for escape

Demands and requests often signal to the individual that something he does not want is about to happen. This in turn often triggers actions (for example, hitting out, screaming or head banging) directed at terminating the aversive situation by the demand or request being withdrawn. Being denied something a person wants is another common situation which may trigger problematic behaviour, aimed at having the denial withdrawn.

Physiological arousal/stimulus overload

A stimulus may trigger or increase physiological arousal and a powerful emotional state. If the person is already experiencing high arousal (for example, tension) or strong emotion (for example, anxiety, anger, distress) then a relatively minor or insignificant event – a request, a disappointment, a commotion – which overloads the physiological system may simply serve as 'the last straw'.

Sometimes a particular event or stimulus (for example, being insulted or thwarted) may cause an immediate surge of strong emotion which rapidly increases physiological arousal to an intolerable level. This in turn may trigger a sudden behavioural response.

Habit

A behaviour may trigger a second behaviour in a sequence which has become automatic through frequent practice (for example, sit down in front of television–bite finger nails; enter room–touch door–touch wall–touch window–lick hand).

Involuntary reaction

A stimulus may directly trigger behaviour in the way that a tap on the knee might elicit a knee jerk. Thus, the experience of pain may trigger screaming, a loud noise may elicit a startle response, a physical threat may trigger an escape response, a hand released from a splint may trigger the response of the hand being pushed down the throat.

ASSESSING ENVIRONMENTAL SETTINGS IMPLICATED IN
PROBLEMATIC BEHAVIOURS

When looking to understand the outcomes which people seek to achieve by acting in ways considered to be problematic – whether the outcome is time with a caregiver, an activity to do, sensory enjoyment or escape from a difficult situation – it is necessary to look beyond the immediate situation and to try to understand the reason for the individual seeking the result that he seeks. Why does the individual need to seek time with a carer? Why doe he need to find something to do to occupy his time? Why does he seek to escape from people to the solitude of his room? One place to look for answers to questions relating to the individual's motivations is within the person's environment. There are a number of features about the person's world and living environment which may have powerful influences upon his motivations.

The physical climate

This relates to aspects of the physical environment which may influence a person's motivations. Such physical factors may influence motivations directly (for example, a crowded and noisy environment may create a high motivation to escape from such a situation). Equally important are the indirect effects of these factors upon motivation. Thus, a crowded and noisy environment may increase a person's anxiety or agitation and in such a context a demand or request which might ordinarily pose no problem for the person, may now elicit an adverse response. Important physical aspects of the environment to consider include temperature, noise level, smell, illumination and crowding.

The social climate

The social climate which the person experiences within his environment is likely to influence the person's needs and desires. Social atmosphere and people's attitudes are especially relevant.

Relationships between carers

The social atmosphere within a residential or day facility may be influenced by:

- the degree of agreement or understanding about an agency's purpose or mission;
- the objectives of staff;
- the understanding and agreement about people's roles within an organization or team;
- the amount of autonomy and personal control which individual staff have in relation to their work;
- the level of participation which staff have in decision-making;
- the resources which are available to staff.

Such variables are likely to influence the level of harmony between carers, the accuracy of communications, the consistency among staff regarding ways of helping individuals in their care, the motivation to work effectively and to give of their best. If conflict exists between carers then exchanges between them are likely to be angry and insensitive. This in turn may increase the tension experienced by the individual.

Attitudes towards the individual

Attitudes towards the person with learning disabilities will have a major influence on the individual concerned. Thus, those people whose carers are authoritarian and controlling may experience frustration and strive for greater independence and control over their own lives. Those people who are treated as children or as incompetent beings may lack the confidence to assert their own independence or the motivation to develop new skills. Those people who experience hostility from their carers may themselves become hostile and angry. Those people who are treated without respect or dignity may start to act in ways which reflect a lack of respect for the self and a lack of personal dignity.

The individual's relationship with his peers

The social atmosphere created by those with whom the individual shares his life may also have a significant influence upon motivation. Thus, living with people whom one fears may increase general anxiety and withdrawal. Living with people with whom one shares no common interests can lead to frustration and an overdependence upon caregivers. Living with people whom one dislikes may lead to resentment and hostility towards them.

The occupational climate

This aspect of the environment is associated with the types of activities and way of life which impinge upon the individual. If a person experiences an unstimulating lifestyle, with little to do and little to look forward to, then this may increase the need to find alternative sources of stimulation and activity. If a person experiences an unpredictable environment, where it becomes difficult to know what to expect, where it is difficult to differentiate morning and afternoon, weekday and weekend, then this may raise a person's anxiety level and increase the need to relieve that anxiety. If a person spends his life in a highly pressured environment, where demands are made of him which he cannot fulfil, where requests are made of him which he cannot understand, where he is continually failing, then this may lower mood, affect the person's self-image and self-confidence and increase the motivation to withdraw from activities and people who place demands on him.

ASSESSING PERSONAL SETTINGS IMPLICATED IN
PROBLEMATIC BEHAVIOURS

Important sources of influence upon the individual's motivations are to be found within the individual himself. Personal settings are those aspects of the person which have a bearing on the individual's motivational state. Such personal setting influences include physical states, psychological states and cognitive factors.

Physical states

A person's physical state may have a significant influence on his motivations. Thus the individual who is unwell or tired will be motivated towards different activities than when he is fit and alert. The relative strength of a person's motivations will differ when he is under the influence of drugs. For example, medication may increase lethargy, which in turn may increase the motivation to opt out of regular activities. Motivations may change under hormonal influences (for example, premenstrual stress or the menopause). When a person is in pain his motivations may be geared towards relieving or otherwise avoiding an increase in discomfort.

Psychological states

A person's mood states may be influenced by immediate or recent environmental events, such as a bereavement, a move, a loss, sexual abuse or other trauma. They may be influenced by longer-term psychiatric problems (for example, schizophrenia or depression) or longstanding emotional difficulties which may result, for example, from childhood abuse or parental rejection.

Mood is closely related to motivation. Thus the depressed individual may seek to spend time on his own, to eat very little, to do very little. The anxious individual may be permanently 'on edge' and easily angered by apparently insignificant matters.

Cognitive factors

A person's interpretation of events that go on around him will have clear implications for his motivational states. Thus the person who believes that people do not like him may become angry and seek to punish those people. The person who believes that he is bad may behave in ways which fulfil people's expectations of him. A person who interprets daily events in negative ways (for example, 'all bad things are my fault/all good things that happen to me are due to the efforts of somebody else') will experience low mood and this in turn will influence his motivations. A person experiencing a psychotic crisis may think others are trying to harm him in some way and may become fearful of people or seek to protect himself more actively from such harm. A person who has difficulty interpreting the social signals of others may be unable to understand the feelings of others and hence may not know when to adjust his own behaviour according to the feelings of those around him.

ASSESSING RELEVANT SKILLS

Skill deficits which are related to behavioural disturbance tend often to occur in the areas of communication, self-occupation and social skills. The person who is not able to express his needs in appropriate ways will do so through alternative methods, such as self-injury or aggression. A person who lacks the skills to occupy himself may rely wholly on others to relieve his boredom (this may be perceived as attention seeking) or he may revert to stimulatory activities, such as finger flicking or rocking at times when he is unoccupied. A person who does not understand social rules or values or who lacks social skills may make gross errors of social judgment or behave in ways which are considered to be socially unacceptable by others (for example, masturbating in public).

Other skills which are relevant to a person's emotional well-being are the skills of problem solving and self-control. A person who is unable to solve simple life problems will continually make errors of judgment and get himself into difficulties. A person who is unable to recognize and control his emotions will be unable to help himself through emotional upsets and will remain dependent upon others for control. Alternatively he may experience frequent loss of control and the feelings of humiliation which may accompany this.

Knowing a person's skills and skill deficits in relevant skill areas will not only help to better understand the reasons why he behaves in ways which appear inappropriate or which directly challenge carers but will also help generate realistic ideas about the kinds of things to teach or encourage in order to help the individual overcome behavioural disturbances and learn more adaptive ways of coping with his world.

ASSESSING MOTIVATORS

The assessment process should include a full assessment of all the things which the person likes and enjoys. Such an assessment is important for three reasons.

1. It may further the understanding of the problematic behaviour itself (for example, the kinds of social attention a person enjoys, the kinds of activities he likes, the kinds of sensory experiences which give him pleasure).
2. It may help to determine the extent to which the things a person enjoys occur naturally in the person's life or whether these things are accessed predominantly through the use of behaviours considered to be problematic.
3. It will be of importance when it comes to planning interventions aimed at helping the individual to change and to develop more adaptive behaviours.

Motivators are those results that a person works to achieve by his actions. Every individual varies to some extent in the things that encourage or discourage his actions. On the whole, the results that people will work to achieve fall into the following broad categories: social, sensory, material or occupational. These categories are the same as the categories of results achieved by problematic behaviour.

ASSESSING CONDITIONS FOR POSITIVE BEHAVIOUR

In addition to developing an understanding of the factors involved in the problematic behaviour, it is important also to develop an understanding of the conditions under which the behaviour is less likely to occur. These include, in particular, the environmental settings (physical, social, occupational), personal settings (physical, psychological, cognitive) and triggers which are most conducive to behaving in ways which are not problematic.

Since much of the intervention work will involve the development of a person's skills, it is also important to know the conditions under which the individual learns most easily. Such information – the best teachers, the best times, the best places, the best ways of presenting instructions or of holding the individual's attention – will generate ideas about the most effective methods for teaching key skills to the individual.

SUMMARIZING ASSESSMENT INFORMATION AND DEVELOPING A
THERAPEUTIC PLAN

Following a full and comprehensive assessment, all the information
which has been gathered should to be analysed and a theory formulated of the various S.T.A.R. factors which may be involved in
maintaining the problematic behaviour. The formulation of the problem becomes the basis from which needs are identified. Second, the
strengths (skills, motivators, conditions for positive behaviour) of the
individual need to be summarized so that they can at a later stage be
used to aid the change process.

Needs are likely to be identified in a number of areas. Some will
relate to altering aspects of the living environment. Some will directly
focus on the person's physical or emotional state. Others will be directed towards teaching the individual better ways of coping with
emotional upset and better ways of achieving looked-for results. Still
others will look to help the individual unlearn maladaptive coping
strategies and responses. Interventions developed from the various
identified needs will together form the therapeutic package. The list of
the person's strengths, which has been drawn up as part of the assessment process, will then be available to ensure that specific interventions
are built and planned around these strengths.

PROCEDURES FOR ARRIVING AT A FORMULATION OF THE PROBLEM AND ESTABLISHING THE THERAPEUTIC PLAN

Step ⟩ 1 ⟨   Define the behaviour

Many people who have behavioural and adjustment difficulties present
their carers with a whole range of challenges – some closely inter-
related, some quite unrelated. The very first step, therefore, even
before assessment is considered, is to clearly define the behaviour
which is to be analysed.

1. The behaviour or behaviours should be defined in clear objective
   terms, free from 'fuzzy' descriptive terms or emotionally charged
   interpretations. Table 2.1 compares definitions of behaviour stated
   in 'fuzzy' or subjective terms and definitions using objective behavioural terminology.
2. A decision needs to be made early on about whether a group of
   behaviours should be analysed as 'one' or as separate behaviours. If
   they are to be analysed as one, the assumption is that they are part

Table 2.1 Describing behaviour

Fuzzy terminology	Behavioural terminology
Naughty	Empties cupboards in the kitchen
Obsessional	Replaces ornaments which have been moved in his bedroom
Attention seeking	Throws equipment at carers
Distressed	Cries and paces about the room
Paranoid	Asks if people are talking about him
Aggressive	Bites others

of the same group and are used interchangeably. Thus, a person's temper tantrum may include a variety of behaviours differing slightly on each occasion – they may include screaming, hitting, kicking, throwing and head banging. A person's 'attention seeking' behaviours may include spitting, shouting, swearing and grabbing – the behaviours being used in different combinations on different occasions. If agreement cannot be reached about whether the behaviours form part of the same 'group', then they should initially be separately analysed until enough information is gathered to enable carers to make this decision.

3. Where several behaviours form part of a sequence, then a description of the person's progression through the sequence may be useful at this stage (for example, a sequence may start by the person becoming very noisy and shouting, it may progress to pacing and swearing and then finally end in hitting).

Step ⧖ 2 ⧖   Assess the function of the behaviour

Table 2.2 presents a summary of the types of results which may be achieved by behaviours identified by others as problematic. For each type of result, the outcomes sought may be positive (access) or negative (escape).

The function which a behaviour serves for an individual may be deduced from analysing the kinds of results which the behaviour achieves for the person and the kinds of triggers which seem to set off the behaviour. For example, if a person frequently screams and hits staff and a consequence of this is that the individual is often removed from the room or is left behind when others go on outings, then it can

Table 2.2 Results which can be achieved by behaviours considered to be problematic

	Gains	Escape
Social	All forms of attention from others	Getting away from people (specific or generally)
Sensory	Pleasing sensory experiences	Relief from aversive sensory experience
Material	Goods	Removal of unwanted goods
Occupational	Activities	Cessation of unwanted activities
Arousal	Physiological stimulation	Emotional release, relief from tension

be deduced from this that one function of the behaviour is to achieve solitude. When one combines information about results with an analysis of triggering events a clearer picture emerges. Thus, in the example above, knowledge that common triggers for screaming and hitting include being in a large group, being close to people and high noise levels, provides a clearer idea about the kinds of situations which prompt the individual to seek solitude. Table 2.3 provides examples of some common triggers associated with problematic behaviour. Different types of assessment tools can be used to gather information about results and triggers for a defined behaviour. Each has its merits and each has its limitations.

Interview/structured discussion

This is, in practice, the most frequently used tool for assessing problematic behaviour and one that is invariably used in combination with the observational methods described below. Nevertheless, as regards the part of the assessment which aims to analyse the function of a behaviour, it remains the most informal and potentially the most unreliable method. It relies on retrospective information. It is based on memory and often on inadequate observations. It can be based on people's preconceived assumptions and biases. In order, therefore, that information gathered about triggers and results using discussion and interviews be as accurate and useful as possible it is important to prepare the content of the discussion in advance and to gather information as systematically and objectively as possible.

1. Questions should be gathered about:
   (a) a definition of the behaviour or behaviours of concern;
   (b) a summary of the history of each behaviour;

Table 2.3 Common triggers for problematic behaviours

Triggers for escape	Being fobbed off
	Being denied something
	Being thwarted
	Being misunderstood
	Being pressurized
	Being insulted
	Being ignored
	Being confronted with 'feared' object
	Pain
	Being threatened
	Routine suddenly upset
	Too much noise
	Too much heat
	Too much pressure
	Overload of arousal
	Overload of emotion
	Obsession interrupted
	Ritual upset
Triggers for gains	Sight of the thing that is wanted
	Smell of the thing that is wanted
	Sound of the thing that is wanted
	Seeing others with the thing that is wanted

(c) the results that each behaviour achieves;
(d) the things that appear to trigger each behaviour;
(e) alternative skills which the individual may possess which he could use to achieve the same results;
(f) current management strategies;
(g) strategies which have been used in the past to try to help the individual with this particular behavioural difficulty.
2. Great care should be taken to try to separate facts from assumptions and answers based on what people believe the interviewer wants to hear. Questions should, as far as possible, be asked using an open format (for example, tell me about . . . ; what happens when . . .) rather than a closed format (for example, does he . . .).
3. To ensure that information is as accurate as possible it is important that people providing the information have had the opportunity to observe the individual in a range of situations. Questions should focus on what people have actually observed and not on what they have heard from others or on their subjective impressions.

Where structured discussion or interview does not provide clear information about triggers and results for problematic behaviour a more direct form of assessment, using observational recording, should be set up.

Observation in the natural environment

This is historically the most frequently used formal tool for gathering information about the possible functions of a behaviour. A large amount of useful information can be obtained through systematic observation and recording of details about the immediate antecedents and immediate outcomes of a behaviour as they occur in the person's natural environment. From these are deduced the triggers and looked-for results. Each time the behaviour occurs the event immediately preceding the behaviour is noted (trigger). The behaviour itself (action) is described in detail (including the length of time for which it continued, the number of times it occurred, its severity). The event which immediately followed the behaviour (its result) is then written down.

A simple observation recording form, as shown in Figure 2.2, can greatly facilitate this method of data collection. The person's name should be clearly written at the top of the recording sheet, together with details of the behaviour which is to be observed and recorded. It is important that each observation is dated and the time of its occurrence recorded.

Figure 2.2 illustrates how details about a behaviour can be recorded. From the few recordings of the behaviour that are shown on the recording chart in Figure 2.2, a picture of the circumstances in which the problematic behaviour occurs is evident. In this example, the behaviour seems to occur when people are sitting or standing next to the person. The result of the behaviour seems to be that people move away. Several more recordings would provide a clearer and more consistent picture of the circumstance in which this behaviour occurs.

The systematic recording of behaviour in the natural environment can provide extremely useful and insightful information about the factors involved in a person's specific behaviour. However, if done badly, the exercise will almost certainly prove useless. The following steps should help increase the accuracy and usefulness of such recording.

1. All those who are involved in the recording process should be clear about the purpose of the assessment (to understand the individual's behaviour better, not the behaviour of the carers).
2. All those who are involved in the recording process should receive some basic training in observation and recording skills and be made aware of the contribution of individual bias, which can influence the things that are observed in any situation (people often see only what they expect to see).
3. When filling in a behavioural recording form, no section of the recording form should be left blank. Thus in response to the question 'What happened immediately before the behaviour started (trigger)'

BEHAVIOUR OBSERVATION CHART

Name LARRY

Date	Time	Setting	Trigger	Behaviour to be Observed SCREAMING		Result
				Action		**Result**
JAN 2ND	10.35AM	GROUP ACTIVITY ROOM. WORKING 1-TO-1-WITH LARRY.	NOTHING SPECIFIC. SITTING NEXT TO HIM, TRYING TO GET HIM TO DRAW A PICTURE.	SCREAMED ABOUT 15 TIMES DURING 10 MINUTE SESSION.		SOMETIMES IGNORED HIM. SOMETIMES TOLD HIM TO CALM DOWN. GAVE UP SESSION AFTER 10 MINUTES.
JAN 2ND	11.20AM	GROUP ACTIVITY ROOM. LARRY SITTING ALONE. WENT OVER TO HIM AND SAT NEXT TO HIM.	STARTED TO TALK TO LARRY.	SCREAMED TWICE.		I TOLD HIM HE SHOULDN'T SCREAM THEN LEFT HIM SITTING ALONE.
JAN 2ND	2.00PM	MINI BUS. SITTING NEXT TO LARRY.	ME BEING THERE. LARRY COULDN'T GET OUT OF THE SEAT. I TRIED TO GET HIM TO LOOK AT THINGS WE WERE DRIVING PAST.	SCREAMED SEVERAL TIMES.		IGNORED SOME SCREAMS. TOLD HIM OFF OCCASIONALLY. WOULD STOP FOR A WHILE, THEN START AGAIN UNTIL I MOVED FROM THE SEAT.
	2.20PM	MINI BUS. HAD COME BACK TO SIT NEXT TO LARRY.	I WAS TALKING TO BILL, TRYING TO IGNORE LARRY'S SCREAMING.	SCREAMED SEVERAL TIMES.		I MANAGED TO IGNORE HIM FOR A TIME. THEN SHOUTED AT HIM. HE STOPPED FOR A WHILE, THEN STARTED AGAIN. KEPT IT UP TILL WE GOT HOME
JAN 2ND	6.25PM	KITCHEN. CAME OVER TO HELP LARRY WITH THE PASTRY.	STANDING NEXT TO HIM, TALKING TO HIM.	STARTED SCREAMING.		I MOVED AWAY AND CONTINUED TO TALK WITH HIM. HE STOPPED.

Figure 2.2 Example of a basic chart for recording observations of a behaviour in the natural environment.

the observation 'the person was sitting in a chair with his eyes closed not moving' should be written rather than 'nothing'.

4. When completing a behavioural recording form observations should be recorded exactly, rather than interpretations from these observations (for example, 'X came into the room and talked with Y' rather than 'A was jealous that Y gave X attention').

5. Observations should be recorded as soon as possible after the behaviour has been observed. The longer the documentation is left the more details will be forgotten by the observer. Waiting till the end of the session/shift to write up one's observations should be strongly discouraged.

6. Observers should, if possible, be independent observers of a situation. It is one of the most difficult tasks of observation to accurately observe one's own behaviour – the tone of one's own voice, the suddenness of one's own movements, the wording of a request. Yet it is often these minute details which are needed in order to obtain a full understanding of a person's behaviour and its triggers. Where relevant, video recordings of the individual and his behaviour should be made and analysed in detail.

Usually about 2 or 3 weeks of data collection will be needed to obtain a clear picture of relevant factors which may be contributing to a behaviour. For behaviours which occur very infrequently, recordings may need to continue for 3 or 4 months in order to obtain adequate information from which an objective and accurate analysis can be made.

Analogue assessment

There may be occasions when, despite a large number of observations, a clear picture still does not emerge about the factors within the immediate environment which are associated with the problematic behaviour. There may be occasions when it is felt that some very specific factors might be involved but the natural environment does not provide the structure within which to test out one's theory. In such cases a more detailed assessment, called an analogue assessment, could be set up to try to obtain more detailed information.

An analogue assessment aims to assess the factors that influence a behaviour by deliberately constructing situations to ensure that particular factors are present (specific triggers, specific results) and systematically measuring the individual's behaviour in each situation. Assessment is conducted on a sessional basis. Sessions are constructed so that:

- sessions are brief (usually not more than 10–15 minutes);
- sessions are highly structured (materials, level and type of social interactions with the person are controlled);

- at least two or three different situations (conditions) are set up in order to compare the person's behaviour in each;
- the length of each session is the same across all conditions, which are kept as constant as possible and only those factors being compared are altered;
- sessions involve the carer systematically and consistently responding to occurrences of the behaviour and recording the frequency of the occurrence of the behaviour;
- all sessions are repeated several times over, each condition being repeated the same number of times (often between six and ten times);
- the different conditions are often presented in sequence during a single time period, each time in a different order;
- the total frequency of the behaviour in each situation is compared – a consistently higher frequency of the behaviour in one condition enables an inference to be made about the function of the behaviour.

An example of the use of an analogue assessment is presented in Figure 2.3. Analogue assessments have the advantage that they can show very clear differences in behaviour across situations, which can make interpretation of the results very straightforward, if the environmental factors have been carefully controlled. They are particularly useful for assessing the function of behaviours which occur at a very high frequency (several times during an hour). For behaviours which occur at low frequencies, analogue assessment is not appropriate. There are ethical considerations, too, when behaviours such as self-injury or physical aggression are involved. It may not be considered to be ethically appropriate to deliberately construct a test situation which 'invites' aggressive or self-injurious behaviour.

Step ⟩ 3 ⟨	Assess setting conditions associated with the problematic behaviour

The purpose of this part of the assessment is to determine what environmental conditions and personal states may be contributing to the behaviour, by creating or strengthening the motivation for the results which the individual seeks through his inappropriate actions.

A summary of some of the general environmental and personal setting conditions which need to be explored is presented in Table 2.4. Methods for assessing and exploring such setting conditions are described below.

Discussion/interview

Some of the setting factors (for example, aspects of the environment, aspects of the person) which increase a person's vulnerability to show-

Neil's shrieking was occurring across a number of day to day situations and the responses and outcomes he was acheiving were very varied, depending on individual carers and their feelings at the time. The behaviour was of a very high frequency (up to several times in a minute on some occasions) and natural observations had not shown any consistent pattern. An analogue situation was set up in which four different conditions were presented.

CONDITIONS	TRIGGERS	RESPONSE TO SCREECHING
1. To test out whether the function of the shrieking was to escape from situations where pressure was put on him to do tasks he did not want to do.	**A high level of demand** Neil is encouraged to engage in a difficult table top activity in the lounge.	**Demand escape** The carer withdraws all attention from Neil for 10 seconds following each incident of shrieking, then resumes the task.
2. To test out whether the function of the shrieking was to escape from situations which involved the social attention of carers.	**High level of attention** Carer continuously talks to Neil. No activity is present.	**Social escape** The carer withdraws attention from Neil for a period of 10 seconds following each incident of shrieking.
3. To test out whether the function of the shrieking was to get people to pay him attention.	**No attention** Neil is left alone with his favourite activity. The carer attends to other people in the room.	**Attention from carer** Carer approaches and talks to Neil for 10 seconds following each incident of shrieking.
4. To act as a 'reference' condition against which the others could be measured. It was constructed in a way which was considered to be the least likely to elicit Neil's shrieking behaviour.	**A low level of help** Neil sits in lounge with a favourite table top activity accompanied by the carer who does not interact with him.	**Help from carer** Carer helps Neil with table top activity for 10 seconds following each incident of shrieking.

Each condition lasted exactly 10 minutes and was repeated successively in a different order each time a total of ten times. This was done over a period of 3 weeks. Each incident of shrieking was recorded during each 10 - minute period.

A total count of shrieking from each of the ten sessions was as follows:

1. Demand escape = 350   2. Social escape = 320   3. Social attention = 50   4. Help with task = 42

These results suggest that a major function of Neil's shrieking is escape from situations which involve both pressure to perform difficult tasks and imposed social contact.

Figure 2.3 An example of the use of an analogue assessment.

Table 2.4 Setting conditions for behaviours considered to be problematic

Environmental setting conditions	Physical	Temperature Lighting Noise Smell Crowding
	Occupational	Level of stimulation Level of personal control Level of predictability and structure Level of aversiveness Appropriateness to life-span stage
	Social	Attitude of carers to client Relationships with other clients Level of harmony between carers Level of consistency
Personal setting conditions	Physical	General health Current medication Hormonal influences Sensory impairments Motor impairments Sleep pattern
	Psychological	Mental disturbance Mood states Anxiety Unresolved trauma from life events

	Cognitive	Self-esteem
		Beliefs about the behaviours/
		    attitudes of others in relation to
		    self
		Thought disorder

ing the behaviour may be obtained by a discussion and exchange of information with the various people who know the person in the different environments in which he spends his time. The person may be able to provide relevant information himself.

Other setting factors (for example, recent life events, past history) may need to be assessed via an interview with carers who have known the individual for some considerable time.

Written records

Written records, for example care and educational records, may provide more historical information (for example, significant life events, early life).

Direct observation

Immediate environmental setting factors may become apparent through direct observation of the environment in which the person spends his time – observation of the interactions between carers, the quality and style of interactions between carers and the individual concerned (for example, very directive, abrupt, unfriendly).

Observational recording forms, such as that shown in Figure 2.2, can be adapted and customized to gather specific additional information about setting conditions which are felt to be important in the assessment. Thus the basic recording form can be adapted to include information about such factors as the time, the place, the people present, the activity in progress, the person's mood state and physical health.

Recording charts can be set up to gather information about the frequency of a person's behaviour in relation to a variety of setting conditions (for example, in relation to a person's menstrual cycle, in relation to *grand mal* seizures, in relation to visits to the family home, in relation to staff changes, in relation to the times of day).

Direct assessment of the individual

Physical, emotional or cognitive states which may be influencing the person's motivations may be assessed through observation of the individual or through talking with him. In some situations a direct assessment by a specialist, such as a doctor, psychiatrist or psychologist, may be required.

Step ⟩ **4** ⟨   Assess skills

In addition to the detailed analysis of the problematic behaviour, as outlined above, an analysis also needs to be made of the person's skills. Whilst a general overview of a person's skills is important, particular attention should be paid to the following.

1. Those skills which could be used by the person to achieve the same results as those achieved by the problematic behaviours (functionally equivalent skills).
2. Those skills whose performance would make the performance of the problematic behaviour more difficult (physically incompatible skills).
3. Those skills whose performance would reduce the motivation for performing the problematic behaviour (functionally incompatible skills).

In addition, information needs to be gathered about the person's

- verbal comprehension and communication skills
- self-occupation skills
- social skills
- problem solving skills
- self-control.

It is deficits in these skills, in particular, which appear again and again to increase people's vulnerability to developing behavioural and emotional disorders.

Aims of assessment

A useful assessment is one that can aid in the planning of a teaching programme. It should therefore aim to answer the following questions.

1. Does the individual have the skill and use it when appropriate without help or prompting?
2. Does the individual have parts of the skill but not the whole skill?
3. Does the individual show the skill if given help?
4. Does the individual show the skill sometimes, but not reliably or all the time?

Such a graded form of assessment provides more information than a Yes/No type of assessment, but is clearly more complicated and time-consuming to carry out.

As with the assessment of problematic behaviours, there are several ways in which skills can be assessed.

Assessment by interview or discussion

The simplest and most informal method of assessing a person's skills is to ask somebody who knows the person well or to ask the person himself. As with all assessments which rely on information provided by other people, care must be taken in the following respects.

1. Ask only those people who have definitely had the opportunity to observe the person in relevant situations.
2. Ask questions in a way which does not suggest that the interviewer has any expectation about what the answer should be, since people may feel obliged to give the answer they think others want to hear. Open questions ('Tell me about . . .') are better than closed questions ('Does he . . . ?') in this respect.
3. Focus only on what the people have themselves observed, rather than on what they have heard from others or what they think a person can do.

Assessment through direct observation

Whenever possible, assessment should be based upon direct observations in the person's natural environment. Thus, to find out the skills a person has in occupying himself, it is best to observe him during 'free' or unstructured times and write down what is observed.

Assessment through direct testing

Although observation in the natural environment can provide a lot of information, some of it may be difficult to interpret: some skills may be difficult to assess, they may be demonstrated only infrequently or there may be no opportunity to demonstrate them. For example, it may be difficult to judge a person's ability to make himself a drink, if he is never allowed into the kitchen. It may take a long time to observe if a person can sign his name if this activity is only performed once a week at the post office. In these cases it is reasonable to 'test out' the person's skills by setting up as natural a situation as possible and observing the individual's response. For example, one could get a form from the post office and ask the person to show how he signs his name.

Step ⟩ 5 ⟨   Assess motivators

Classes of motivators to be assessed are presented in Table 2.5. The methods for assessing motivators are essentially the same as for skills and problematic behaviours.

Interview/discussion

Important information can be obtained by asking people who know the individual well or asking the person himself. When interviewing other people about an individual's preferences, it is important to focus the interview around what they have observed and not around what they have heard from others or what they think the individual may like or dislike.

Observation in the natural environment

Observation of a person in his natural environment can provide a lot of information about the things that encourage his actions. Things that are likely to prove useful for encouraging new learning or building up

Table 2.5 Categories of positive reinforcement which people will work to achieve

Category	Examples
Social	Praise, physical closeness, smiles, eye contact, social recognition, a chat, sharing experiences
Sensory	Pleasing sights, sounds, smells
	Pleasing tactile sensations, e.g. stroking, tickling, massaging, being held, being rocked
Material	Food, drink, personal possessions
Complex	Activities or treats which may have a social, sensory and material component, e.g. going to a concert, playing board games, going to a disco
Symbolic	Money, tokens, stars
Self-esteem	A sense of achievement, of importance, of competence, of self-worth, of control

existing skills are things that the person spends a lot of time with, given the opportunity, and things that a person works hard to achieve.

Emotional responses, such as laughing or crying, do not always provide reliable evidence that a thing or activity is likely to encourage behaviour. Anxiety and excitement may look very similar and even when they are interpreted correctly their exact significance may be uncertain. For example, people will often do things they find frightening ('thrills') and may repeat actions that get them into trouble, since 'trouble' can often mean a lot of attention even though it may make them cry. The most reliable information obtained by observation is obtained from observing the length of time people spend on various activities and how hard they work to achieve these activities and other events.

Testing

Although observation can provide a lot of information, some of it can be difficult to interpret. Some events may be very rare or may not be available at all. Sometimes a person may have a range of preferences but it is unclear from mere observation which of these are more important to the individual. In such situations it is possible to formally test out an individual's preferences in relation to positive motivators. A structured method for testing out a person's reinforcer preferences is shown below.

1. Select a range of potentially reinforcing items, from the things the person appears to enjoy or which you believe he might enjoy given the opportunity.

2. Offer the individual two or three items together to choose from and allow one choice only. Record the item selected.
3. When the person has finished with or tired of the reinforcer, offer another two or three items in the same way and record the item selected.
4. Systematically work through all the items which you wish to test out (this may take several short sessions), ensuring that each item has been offered in combination with all other items. Record the item selected.
5. Review selections from each pairing or combination to see if any clear preferences emerge. The most frequently selected items are likely to be the preferred items.

This method may be particularly useful with individuals who are unable to show clearly their preferences, or for whom important reinforcers appear to be material items or sensory stimulation.

Step ⟩ 6 ⟨   Assess conditions for positive behaviour

Time needs to be given to gathering information about conditions under which the individual is less likely to show problematic behaviour. These include:

- environmental setting conditions (physical, social, occupational) in which the behaviour rarely occurs;
- personal setting conditions (physical, psychological) in which the behavioural rarely occurs;
- methods of presenting triggers which will not lead to the problematic behaviour.

Any of the methods described above in STEP 2 can be used for this purpose – discussion, observation in the natural environment or direct testing.

Spending time considering the conditions for positive behaviour not only provides useful information, which can be used subsequently to facilitate the change process, but it can have a positive impact on the attitude towards the individual of those working with him.

Step ⟩ 7 ⟨   Summarize the person's strengths

The outcome of the assessment of the person's skills and motivators, and information about the conditions for positive behaviour (including

optimal conditions for learning and conditions for appropriate behaviour) need to be condensed into a summary form. The summary
will include a list of the following:

- the person's skills;
- the person's preferences;
- the conditions for the person's positive behaviour;
- the conditions under which the person learns best.

An example of a strengths list is shown in Figure 2.4.

Step ⟨ 8 ⟩   Make a formulation about the problematic behaviour

---

All the assessment information which has been collected about the
problematic behaviour needs to be analysed and a formulation made
about the factors involved. Analysis is conducted by carefully inspecting
the data.

1. **Triggers.** Information from the structured discussions will be sup-
   plemented by a count of the various triggers noted on the charts
   collected during natural observation in the person's environment.
   This may show whether any specific triggers occur more often than
   do others (for example, when activities are cancelled, when the
   person is told to wait, the presence of specific people). The results
   from analogue assessments will supplement observational and informally collected information.
2. **Results.** Information from the structured discussions will be supple-
   mented by a count of the various outcomes for the behaviour, which
   have been noted on the charts collected during natural observation
   in the person's environment. Some results may occur more frequently than others. The results of analogue assessments may be
   added to this information.
3. **Trigger–action–result sequences.** Discussions and observational
   data may have shown some consistent trigger–action–result sequences (for example, someone starts to scream–person slaps
   face–person taken to quiet area). The regular occurrence of such
   specific sequences will help further pinpoint the problematic triggers
   and associated results.
4. **Environmental setting factors.** Information from structured discussions, from interviews with other significant people, from observation charts and from frequency charts may reveal some consistent
   environmental situations (physical, social, occupational) in which
   the behaviour is more likely to occur (for example, noisy rooms,
   crowded shops, specific carers, unstructured times of day).

STRENGTHS LIST
Name *LARRY*

Skills

LARRY CAN OPERATE A CASSETTE RECORDER
LARRY MAKES NEEDS KNOWN BY POINTING, PULLING PEOPLE TO WHAT HE WANTS
LARRY USES THREE MAKATON SIGNS SPONTANEOUSLY (DRINK, BISCUIT, MORE)
LARRY SEEMS TO UNDERSTAND INSTRUCTIONS IF THEY ARE SIMPLY STATED
LARRY MAKES GOOD EYE CONTACT IF HE WANTS TO
LARRY APPROACHES CARERS IF HE WANTS THEIR ATTENTION OR TIME
LARRY CAN RIDE A BIKE
LARRY CAN SET THE TABLE FOR A MEAL
LARRY CAN TAKE THE DIRTY DISHES INTO THE KITCHEN AFTER A MEAL
LARRY CAN WASH AND DRESS INDEPENDENTLY (EXCEPT BUTTONS AND FASTENERS)
LARRY CAN MAKE HIS BED WITH HELP
LARRY CAN WASH DISHES WITH HELP
LARRY CAN RUN SIMPLE ERRANDS AROUND THE HOUSE

Preferences

LARRY LOVES FOOD, ESPECIALLY PARTY FOODS (CRISPS, FIZZY DRINKS, COCKTAIL
SAUSAGES, SANDWICHES, SAUSAGE ROLLS, SWEETS, CHOCOLATES)
LARRY ENJOYS RIDING HIS BIKE
LARRY ENJOYS RUNNING
LARRY ENJOYS A BATH
LARRY ENJOYS WASHING UP, SPLASHING WATER
LARRY ENJOYS TEARING PAPER, ESPECIALLY WHEN HE IS AGITATED
LARRY ENJOYS SPENDING TIME IN HIS ROOM ALONE
LARRY ENJOYS VISITING HIS MOTHER AT HOME
LARRY ENJOYS DRAWING
LARRY ENJOYS JIGSAW PUZZLES
LARRY ENJOYS BEING OUTDOORS
LARRY ENJOYS SWIMMING
LARRY ENJOYS MUSIC

Conditions for Positive Behaviour

LARRY FEELS SAFER WITH PEOPLE HE HAS KNOWN A LONG TIME
LARRY IS CALMER WHEN HE KNOWS THE ROUTINE
LARRY IS CALMER WHEN HIS TIME IS STRUCTURED
LARRY IS HAPPIER IN A QUIET, UNCROWDED ROOM

Conditions for Learning

LARRY CAN CONCENTRATE FOR UP TO 5 MINUTES
LARRY CAN SIT FOR LONG PERIODS OF TIME
LARRY IS MORE CO-OPERATIVE IF HE IS REWARDED WITH ONE OF HIS FAVOURITE FOODS

Figure 2.4 An example of a strengths list.

5. **Personal setting factors.** Information from historical records, from structured discussions, from interviews with other significant people, from observation charts and frequency charts may reveal some clear relationships between personal setting conditions and the behaviour (for example, an increase in the behaviour premenstrually or in the days leading up to a *grand mal* seizure, following a poor night's sleep, when low mood is experienced, when a key worker leaves for another job).

6. **Related skills deficits.** Information about the individual's skills may show that the person lacks the specific communication, social or occupational skills to achieve the results that are currently being achieved by the problem behaviour (for example, the skill of communicating 'I don't want to', 'spend some time with me'; the skill of doing something constructive with one's hands; the skill of waiting one's turn in the normal flow of a two-way conversation; the skill of sharing). It may reveal a more general deficit in a skill area which appears related to the problem behaviour. For example, a poor concept of time and inability to sequence events in time may be an important factor in a person having outbursts of anger or agitation when unreasonable demands (for example, lunch at 11 a.m., going to the day-centre on Sunday morning) are not met.

A formulation of the problem can now be made using the format illustrated in Figure 2.5.

The case study on which the formulation is based (Larry) appears in Chapter 13. It will be noted from Figure 2.5 that the statements made about the factors implicated in the problematic behaviour all start with the words 'seem to . . .', 'appear to be . . .', which reflects the fact that there can never be any absolutely certainty of the specific factors involved and their relative contribution but only an informed judgment, which subsequently may or may not prove to be accurate. Only the success or failure of the interventions which follow from the assessment will attest to its accuracy. Nevertheless, this summary can now lead to some general statements about the issues which need to be addressed in order to help the individual overcome his difficulties.

Step ⟩ **9** ⟨	**Make a general statement of needs in relation to the behaviour of concern**

The formulation of the problem should now be reviewed and a list of needs generated from each section where relevant factors have been identified. Figure 2.6 shows an example of a needs statement which has been generated from the formulation shown in Figure 2.5. It is

A S.T.A.R. ANALYSIS OF PROBLEMATIC BEHAVIOUR THE FORMULATION

Name *LARRY*

Definition of Behaviour

SCREAMING
RUSHING ABOUT
PULLING THINGS OFF WALLS AND SHELVES
PUSHING ANYONE IN HIS WAY

Appears to achieve the following results

RELEASE FROM HIGH LEVEL OF AGITATION
EXPRESSION OF HIGH LEVEL OF ANXIETY

Appears to be set off by the following triggers

AN OVERLOAD OF AGITATION/EMOTION
(TRIGGERS WHICH INCREASE AGITATION – WAITING, NOISE, A COMMOTION, BEING
TOLD NOT TO TOUCH THINGS)
PEOPLE SITTING NEXT TO HIM
BEING REFUSED MORE FOOD

Seems to occur in the context of the following environmental setting conditions

Physical	Occupational
NOISY, CROWDED PLACES (ESPECIALLY	*UNSTRUCTURED TIMES OF DAY (ESPECIALLY*
MINIBUS, DINING ROOM)	*ON RETURN FROM DAY CENTRE)*
LARGE GROUP ACTIVITIES	*MAJOR CHANGES IN HIS ROUTINE*
	(HOLIDAYS, STAFF CHANGES)
	BIRTHDAY PARTIES

Appears to be related to the following personal setting conditions

Physical	Psychological
HIGH LEVELS OF AGITATION WHICH	*CONSTANT STATE OF ANXIETY*
CAN LAST SEVERAL MONTHS	

Appear to be associated with a deficit in the following skill/skill areas

INABILITY TO WAIT FOR MORE THAN 4 SECONDS
INABILITY TO CONTROL HIS OWN HIGH AROUSAL
DOES NOT KNOW HOW TO ASK PEOPLE TO MOVE AWAY

Figure 2.5 An example of a S.T.A.R. formulation of a problematic behaviour.

NEEDS LIST
Name *LARRY*
Description of behaviour *AGITATED OUTBURSTS = SCREAMING, RUSHING ABOUT, PULLING THINGS OFF WALLS AND SHELVES, PUSHING ANYONE IN HIS WAY*

1. *LARRY NEEDS AN APPROPRIATE MEANS OF REDUCING HIS AGITATION*

2. *LARRY NEEDS TO BE ABLE TO WAIT FOR THINGS WITHOUT BECOMING AGITATED*

3. *LARRY NEEDS TO BE ABLE TO REMAIN CALM WHEN TRAVELLING USING TRANSPORT*

4. *LARRY NEEDS TO REMAIN CALM DURING MEALTIMES*

5. *LARRY NEEDS TO REMAIN CALM DURING THE TIME BETWEEN RETURNING HOME*

    FROM THE DAY CENTRE AND HAVING HIS EVENING MEAL

6. *LARRY NEEDS TO BE LESS ANXIOUS*

7. *LARRY NEEDS TO COPE BETTER WITH HOLIDAY PERIODS*

8. *LARRY NEEDS TO COPE BETTER WITH NEW STAFF MEMBERS*

9. *LARRY NEEDS TO HAVE FEWER OUTBURSTS OF AGITATION*

10. *LARRY NEEDS TO BE ABLE TO TOLERATE PEOPLE BEING NEXT TO HIM*

11. *LARRY NEEDS AN APPROPRIATE MEANS OF ASKING PEOPLE TO MOVE AWAY*

Figure 2.6 An example of a needs list which relates to a person's problematic behaviour.

important that needs should be stated in terms of positive behavioural outcomes which would occur if the need was met. From the list of needs priority interventions will be set.

- Some interventions will require few or no additional resources and will simply require minor adjustments to be made within a person's environment.
- Some interventions will have major resource implications (staffing and financial).
- Some interventions may require input from an external agent (for example, counsellor, speech therapist).
- Some interventions will be expected to have a fairly immediate impact upon the behaviour.
- Some interventions will be expected to show long-term gains for the individual rather than have an immediate impact upon the behaviour.
- Priorities will depend on available resources, access to professional support services and the urgency of the problem.

The needs list is intended to be the basis of a long-term strategic plan aimed at helping the individual overcome the immediate problem and to decrease his vulnerability to developing new problems or of the problem recurring in the future.

SUMMARY

When a person who has severe learning disabilities is identified as having a serious behavioural problem with which he requires help, a considerable amount of preparatory work needs to be completed before a useful therapeutic package can be put together. Hasty decisions based upon inadequate information and prompted by a feeling of urgency will fail in the long term.

A long-term perspective is essential, not least because problematic behaviours are likely to serve important functions in the life of the individual concerned. Thus, if they are to be reduced then other skills must be encouraged and new skills developed to replace less appropriate actions. Environments may need to be adapted to meet the individual's specific needs. Physical, emotional and cognitive issues may need to be addressed. All this requires a period of assessment of the problematic behaviour itself, of the person's skills, of the environments in which the behaviour occurs, of the person himself and the person's history. From such an assessment, priority needs can be established which will form the basis of a comprehensive package of therapeutic interventions.

ASSESSING THE PROBLEM

SUMMARY OF STEPS

1

Define the behaviour

2

Assess the function of the behaviour

3

Assess setting conditions
associated with the problematic behaviour

4

Assess skills

5

Assess motivators

6

Assess conditions for positive behaviour

7

Summarize assessment information

8

Make a formulation about the problematic behaviour

9

Make a general statement
of needs in relation to the behaviour of concern

Defining goals

3

The approach to behavioural change which is presented in this book stresses the need for clarity – clarity with respect to what is to be achieved, clarity with respect to how it is to be achieved. This basic principle is central to both motivation and to efficiency.

People who have learning disabilities cannot afford inefficiency on the part of those paid to help them. Progress for them is hard won. It is vital that the resources of whoever is involved and whatever the context (student–teacher, client–counsellor, resident–carer) be directed with maximum precision. Clarity of purpose will encourage efficiency of approach. It will also assist the motivation of all those involved as it will enable them to see clearly when goals have been achieved.

The assessment of a person's difficulties with respect to his behaviour will have led to a summary of needs. Some of these will have been stated in very general terms, indicating areas in which work needs to take place (for example, communication, self-occupation). Others will be less general, though still lacking precision (for example, to reduce self-injury). These general statements need to be translated into specific goals or action targets. These goals in turn will require further analysis into sub-goals. Behavioural change, as was stated in Chapter 1, is usually best effected in a graded, step-by-step manner. Goal-setting is thus relevant to the development of virtually all aspects of the therapeutic package, which are detailed in subsequent chapters of this book. When developing programmes of change, therefore, the reader should use this chapter in conjunction with other relevant chapters.

GOAL-SETTING – GENERAL PRINCIPLES

DEFINING GOALS IN ACTION TERMS

Maximum clarity is achieved when goals are expressed in terms of observable and specific actions rather than in terms of unobservable

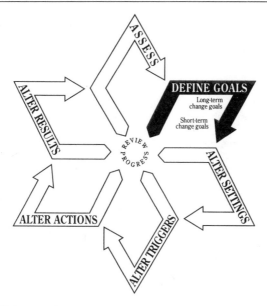

Figure 3.1 Defining goals.

inner states or abstract generalizations. For example, the goal of helping an individual to 'be more sociable' is a general statement about an abstract notion of 'sociability' – it could be interpreted in many ways. The possibility of people making personal interpretations of such a goal reduces the likelihood of a coherent, consistent approach. Furthermore, it would be difficult to know when or whether such an abstract goal had been achieved. This, in turn, does little for the motivation of the individual in difficulty or those trying to help him. Lack of clarity is likely to decrease the sense of achievement of all involved and to create disagreements, which in turn may impair the effectiveness of planned interventions.

Precise goals are ones that refer to a specific action or actions which can be observed and agreed upon. For example, 'Being more sociable' could be defined as:

Initiating conversation at the dinner table.
Playing football with other children in the playground.
Saying 'Good morning' on arrival at the day-centre.

Goals will sometimes be defined in terms of an absence or reduction in behaviour. The emphasis nevertheless remains upon that which can be observed and easily agreed upon. Thus being more sociable might also be defined as:

Table 3.1 Examples of long-term goals relating to observable behaviours vs. less observable states

Abstract goals	Action goals
Improve social relationships	Roll a ball back and forth with another child
Be more co-operative	Wash dishes after lunch
Improve emotional adjustment	Have temper outburst less than three times a week
Improve concentration span	Stay in kitchen for 10 minutes during preparation of meal
Improve sexual adjustment	Masturbate only in own room or toilet cubicle
Develop potential	Master five new skills on community living checklist
Understand the concept 'three'	Put three packets of cereal and three tins of beans into shopping trolley when requested

Not hitting people unless attacked first.
Not biting fellow residents when they approach.

Only by being precise and specific about goals of change is it possible:

- to know exactly what one is trying to achieve;
- to know whether or not achievement has occurred.

Precision in goals can also help to clarify how change can be effected. A clear aim often makes the route to change more obvious. Further examples of the differences between action goals and 'fuzzier' aims are given in Table 3.1.

IDENTIFYING ACHIEVABLE LONG-TERM GOALS

It is important to have some idea of the time-span involved in achieving goals that are set. Translating statements of needs into specific goals will identify objectives that are relatively long-term. Such long-term goals are important because they give overall purpose to the day-to-day activities of service provision. However, the estimated time-span for a long-term goal should not be excessive. Goals that might take several years to accomplish tend to be forgotten or to lose their capacity to guide and to motivate.

As a rule of thumb, long-term goals should be those that might be achieved within a 6–12-month period.

An estimate of what is achievable over the time-span will depend upon characteristics of the individual and the resources available to assist development. Thus the first step in goal-setting is to translate statements of needs into action objectives achievable within a 6–12-month period. These then require further analysis in order to inform more day-to-day practice.

BREAKING LONG-TERM GOALS INTO STEPS

Skill-teaching

Long-term skill-teaching goals are likely to involve a task too complex to be mastered at one go. In order to make it easier for the individual to learn, the task needs to be broken down into small steps which can be taught one at a time. Many complex skills are taught in this way. Driving a car, for example, involves a number of skills such as starting, accelerating, braking, steering and clutch control with each skill integrated into a series of performances such as reversing or parking. These many skills, which combine to form the very complex task of driving, are rarely taught to drivers during their first lesson. They are broken down into a series of tasks and steps within tasks, which are taught over a number of lessons. As each task or step is mastered, another is introduced.

For people with learning difficulties the skills which need to be acquired to help them cope better with their world, and thereby reduce the need to behave in challenging or inappropriate ways, are likely to prove equally complex. It is important, therefore, to simplify the learning process by breaking the skills down into steps and teaching them one step at a time, in a graded way.

Breaking complex skills down into their component skills and breaking component skills into steps has many advantages.

1. It enables the person teaching to assess more accurately how much of the task the individual can already perform.
2. It enables the person teaching to assess which aspects of the task still need to be learned.
3. It enables the actual teaching to be organized into manageable 'chunks' and a skill to be taught systematically in a step-by-step manner.

Problematic or inappropriate behaviour

The process of breaking down behaviour considered to be problematic into longer-term change goals is not quite the same as the task analysis of skill-teaching goals. It is about reducing rather than building behaviour, which can be a long-term process and is rarely a matter of sudden change. There are a number of reasons for this. It is not that the behaviour itself is complex, rather it is because it usually has many contributing causes that are not always easy to identify. In addition, the methods for effecting change can be less precise than in the skill-teaching situation. It is a 'messier' business than skill-teaching.

Task analysis of skills makes the actual teaching easier and more efficient. Breaking down goals in relation to behavioural problems makes objectives more realistic and helps to sustain the motivation of those involved.

There are two common ways of breaking down goals related to the reduction of behavioural problems.

1. A breakdown in terms of frequency. This involves taking the present frequency of the behaviour and the desired frequency in terms of final outcome. The difference between these two frequencies is then split into a series of intermediate goals. For example, if an individual currently hits out on average ten times a day and the aim is that this should be reduced to zero, then targets could be set in terms of successive reduction by two (eight, six, four, two, zero). Such a graded approach to behavioural reduction is the basis of some of the work described in Chapter 8 (differential reinforcement of low rate of problematic behaviour).

2. A breakdown by situation. For example, if an individual spits at very high frequency onto solid surfaces in all situations and it is desired that the spitting be confined to private areas, then goals can be set in terms of changes in specific situations until the end-point is reached. Thus the first step might be to eliminate spitting in one-to-one teaching, then at meal times, then in unstructured group leisure activities and so on.

Breaking down problematic behaviours in this way sustains motivation and encourages appropriate expectations in terms of progressive rather than spectacular change. Unlike skill-teaching, however, it does not make the process of change easier or give any pointers as to how progress is to be made.

ORGANIZING SKILL-TEACHING STEPS INTO CHANGE SEQUENCES

Effecting change using a graded approach, which involves breaking tasks and goals into small steps, requires consideration of the order of teaching the steps and of the number of steps which can be taught at any one time. There are a number of ways in which steps can be organized for skill-teaching.

Part-task chaining

This involves teaching a task one step at a time. As one step is mastered another is added and this process continues until the learner can manage the whole task. For example, learning to operate a video recorder could start with the learner selecting the assigned channel on the TV while the rest of the task is completed by the person teaching. Once the first step is executed successfully a new one is added. Thus, the second step might involve the learner loading the tape into the video recorder. The third step might involve the learner pressing the 'record' button.

The steps in the task are seen as links in a chain. As one link is forged another is added and so on until the chain (skill) is complete. There are two ways in which a skill can be built up step by step:

1. Forward chaining. This involves teaching the first step in the sequence with the teacher then completing or helping the individual to complete the remainder of the sequence. Once the first step is mastered, the second step is added to the first and the two steps are taught together, with the teacher completing or helping the individual through the remaining steps. Then the third step is added and so on, until the final step is reached. A skill such as pointing, for example, might be taught using a forward-chaining sequence: the learner is taught first to stretch out the arm, then to shape the hand correctly and finally to line up the outstretched arm with the object, hand shaped correctly in a pointing position.
2. Backward chaining. This involves teaching the last step in the sequence first. Once this step is mastered, the penultimate step is linked with the final step and so on, until all steps have been learned. Learning to operate the video recorder could thus be taught using a backward-chaining method. The learner is taught to press the 'record' button on the video recorder, the teacher having selected the appropriate channel and loaded the tape. Once this task is mastered the learner is taught to load the tape (and press the 're-cord' button), the teacher having selected the appropriate channel. Finally the learner is taught to select the channel, (then load the tape and press the 'record' button).

There are two important points to be made about a chaining approach:

1. The number of links in the chain or steps in the sequence is varied according to the needs of the learner. The more difficult the task for the learner, the smaller the steps required and hence the greater the number of steps.
2. Where feasible, a backward-chaining approach should be selected because the learner's contribution always leads to task completion.

This will often enhance the motivation to continue working at the task. This is because the learner's action always achieves a purpose, a result natural to the task in question.

Whole-task teaching

Whole-task teaching takes the learner through the whole skill every time that it is practised. As much (or as little) help as needed is given at every stage. Thus, in the example given earlier, the learner would participate actively in all aspects of operating the video recorder. Progress would be effected by a gradual reduction in the amount of help given at each stage in the task (Chapter 6).

Whole-task teaching has the advantage of teaching a skill in a more integrated, naturalistic manner. It encounters difficulties where the sequence is long and/or steps are especially difficult for the person. This may lead to frustration and impatience on the part of the learner or teacher and this will interfere with the learning process.

Shaping

Shaping (sometimes known as response shaping or successive approximation) is a method of building up a skill using only reinforcement, initially to reward behaviour that is closest at the time to the desired objective. As the use of this behaviour becomes the norm for the individual concerned the basis of reinforcement is shifted to an action that is a bit closer to the desired objective. In other words, the person now needs to do a little more or a little better in order to receive reinforcement. In this way the individual learns, little by little, to act in a way that is more and more like the skilled outcome desired.

For example, an individual may never sit next to others in group activities and resists any prompting to trigger this behaviour. The person may, however, sometimes sit on a chair about 10 feet from the group. The desired objective is for him to sit with a group for the duration of a whole activity. A powerful reinforcer would initially be given each time the person remained seated for a predetermined time (for example, 1 minute) at a distance of 10 feet from the group. Once this was occurring regularly the chair could be moved a little closer and the reinforcement given for sitting 9 feet from the group for a given period of time. No reinforcement would be given if the student moved the chair back or left the seat before the target time had elapsed. In this gradual way, time seated and closeness to the group could be built up until the person was sitting with the group for the duration of the activity. Shaping is particularly helpful where an action is difficult to trigger directly (for example, speech) or where a person resists triggers provided by others (the commonest resistances are to instructions and to physical prompts).

ORGANIZING THE REDUCTION OF PROBLEMATIC BEHAVIOUR INTO CHANGE SEQUENCES

As discussed earlier, breaking down goals related to behavioural problems is rather different from breaking down skill-teaching tasks. However, the idea of a series of intermediate goals as a strategy for assisting larger changes remains valid. The need for such an organized strategy is greatest when seeking to change a very high-frequency behaviour or when working in conditions where resources are extremely limited. In these circumstances it may be useful to focus efforts for change into specific, discriminable situations ('sessions'). A systematic way of working is applied in these situations and its effectiveness assessed. If progress is made, then the way of working can be extended to another specific situation. This process continues until change has been effected in all those situations where it is important for change to occur.

The second strategy, mentioned earlier, is to break down the long-term goal into a logical series of graded reductions in frequency. This takes account of motivational considerations rather than the process of behavioural change itself. Motivation to persist with long-term therapeutic interventions is often sustained only as long as progress is evident, as long as goals are being achieved. Thus, setting small modest goals in a step-wise fashion is more likely to have a positive impact on the motivation of those working to effect change.

SETTING SHORT-TERM OBJECTIVES

Teaching skills step by step reduces the risk of failure and increases the chance of success. Working to reduce inappropriate or unhelpful behaviour in stages increases the perception of progress and the 'sessional' approach provides ready feedback on the effectiveness of specific ways of working.

Experiencing progress is important for all those involved in the process of change. Breaking down long-term goals raises the likelihood of this experience. This is consolidated by formalizing shorter-term goals. Having a series of shorter-term objectives provides a more continuous sense of achievement and encourages persistence, which is so essential to overcoming serious learning and behavioural difficulties; it also helps to refine the approaches used for teaching and behaviour reduction. It is most unlikely that the 'right' approach to achieving a long-term goal will be found straight away. In setting short-term objectives one is providing the opportunity not just to review achievements regularly but, in the light of this, to review the means being used to reach objectives. This allows intervention programmes to be modified and adjusted regularly in line with progress made.

The final step in a comprehensive plan is to set clear and precise short-term objectives. These will be based upon the breakdown of the targeted skill or behavioural problem, and the strategy that is to be used in presenting the skill or in effecting behaviour reduction. As a rough guide, such short-term objectives should be achievable within a 1–6-week period.

SUMMARY

There are a number of steps that need to be taken after a management plan has been drawn up. 'Needs' which have been identified must be translated into long-term goals. The tasks involved must be analysed and broken down into a series of small steps linked by a sequencing strategy. Finally these steps must be translated into very precise short-term objectives, which will be the immediate focus of programmes of change.

In the first part of this chapter the principles involved in establishing specific short-term goals have been outlined. In the second part, the steps that need to be followed to establish such specific and immediate goals are detailed.

PROCEDURES FOR ESTABLISHING SPECIFIC GOALS

Having listed a person's strengths and identified priority areas of work in the form of 'needs', the next stage is to decide how these needs can be met and to set specific goals in areas of skill building and problem behaviour reduction.

Step ⟩ **1** ⟨ **Translate needs into long-term goals**

Select long-term goals

There are usually a number of possible ways of meeting a person's identified needs. For example, the expressed need 'To use appropriate means of letting people know what he wants' could be met by teaching the person names of objects, by teaching the signs for specific objects, by teaching a more general sign for 'please' or by teaching the learner to take others over to what is wanted. If long-term goals are to have an impact upon the problem behaviour, they need to be achieved as quickly as possible. In terms of skill development, the best approach to selecting goals is to look at the skills which the person already has (summarized in the strengths list) and, if possible, to **build on these existing skills** by encouraging their increased usage or to use them as a foundation for new skills. Thus, if the person uses a lot of gestures but has no speech sounds, then it would be more appropriate to teach signs rather than spoken names of objects.

As regards problematic behaviour, the long-term goal will inevitably involve some level of reduction. However, most behaviour is acceptable under some circumstances and if the individual already has an acceptable element in the behaviour it will be important to target this for an increase as well as the decreases required. For example, if a person does masturbate in private then it is as important to encourage this as a goal of change as it is to see a reduction of masturbation in public areas.

Write long-term goals

Long-term goals describe in specific terms what the person will be doing after the programme of change. They are written in language that refers as much as possible to easily observed actions rather than to unobservable inner states or dispositions. Table 3.1 illustrates the differences between long-term goals expressed in action-oriented terms and those expressed less precisely, in abstract terms.

Long-term action goals state **who** will do **what** under what **conditions** (and with how much **help**).

Who	The name of the person who will achieve the action goal.
Will do what	The action that the person will be observed to carry out (or not carry out, in the case of an inappropriate behaviour).
Under what conditions	The conditions under which the action is to be performed. This includes information about the settings (for example, time, place, situation).
With how much help (optional)	The level of independence with which the skill is to be performed. This includes information about the triggers (prompts) which need to be provided.

Table 3.2 gives examples of how needs can be translated into long-term action oriented goals.

Table 3.2 Translating needs into long-term goals

Need	Who	Will do what	Under what circumstances	With how much help
To stop throwing objects at people	Joan	will not throw things at people or on to the floor	when in the lounge	
To calm himself when agitated	Fred	will practise relaxation	for 10 minutes each day	when reminded
To come away from dangerous activities	Tina	will respond appropriately to the instruction 'Come here'	when out for walks with staff	
To indicate appropriately if he does not want to do something	Peter	will sign 'No'	if he does not want the activity which is offered	without help

Step ⟨ 2 ⟩   Break long-term goals into achievable steps

Long-term goals are set for a 6–12-month time period. The next step is to break down these longer-term goals into sub-goals that are small enough to achieve within a 1–6-week period.

Skills

Skill development goals need to be analysed at two levels: complex tasks as component skills and component skills as steps.

Complex tasks as component skills

The first level of analysis looks at whether a targeted skill can be broken down into a number of individual skills. For example, the task of playing ludo involves the following separate skills:

- sitting in one place for at least a few minutes;
- looking at dice and board;
- counting up to six;
- turn-taking;
- recognizing and matching colours;
- picking up counters and dice.

The task of crossing the road safely involves at least the following skills:

- recognizing the kerb side;
- stopping at the kerb side;
- looking to both sides;
- listening for the noise of cars;
- responding to the triggers 'no cars, no sound of cars' by crossing the road;
- responding to the triggers 'moving car approaching, sound of car' by standing still.

Component skills as steps

Once a task has been analysed into its component skills, each component skill can then be broken down into a series of small steps, which will take the individual from his present level of skill to the desired level. The component skill of 'looking at the dice and board' during a game of ludo can be broken down as:

- looking at the dice and board briefly when it is taken out of the box;
- looking at the dice as it is thrown;
- looking at the dice as it is thrown until it settles on the table;
- looking at the dice long enough for the spots to be counted and observing the counter being moved;
- looking at the dice and board while two people have a turn at throwing the dice and moving their counters.

The component skills of stopping at the kerb side can be broken down into:

- stopping at the kerb when the carer, who is walking with arms linked with the learner, stops;
- stopping at the kerb when the carer, who is walking alongside the learner, gives a verbal instruction to stop;
- stopping at the kerb when the carer, who is walking alongside the learner, verbally reminds the learner that he should stop at the kerb side whenever this is encountered;
- stopping at the kerb with no verbal reminders from the carer, who is walking alongside the learner;
- stopping at the kerb when walking independently.

There are no 'right' number of steps into which a task can be broken down. The important point is that steps are small enough for the individual to master them within a short space of time – no more than 6 weeks. If steps are mastered very quickly, then subsequent steps can be made larger. If, on the other hand, the individual experiences considerable difficulty in learning a step, then it may be necessary to break that step down into even smaller steps.

Just as there is no 'right' number of steps into which a task can be broken down, so too there is no 'right' way to perform a task. Most skills can be performed in a variety of ways. For example, dice can be thrown downwards from a clenched fist, they can be thrown upwards from a flat palm or they can be thrown outwards from a clenched fist with a pushing movement of the arm. The choice of approach should be dictated by the current abilities and preferences of the learner relevant to the task in hand. If the learner has already made some progress using a particular method it will usually be better to build on this rather than to 'impose' a 'textbook' approach.

Some complex skills will require a good deal of imagination on the part of the person carrying out the teaching to get the learner from the present level to the desired objective. In deciding how to analyse a task it is important to identify what is realistic for the individual, to build on existing skills where possible and to incorporate the learner's preferences as much as possible.

Problematic behaviour

Behaviour may be judged as problematic because it occurs too frequently, because it occurs in too many situations, because it goes on for too long and/or because it is too severe. The long-term objective will identify the key 'dimension' which makes the behaviour problematic to others (frequency, extensiveness, duration, severity). This can then be broken down into steps along that dimension. A behaviour may be targeted to occur less and less frequently, in fewer and fewer situations, to last less and less time or to be expressed less and less severely. This breakdown will make it easier to see progress and this in turn will encourage persistence and refinement of intervention programmes.

Step ⟩ 3 ⟨   Organize steps into change sequences

Having analysed the skill or the problematic behaviour into smaller change steps it is necessary to identify a strategy for implementing change.

Skill-teaching

Whole-task teaching or part-task chaining

There are no rigid rules for selecting whole-task as opposed to part-task approaches. A whole-task strategy will be preferred when:

- the individual can already perform several parts of the skill;
- the individual enjoys the task in question;
- the task can be completed with the individual's usual span of concentration.

If these conditions are not met then a part-task approach is to be preferred. For example, if the person can sustain looking for several minutes and can be prompted to take turns, can count to three and can pick up small counters and a dice, then whole-task teaching of the game of ludo will be appropriate. If, on the other hand, the person's skills are more limited, such that even picking up the counters and dice poses problems and/or his concentration span is very short, then part-task teaching may be more appropriate.

Backward or forward chaining

Logic requires certain skills to be taught in a fixed sequence. For example, it is necessary to stop at the kerb side in order to look in both directions and listen for oncoming traffic. In such cases the skill itself determines the order of teaching. With other skills there is more choice. For example, a person could be taught to play ludo by being taught first to move the counter the required number of places or the teaching could start with learning to throw the dice. In general, when there is a choice, backward chaining is to be preferred because teaching the final step first means that the learner always completes the task in the course of learning. This itself can be a powerful source of encouragement.

Chaining or shaping

Chaining procedures tend to be more efficient for new skill-teaching as the person carrying out the teaching is able to manage directly the learning process. Shaping requires waiting for the learner to perform the target behaviour or skill in question. This may limit the number of teaching opportunities and reduce the learning impact of the opportunities that do occur if the person carrying out the teaching is not able to respond immediately. Shaping is most likely to be of use when there are difficulties in prompting: some tasks are difficult to prompt, some learners ignore or resist prompts. In general, chaining procedures are to be preferred for teaching new skills.

Analysis of problematic behaviours

There are two major strategies in problem-behaviour analysis: goals may be set in terms of reducing frequency, duration or severity across all situations; alternatively goals may be set in terms of change within a limited situation (time, place, activity). The number of situations in which change is targeted are then progressively expanded. Breakdown by situation is likely to be more helpful with very high-frequency behaviours or where resources such as staffing levels are spread very unevenly across situations so that initial efforts need to be focused onto the best resourced situations.

Step ⟨ 4 ⟩   Set short-term change objectives

Having organized a strategy for presenting the steps that will lead to the long-term goals, the final step in planning an intervention programme is to establish the immediate goal of the intervention – in other words to specify a short-term change objective.

Short-term change objectives are statements about the immediate goal of any intervention programme. A person should be able to achieve such objectives within 1–6 weeks. Achievement of a series of short-term objectives will lead to the ultimate attainment of the long-term goal. It is essential that short-term objectives are stated very precisely so that there can be no doubt when they have been achieved. Achievement of one short-term objective is a prerequisite for moving on to the next objective.

Write short-term change objectives

A precise objective will state: **who** will do **what** under what **conditions** with how much **help** and to what degree of **success**.

Who	The name of the individual who will be performing the action in question.
Will do what	The action that the person will be observed to carry out (or not carry out in the case of a problematic behaviour).
Under what conditions	The conditions under which the action is to be performed. This includes information about the settings (especially time, place, situation) under which the action is to occur.
With how much help	The level of independence with which the action is to be performed. This provides information about triggers which will be

	provided to enable the individual to perform the action.
To what degree of success	The frequency or duration of an action that needs to be achieved under the given circumstances if one is to be sure that the step has been mastered.

Examples of precisely stated short-term objectives are given in Table 3.3. An illustration of how a single long-term goal can be achieved via a series of specific short-term objectives is shown in Table 3.4. Programmes based upon short-term objectives are reviewed regularly (1–6 weeks) to see whether success has been achieved according to the criteria stated. If progress does not occur it may be necessary to persist a little longer or to set more limited short-term objectives. If objectives are achieved in less than the review period then subsequent steps can be made larger.

SUMMARY

Before implementing any behavioural change plan there must be clear and concrete goals: these need to be both long- and short-term goals and to be realistic in terms of both the learner and the available resources. Setting such goals requires analysis of the task involved and identifying a sequence whereby individual steps can be organized to

Table 3.3 Examples of short-term behavioural objectives

Who	Will do what	Under what circumstances	With how much help	To what degree of success
Peter	will come to his teacher	during play time	on request	three times out of three for 2 weeks
Mary	will sign 'No'	if offered an activity she does not want	without prompting	three times during morning work
John	will draw in his colouring book	alongside Mark	with occasional reminders from his mother	for 15 minutes three times in 1 week
Maggie	will lie on the floor with eyes closed	in her bedroom each evening	with reminders to stay 'calm' and relaxed	for 10 minutes on five consecutive days

Table 3.4 Reaching a long-term goal by a series of short-term objectives: Peter will practise relaxation for 10 minutes each day when asked

Who	Will do what	Under what circumstances	With how much help	To what degree of success
Peter	will lie on the floor	in a darkened room	with a carer continually talking in a soothing voice, physically prompting him to remain still	for 30 seconds on five successive sessions
Peter	will lie on the floor	in a darkened room	with a carer continually talking in a soothing voice, verbally prompting him to remain still	for 30 seconds on five successive sessions
Peter	will lie on the floor, his eyes closed	in a darkened room	with verbal prompts to be 'calm' and 'relaxed' every 5 seconds	for 30 seconds on five successive sessions
Peter	will lie on the floor, his eyes closed	in a darkened room	with verbal prompts to be 'calm' and 'relaxed' every 5 seconds	for 1 minute on five successive sessions
Peter	will lie on the floor, his eyes closed	in a darkened room	with verbal prompts to be 'calm' and 'relaxed' every 5 seconds	for 5 minutes on five successive sessions
Peter	will lie on the floor, his eyes closed	in a darkened room	with verbal prompts to be 'calm' and 'relaxed' every 10 seconds	for 5 minutes on five successive sessions
Peter	will lie on the floor, his eyes closed	in a darkened room	with verbal prompts to be 'calm' and 'relaxed' every 20 seconds	for 5 minutes on five successive sessions
Peter	will lie on the floor, his eyes closed	in a darkened room	with verbal prompts to be 'calm' and 'relaxed' every 20 seconds	for 10 minutes on five successive sessions

produce progress towards a long-term goal through a series of short-term goals. This will require effort to complete but investment at this stage will save time in the long run and enhance the efficiency of work to teach new skills and to reduce problematic behaviours.

DEFINING GOALS

SUMMARY OF STEPS

1

Translate needs into long-term goals

2

Break long-term goals into achievable steps

3

Organize steps into change sequences

4

Set short-term change objectives

Altering setting conditions

4

Setting conditions are those factors that act over time to create and strengthen motivations for achieving particular results which meet the individual's wants and needs. Settings influence the power and priority of motivations: observed behaviours are the means whereby the individual seeks to get these wants and needs met. The present chapter is concerned with the setting conditions which have been identified as relevant to the person's inappropriate or disturbed behaviour and with methods for reducing the strength of the motivation that the behaviour seeks to satisfy. If a means can be found of altering the relevant setting conditions, then this is likely to reduce the need to act in ways that others find disturbing.

It must be remembered, however, that addressing setting conditions is only one part of the therapeutic package. Interventions at this level alone are unlikely to lead to permanent elimination of a behavioural difficulty. Many, though not all, setting conditions represent some form of adversity (for example, pain, emotional distress, trauma). Even if the adversity is eliminated it is unlikely, in the longer term, that any ordinary life can be constructed without another form of adversity being experienced at some time or another during the person's lifetime. The long-term resolution of behavioural difficulties is, therefore, bound to involve the person learning better ways of expressing his wants and needs and of handling the adversity and discomfort that he experiences during the course of everyday life.

Work on setting conditions must, therefore, be considered alongside the work discussed in subsequent chapters. It is an adjunct not a replacement for that work. It is a feature of the S.T.A.R. approach that work is needed at every level involved in a particular problem in order that a long-term resolution can be effected.

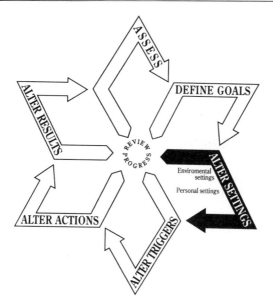

Figure 4.1 Altering setting conditions.

ALTERING SETTING CONDITIONS–GENERAL PRINCIPLES

The term 'setting conditions' refers to a variety of factors that affect behaviour. It is a general category that incorporates diverse influences, both environmental and personal. Interventions at the settings level are likewise varied, ranging from very practical, easily made alterations in everyday life (for example, making more activities available), to complex and specialized interventions (for example, psychotherapy). It is hard to generalize across such a range of work and the level of precision is not nearly as great as that to be found in subsequent chapters.

It should also be noted that there is far less research information about how to work effectively at the level of personal settings to help people with learning difficulties, compared to the information available about how to work at this level with people who do not have learning difficulties. For example, there is relatively little research work available on the best ways to provide bereavement counselling for people with learning disabilities, or on how to provide cognitive therapy for depression or on how to provide psychotherapy for those who have been victims of childhood abuse. Nevertheless, while there may be less certainty about how best to proceed in some situations, it would be unjust and inappropriate to deny people with learning difficulties access to such forms of help. Well thought out experimentation and evaluation is the only way in which knowledge can advance.

Interventions at the setting-conditions level can, in general, be divided into two categories.

1. Interventions which seek to eliminate or alleviate environmental setting factors by work on the relevant environmental conditions.
2. Interventions which seek to eliminate or alleviate personal setting conditions by direct work with the individual.

WORKING TO ELIMINATE OR ALLEVIATE ENVIRONMENTAL
SETTING CONDITIONS

Some environmental factors that may be involved in the development and maintenance of disturbed behaviour can be removed altogether from the individual's life. For example, if a person lives in a residential setting where there is continual conflict and an overall poor quality of relationships, and this is reflected in the person's emotions (anger) and behaviour (aggression), an alternative placement in a better quality social environment may be one option for help.

It is not usually as easy as this: sometimes such elimination is not possible, sometimes it is possible but only at a high cost to the long-term prospects of the person concerned. For example, if a person's behavioural outbursts only occurred in situations outside the home setting, then it would be possible to resolve the problem by the individual not going out at all. (Indeed such temporary elimination of a problematic setting condition is often useful when things are at crisis level and everyone needs some breathing space.) However, as a long-term solution it would be unacceptable: the restrictions on the development of the individual and of others who share in the life of the individual would be too high a price to pay for this approach to behaviour change. There is, therefore, a need to consider other, less dramatic ways of working at the setting-conditions level – alleviation rather than elimination.

Alleviating adverse physical setting conditions

Physical settings associated with an increased risk of behavioural difficulties include factors such as temperature, illumination, smell, crowding and noise. Adverse physical setting conditions can influence general stress and anxiety and can decrease tolerance levels to daily pressures. Some physical setting conditions tend to be relatively permanent features of the environment (for example, illumination, temperature), others are associated with the presence of other people (for example, crowding, noise) and may, therefore, be more transient features of the environment. Where adverse physical setting conditions have been identified as having an influence upon a person's mood and consequent behaviour, then it becomes important that these conditions are alleviated. (The alternative is to teach the person to accept them!) Sometimes the task of alleviating adverse aspects of the physical environment may require a large financial outlay, which may be out of the immediate control of carers working within a care organization (for example, building an extension onto a lounge, in order to provide a quiet room within a house shared by several residents, or providing thick carpets and curtains to dampen loud noise). Sometimes changes may simply require a little ingenuity or reorganization of a physical environment (for example, staggering mealtimes to minimize crowding and noise).

One aspect of the physical environment which often needs to be addressed with respect to people who have behavioural difficulties, and particularly those whose behaviour is associated with agitation and high levels of emotion, is physical space. A number of such individuals seem to feel uncomfortable when others are too close or when too many people are together in one place. They seem to require a greater area of personal space around them than do other people. It is often important for them also to have a quiet area within the place where they spend their day or where they live, to which they can retreat if they become anxious or agitated and which is readily available to them. In the person's living environment, this area is often the person's own bedroom. In services providing day-time occupation for people with learning difficulties, in may be more difficult to find a quiet and safe area to which people can retreat when they feel the need to. However, where the need for such an area is recognized then it is important that this need is addressed.

Many adverse physical setting conditions are likely to influence the well-being of all those who have to spend time within those settings. Poor lighting or unacceptable levels of noise, for example, are likely to affect both service users and service providers. If everybody's stress levels are increased as a result, the quality of social interactions is likely to be impaired (see below). It is therefore important that when such adverse physical setting conditions are identified, a way is found to reduce them.

Alleviating adverse social setting conditions

Where social climate factors are relevant to the behavioural difficulty in question and a whole new (and perfect) social system cannot be created, then ways need to be found of working with the social system in order to effect the relevant change.

Attitude to the person with learning difficulties

Some of the setting conditions implicated in behavioural difficulties have their roots in the ways that other people in the life of the individual concerned relate to that person. The quantity and quality of social interactions and supports are essential to the well-being of any human being. Table 4.1 indicates some of the ways that patterns of social relationships might impact upon the individual's feelings (and consequent motivations).

Everyone behaves in these ways some of the time. Problems arise when some or most of the people in a social group behave like this for much of the time. When most staff in a residential home or day service, or when most family members, are responding to the individual with learning difficulties (or for that matter any other group member) with hostility, criticism, bossiness or inconsistency for much of the time, then the individual is likely to experience serious discomfort and this in turn will be reflected in his behaviour.

Sometimes such patterns of relating towards the person with learning difficulties may reflect the learning experiences of carers over time. For example, working with people who have profound learning disabilities or major problems in tolerating social contact can be very discouraging. The social approaches of carers may draw no response or they may

Table 4.1 Relationship between social system characteristics and individual experience

Social climate	Individual experience
Lack of contact	Boredom, loneliness
Hostility, criticism	Anger, sadness, guilt
Bossiness, total control	Frustration
Inconsistency, unpredictability	Confusion, anxiety

Table 4.2 Examples of why work groups may develop inappropriate ways of relating to one another

Social condition	Effects on interpersonal relationships
Lack of direction/leadership	Confusion, inconsistency
Lack of skills	Errors, conflicts
Lack of resources	Frustration, anger, helplessness
Lack of emotional support	Stress, withdrawal, poor communication
Lack of valuation	Apathy, mistrust
Personal difficulties at home	Loss of energy, reduced tolerance

elicit active rejection. Over time this may mean that social contact between staff or family members and the person with learning difficulties may be avoided, with the sorts of effects upon the person outlined in Table 4.1. Negative attitudes of carers towards the person may also reflect shared prejudices which act to the disadvantage of the person or other group members. If there is a belief among carers that people with learning difficulties are inherently unreasonable and unreliable then it will become important for them to keep control at all times and ignore any initiation by the individual.

Relationships between carers

Some of the setting conditions implicated in the behavioural difficulties of the individual may originate from the way that the carers who are involved in the person's life relate to one another: conflict and tension may exist between carers; there may be mistrust, dislike and a general lack of interpersonal communication. The reasons why a social group gets into these ways of relating to each other are varied. Table 4.2 indicates some possible reasons why adverse social relationships may develop within a working group.

Whatever the causes, the effects on the relationship between carers can be damaging. This in turn affects the quality of their work and the quality of their relationships with the people for whom care is being provided. Adverse patterns of social relationships with service users are likely to impact upon the feelings and consequent motivations of the individual, as outlined earlier.

Resolving social system difficulties

The origin of social system difficulties may be many and varied. Resolving these difficulties may be straightforward or complex. Whoever is trying to tackle these issues will need to work with the social group as a whole (not necessarily all at once) and take the group through a series of steps using a problem-solving approach.

1. Develop a shared awareness of the problem.
2. Define the outcome to be achieved.
3. Brainstorm the options for change.
4. Evaluate the options identified.
5. Select the most appropriate course of action.
6. Implement, monitor, review.

The first step, which is the development of a shared awareness of the problem, is often the most difficult. A shared understanding of the problem may be reached through a number of ways:

- by group discussion;
- by individual discussions with group members;
- by anonymous questionnaires (for example, about relationships within the group);
- by collecting observational data (for example, about the level and type of social contact in a system, about the level of engagement in meaningful activities by service users). Data collected can then be fed back to the group as a means of raising their awareness of the nature of the problem.

Once there is a shared view of the problem (STEP 1) then it becomes possible to define the outcome which needs to be achieved (STEP 2) and progress towards a solution: this is rarely an easy endeavour. Critical to this progress is to generate as many ideas as possible (STEP 3) and to allow conflict and controversy to occur as each idea is discussed in turn (STEP 4), before moving towards a plan of action (STEP 5). Whatever is decided needs then to be monitored and reviewed (STEP 6) to see if the desired changes have occurred.

A social group needs to develop a consciousness of itself as a group and to get into the habit of reflecting upon the state of group relationships. This is a great challenge both for professional and for family caregivers. It is as important for a staff group in a residential home to consider the quality of relationships within the home as it is to consider the activities carried out by the staff. This type of group problem-solving approach is something that can be undertaken by most people who have some experience of working with groups and who have some credibility with the group in question. It is a reasonable approach that should always be the starting point in trying to resolve social system difficulties.

When social system difficulties cannot be resolved

Group dynamics can sometimes be very complex and the common-sense approach described above can make no headway. In these cases it will be useful to refer to someone who has specialized training in group dynamics: family therapists and people who run therapeutic groups are the most obvious source of such expertise. However, within any organization there may be individuals who have undertaken special training in this area, often at their own initiative, whose job titles may not readily reflect this. Sometimes people who work in personnel and training have this sort of background. Such expertise may be a source of guidance and support to the individual working to effect systemic change. On occasions it may be possible to use specialists more directly in the change process.

Alleviating adverse occupational setting conditions

Each individual has different needs in relation to the type of occupations and activities in which they engage on a daily basis. The appropriateness of activities which are available and which may be required will affect the individual's well-being and satisfaction. When many people live together or spend their day time in group activities, the needs of the individual may not be considered as fully as might be desirable.

Occupational setting conditions may become adverse for a number of reasons.

1. Occupational activities and daily routines may be inappropriate given the life-stage developmental level of the individual. Thus, young adults may enjoy more vigorous and energetic activities, requiring a full daily programme to keep them occupied. Elderly people, on the other hand, may prefer a slower pace of life, activities which do not require so much physical exertion and time to sit around quietly. If occupation is forced upon the individual which is inappropriate, given the life-stage development of the person, this may cause frustration, anger or withdrawal.

2. Everyday routines and activities may be aversive because they are too difficult or unpleasant. When people spend long periods of time in environments where they are required to do tasks which are aversive for them, this will cause stress. It may create anxiety because the individual does not understand what is expected. It may create anger because the individual is forced to spend a lot of time doing activities he does not enjoy. It may cause helplessness because the individual cannot succeed in the tasks which are set for him.

3. The person's environment may not provide an appropriate level of structure. Some people may be unable to cope successfully when their time is not structured for them, when they are not occupied or directed in some way and when they cannot predict what is to happen next. Others may find structured timetables and regular activities too pressured and monotonous; they may prefer more spontaneous and relaxed environments.

When activities and daily routines are assessed as being implicated in a person's behavioural difficulty, then appropriate action may require:

- addressing life-span developmental needs;
- adjusting the level of structure and predictability;
- reviewing the types of activities, demands and pressures placed on the person on a daily basis.

Adjusting daily routines and activities to meet a person's special needs may be achieved in a number of ways.

1. Through the reorganization of general activities and routines of an establishment to ensure that each person's needs are being met within the general structure of things (for example, allocating domestic tasks according to interests rather than insisting that each person has a regular turn at washing the dishes, or ensuring that leisure activities which are offered cover the range of interests within the group).
2. Through the setting-up of an individual timetable of activities for the person, different from that of other service users.
3. Acceptance of the fact that the environment (day-time or residential) may be unable to meet the person's needs, in which case an alternative and more appropriate environment may need to be found.

Perceived structure and predictability can be increased by providing the person with regular information.

1. Information can be given verbally about the day's forthcoming events and about any changes in routine.
2. Information can be presented in written form.
3. Information can be presented using pictorial representations (timetables and calendars). Such information can be given on a daily, weekly or monthly basis. Visually presented information provides the person with a permanent reference to which he can turn whenever he becomes anxious about his routine. Calendars provide a means of helping people with a poor sense of time to count the days to important forthcoming events (visits home, holidays), thereby reducing anxiety associated with unpredictability.

WORKING TO ELIMINATE OR ALLEVIATE PERSONAL SETTING CONDITIONS

In the preceding paragraphs consideration was given to how changes might be made in the person's environment so that its influences can be more helpful and conditions are not created in which behavioural difficulties are encouraged. The paragraphs which follow consider ways in which direct work with the individual may serve to alter the impact that the environment has upon the person by addressing those setting conditions that arise from within the individual.

A wide range of interventions are available to alleviate physical and emotional distress and to alter ways of thinking about the world that may be inaccurate or which increase experienced distress. Any of these – physical distress, emotional distress, inappropriate perceptions about one's world – can be important setting conditions for behavioural difficulties.

Alleviating physical distress

It may in some cases be possible to eliminate the source of physical distress. For example, if there is a particular food item to which the person is very sensitive and this shows in irritability and shouting and screaming whenever routine requests and demands are made, then the substance might be withdrawn from the person's diet. If an individual experiences recurring difficulties with wisdom teeth and the pain causes self-injurious outbursts, then dental treatment may eliminate the problem.

Health problems and health interventions are far too numerous to discuss here. This paragraph serves merely to stress the importance of physical well-being, as physical difficulties are all too easy to miss in people who are unable to communicate about themselves. These include general health needs such as infections or inflammations, and more specialized health needs such as those related to the management of epilepsy and deteriorating conditions such as Alzheimer's disease. They will require the support of a range of health-care professionals to guide assessment and intervention work. Where behavioural disturbance is of recent and sudden onset, then the possibility that some kind of physical distress is involved is high and needs to be thoroughly investigated.

Helping the person to maintain a healthy lifestyle, with an appropriate diet and regular exercise, will enhance his sense of well-being. Regular exercise is likely to have a positive effect on general anxiety and may decrease the overall frequency of behavioural disturbance.

Alleviating emotional distress

Emotional distress can take many forms, for example, anxiety, sadness, fear or depression. Such distress can be manifested as behavioural disturbance (for example, aggression, self-injury, withdrawal). Some forms of emotional distress are accessible to direct intervention.

General anxiety

General anxiety can be alleviated by regular induction of a relaxed state. This can be effected in at least three ways.

1. Teaching relaxation exercises, such as progressive muscular relaxation (Chapter 9), transcendental meditation and yoga.
2. Direct induction of relaxation using such methods as music, massage and aromatic oils.
3. Prescription drugs given under the direction of a medical practitioner. These can be useful in extreme cases to help relieve high levels of tension and anxiety.

If relaxation methods are to be used to help alleviate general anxiety then these should be practised on a regular basis (at least daily) and become part of the person's regular routine.

Sadness and low mood

Anxiety is not the only emotional state open to direct alteration. Sad feelings can be alleviated as well. There are several ways of achieving this for the individual.

1. By getting the person active and scheduling regular access for the person to activities that are currently or have in the past been enjoyed. The aim is to increase the amount of pleasurable experiences and, thereby, the density of positive reinforcement. Activity also increases a sense of personal control, so frequently lost when a person becomes sad or depressed.
2. By increasing access to pleasurable memories (something which is difficult when sad). This may be done by discussion, photo albums, home movies, getting out mementos and souvenirs.
3. By diverting the person's thoughts away from unhappy ones and onto more positive ones. This may be done by getting the person to recall positive experiences which have happened during the day and to discuss positive experiences which are due to happen (for example, outings or special activities).
4. By increasing the level of achievement being experienced by the individual so that he begins to regain a sense of personal control. This may be done by reducing pressures and demands to ensure that success occurs when the person does engage in daily tasks.
5. By ensuring that the person is made aware of his daily successes and achievements. This can be done through verbal feedback or through the encouragement of self-monitoring (Chapter 9).

All these interventions are relatively easy to construct once the nature of the difficulty (feeling sad) is identified. There are also drug interventions that help to lift mood and these can be particularly helpful in serious depression. For these, of course, medical support must be sought.

Dealing with the effects of trauma

Traumatic events in a person's life (abusive experiences, leaving home, being moved from one residential placement to another, bereavement) may continue to trouble the person and influence his wants and needs if these events have not been properly 'processed'. The nature of such 'processing' is not fully understood but it is thought that if highly distressing events are stored in the memory without having been fully understood and without the level of distress having been reduced, any individual can continue to experience emotional disturbance. Past events may intrude vividly on everyday life and general emotional well-being will be damaged.

When it is felt that traumatic past events are troubling the individual and affecting emotional well-being, then the help of a qualified psychologist, psychiatrist, psychotherapist or counsellor should be sought. The professional practitioner may work with the individual directly or guide the carer through the steps of assisting the individual to work through the traumatic event.

Alleviating inaccurate thinking

The emotions that an individual experiences and the behaviour considered appropriate depend very much upon how the world is interpreted. This interpretation is not necessarily something conscious. On first meeting a new person an individual will make all sorts of rapid judgements in terms of age, appearance and status which will guide what he says and how he interacts with that person, his body language and many other kinds of behaviour – most of this occurring without conscious awareness. Other kinds of interpretation are more conscious. How a person feels and acts when faced with another person running towards him, arms waving and shouting, will depend very much on whether he recognizes the other person as someone he knows. If he recognizes the person as a friend he is likely to interpret the approach as an enthusiastic greeting. If he does not recognize the person at all, he is likely to interpret the approach as an assault. These examples illustrate how the registration and interpretation of events guides how people feel and how they act and react to everyday situations. A person's attention is always selective and information is always filtered through some form of analysis. Some of these analyses may be conscious, many are not.

Once this general principle is understood then it becomes clear that the way in which situations are read and interpreted will play a large part in determining motivation and behaviour. People with learning difficulties by definition struggle to understand the world around them. They are thus vulnerable to difficulties arising from misunderstanding the meaning of events. If this is identified as one of the setting factors involved in a behavioural difficulty there are two ways of addressing this.

1. Increasing the amount of information available. If a person becomes upset whenever activities are changed then one way of making this

more comprehensible would be to give the person a timetable that he could relate to. If anger occurs whenever a request is denied, then improving the explanation given would be a way of helping the person cope by enabling him to understand why something is refused and when it might be available. This might make the critical difference between being cross and being in a rage.

2. Making relevant information more obvious. For example, allowing a person to see the dead body of a relative or friend, attend the funeral and have some explanation of death might make it easier to understand why he no longer sees a person who has hitherto been an important part of his life.

At one level these examples are very obvious but getting information over to someone whose central difficulty is handling information can be very challenging and will require great ingenuity. There are some forms of inaccurate thinking that are part of a major mental illness such as the schizophrenic disorders or severe depression. These will usually require drug interventions under psychiatric supervision in addition to the kinds of help outlined here.

Personal counselling and individual therapy

There are many ways in which intervention with the individual can help to alleviate the setting conditions involved in behavioural difficulties. Some kinds of interventions are readily accessible, others are highly specialized. Many of the approaches used to help alleviate emotional distress and inaccurate thinking are used in the processes of counselling and psychotherapy. This way of working involves a qualified helper meeting regularly with a person experiencing emotional distress. The role of that helper is to enable the individual to understand his distress and to find constructive ways of coping. The process often incorporates a positive valuation of the person (more positive input), careful exposure to distressing events and the correcting of inaccurate thinking. There may be other elements too. A personal counselling service for a person with learning difficulties should only be carried out by someone trained in this way of working.

DEVELOPING PROGRAMMES FOR SETTING-LEVEL CHANGES

The assessment process may have highlighted setting conditions which seem relevant to the occurrence of a person's behavioural difficulty. Sometimes these changes may seem desirable in and of themselves: that people should experience positive value and respect, that they should have choices about their lives and that they should have available interesting things to do are matters about which there is little dispute. However the perspective of this book is very much about help that specifically targets the disturbance and distress of an individual. It may be laudable to reduce authoritarianism and to increase an individual's control but if it makes no difference to the number of times the person punches and kicks other people then his individual needs have not been met. It is entirely desirable to lift a person's depression but if that person continues to injure himself then, again, the work is not completed. The focus of this chapter is upon those setting conditions that have been identified as being relevant to the problematic behaviour of the individual.

Step ⟩ 1 ⟨ Identify the need

The needs list which summarizes the assessment phase may contain needs that require intervention at the setting-condition level. Figure 2.6 contains several examples of such needs. Two of these are:

> Larry needs to be able to remain calm when travelling using transport.
> Larry needs to be less anxious.

Each identified need should be addressed separately.

Step ⟩ 2 ⟨ Review the options for achieving the specified outcomes

There may be a number of ways to tackling a setting-level problem and these need to be reviewed before a decision is made about the most appropriate approach. For example, 'Becoming less anxious' might be effected by:

- regular relaxation induction;
- a course of an anti-anxiety drug;
- some form of counselling/psychotherapy input;
- the scheduling of regular exercise.

and 'Remaining calm when travelling using transport' might be effected by:

- travelling in a taxi rather than a crowded minibus;
- never travelling with more than two other people;
- practising relaxation-inducing exercises while travelling on crowded transport.

Some of these interventions might require specialist input in terms of consultation or direct work with the individual. It is important at this stage to identify the need for any specialist input for the options under consideration. Other interventions might require other additional resources (for example, funding). Such resources must be identified at this stage.

Step ⟩ 3 ⟨   Consult with specialist resources

Before making any final decision about a plan of action the specialist resources identified as helpful or necessary in STEP 2 should be consulted for their opinion as to the desirability or feasibility of the options under consideration. They may also have new ideas about ways of meeting the identified need. The availability of other identified resources should also be checked.

The move to STEP 3 is of course accelerated where a highly specialized need is identified. For example, a need to experience clearer consciousness and less disruption from epileptic activity is not met by everyone involved on a daily basis getting together and swapping ideas. In this case, the advice of a neurologist is the key determinant of what should be done.

This point is perhaps obvious to those accustomed to working in multi-disciplinary settings where specialists feature prominently in the lives of people with learning difficulties. However, the trend is to move away from such models, towards the lifestyles led by others in the community. This places an increasing burden on those in daily contact, whether in day or residential settings, to be aware of when specialist help is needed and to know where to find it.

Step ⟩ 4 ⟨   Set long-term goals

The selected option must now be translated into a clearly stated long-term goal, using the format described in Chapter 3 (STEP 1). For example, the need for Larry to 'remain calm when travelling on transport' could be translated into the following long-term goal.

Who	Larry
Will do what	will use a taxi
Under what circumstances	to travel to and from the day-centre.

The need for Larry to 'be less anxious' could be translated into the following long-term goal.

Who	Larry
will do what	Will have a massage using aromatic oils
Under what circumstances	each morning before breakfast.

Having clear goals makes it easy to judge if the goals have been achieved.

Step 5   Formulate the action plan to be followed

The action plan should specify which actions are to be taken and by whom, if the desired outcome is to be achieved. For example, ensuring that Larry has a massage using aromatic oils each morning may involve the following action plan.

1. Key worker to consult with aroma therapist about appropriate oils.
2. All carers to be shown how to use oils and implement massage.
3. Manager to timetable named individuals for half-an-hour each morning to give massage.

Helping Larry to travel successfully to and from the day-centre in a taxi may involve the following action plan.

1. Manager negotiating with local minicab firm to identify no more than three drivers to transport Larry.
2. Manager timetabling named staff to accompany Larry in the mornings and to travel back with him in the evenings.
3. Key worker providing Larry with something he can use as a comforter should he become agitated.
4. Key worker teaching Larry to use the comforter at times when he is agitated.
5. Key worker to discuss with all staff at staff meeting how to help Larry keep calm in the taxi.

In brief, an action plan states **who** has to do **what** in order for the specified outcome to be achieved. Some parts of the plan may then need to be further broken down into smaller action steps, using task analysis and goal-setting (as described in Chapter 3).

Step 6   Plan the record of progress

Any intervention needs to be monitored and setting-level interventions are no exception. It is vital to know if the outcome has been achieved, if needs identified at the setting level have been met. Such records can be set alongside records of the behaviour that is the main focus of concern to establish the impact of the intervention on the behaviour itself. When planning the record of progress it is important first to identify what is to be measured. For example, 'anxiety' may need to be measured in terms of observable behaviour, such as pacing, screaming, hitting out (Chapter 11, STEP 1). Second, an appropriate method of data collection should be planned (Chapter 11, STEPS 2, 3, and 4) and a recording form should be prepared (Chapter 11, STEP 5).

Step 7   Set the review date

As with all the programmes discussed in this book, a plan is much more likely to be implemented and sustained if a date for review is fixed at the time that the plan is set up. Intervening in setting conditions tends to involve complex interventions which need to be sustained over time if any effect is to show. Thus, a very short-term review is unlikely to be helpful. On the other hand momentum is lost if review dates are too far ahead. A sensible review date will allow time for the action steps to be organized and implemented and time for the individual to experience the effects of the actions over a 6–8-week period.

Step 8   Write the action plan

The action plan for setting-level interventions should contain the following.

1. The behaviour reduction target. This is a statement of the long-term goal of work with the individual in terms of the target behaviour that it is intended should reduce. This should be specified in the ways outlined in Chapter 3 (STEP 1). For example, Larry will have an outburst of agitation no more than once per month.
2. The specific goal of the intervention.
3. The action plan.

4. Recording procedures and recording chart.
5. Review date.

An example of a written plan for a setting-level intervention is shown in Figure 4.2.

Step ⟩ **9** ⟨   **Take baseline measure**

A measure of the target behaviour should be taken before any intervention is implemented. This will provide an objective basis against which progress can be measured. The reader should consult Chapter 11 (STEP 6) for information about how to set up appropriate baseline measures. When work around the problematic behaviour of an individual continues over a long period of time, the original severity of frequency of a behaviour is bound to be forgotten. This is why an objective baseline measure is essential. Without such a measure, only a guess will be possible about the extent of progress which has been achieved.

Step ⟩ **10** ⟨   **Implement, review and move on**

The review is based on objective records of progress which have been kept and which have been summarized, where appropriate, as a graph or chart (Chapter 11, STEPS 8 and 9). The review process will identify the need for changes or additions to the intervention plan that will themselves be incorporated in subsequent written plans. Other setting-level difficulties will require their own action plans. Reviews will also highlight the relationship between changes in setting conditions and changes in behaviour as discussed above. This may have implications in terms of further assessment work and subsequent action plans.

SUMMARY

This chapter has described how the broad concept of setting conditions can guide the development of interventions relevant to individual needs. These interventions may involve the elimination of an identified setting condition or its alleviation through work at the environmental or the personal level. Altering setting conditions is intended to decrease the strength of the motivation involved in the behavioural difficulty. It is unlikely, on its own, to achieve complete elimination of the problem.

INTERVENTION PLAN

Name *LARRY*	Date *FEB 6TH*

Need

LARRY NEEDS TO REMAIN CALM DURING TIME BETWEEN RETURNING HOME FROM DAY CENTRE AND HAVING HIS EVENING MEAL

Behaviour Reduction Target

LARRY WILL HAVE NO MORE THAN ONE OUTBURST OF AGGRESSION EACH MONTH

Setting Alteration Target

LARRY WILL HAVE HIS TIME STRUCTURED BETWEEN 5.00 - 7.00 EACH WEEKDAY EVENING

Action Plan

1. LARRY TO HAVE HALF HOUR AROMATHERAPY SESSION ON RETURN FROM DAY-CENTRE

2. 3 X HALF-HOUR ACTIVITIES TO BE PLANNED FOR EACH EVENING (KEY WORKER) TO FOLLOW AROMATHERAPY

3. KEY WORKER TO PREPARE WEEKLY TIMETABLE OF ACTIVITIES USING PHOTOGRAPHS TO SHOW EACH ACTIVITY

4. STAFF TO BE ALLOCATED EACH MORNING TO EXPLAIN THE EVENING ACTIVITIES TO LARRY

5. PERSON DOING AROMATHERAPY TO TALK LARRY THROUGH TIMETABLE FOR REST OF EVENING WITH LARRY

6. MANAGER TO ENSURE STAFF ARE ALLOCATED TO EACH EVENING'S ACTIVITIES

Recording Procedure

ANY EPISODES OF SCREAMING, PUSHING, PULLING THINGS OFF WALLS AND SHELVES SHOULD BE RECORDED ON THE CHART PROVIDED

Review Date   *APRIL 14TH*

Figure 4.2 Example of a written plan for a setting-level intervention.

Interventions at the level of settings need to be combined with the sorts of work described in subsequent chapters. This other work will enable the person to learn better ways of coping with difficult situations and will encourage him to leave behind the old ways that others find problematic.

ALTERING SETTING CONDITIONS

SUMMARY OF STEPS

1

Identify need

2

Review the options for acheiving the specified outcomes

3

Consult with specialist resources

4

Set long-term goal

5

Formulate the action plan to be followed

6

Plan the record of progress

7

Set the review date

8

Write the action plan

9

Take baseline measure

10

Implement review and move on

Altering triggers associated with problematic behaviour

5

Helping people with behavioural difficulties is a multi-dimensional endeavour which requires a problem-solving approach. Which specific methods will be adopted for a given individual will largely depend upon the initial assessment and analysis of the problem. The previous chapter focused on interventions aimed at altering setting conditions which create or strengthen the motivations for particular outcomes and which then lead on to problematic or disturbed behaviour. The present chapter is concerned with the more immediate antecedents of problematic behaviour – its triggers. Interventions at this level aim to reduce the incidence of problematic behaviours by working directly on the trigger–action sequence. This contrasts with the work described in Chapters 8 and 10, which focuses directly on the action–result sequence.

TRIGGER-LEVEL INTERVENTIONS – GENERAL PRINCIPLES

IDENTIFYING PROBLEMS WITH THE TRIGGER–ACTION SEQUENCE

The triggers for problematic behaviour can be any stimulus within a person's external environment, such as the sight of something, a specific sound or smell, specific people or places, the things people say. Triggers can also come from within the person, for example, a sharp pain, a sudden memory. A stimulus triggers a behaviour because:

- it may signal to the individual that something that he wants has become available;
- it may signal to the individual that something that he fears or dislikes is about to happen;
- it may produce within the individual an intolerably high level of negative emotion or physiological arousal;

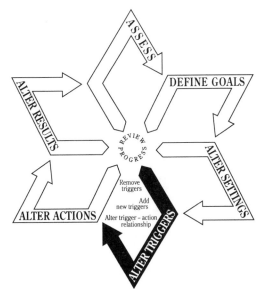

Figure 5.1 Altering triggers.

- it may trigger an action out of habit;
- it may elicit a reflex reaction.

These situations seem to be fairly clear-cut: a stimulus occurs and this triggers a behaviour considered to be problematic. Triggering problems are not always so clear-cut: problems may arise, not because the behaviour itself is inappropriate, but because the circumstances in which it is performed may be inappropriate.

- Actions may be under the control of the wrong triggers. For example, taking one's clothes off in the high street may be considered to be inappropriate. However, taking one's clothes off in the bedroom or bathroom may be considered to be quite appropriate.
- Actions may be under the control of too many triggers. For example, spinning objects for stimulation may be considered an acceptable thing to do. Spinning any object which comes to hand, however, renders the behaviour a problem.
- Actions may be under the control of too few triggers. For example, an individual may always remain calm and co-operative in the presence of one or two carers but always appears agitated and non-co-operative in the presence of all other people.

In these cases the problems are ones of discrimination (not knowing the situations in which the behaviour is/is not appropriate) and generalization (failure to extend appropriate behaviour and rules of behaviour across environments). Still other problems arise when no triggers exist which can enable a person to control his behaviour with the result that, once started, the person finds it difficult to stop. Thus people who engage in obsessional or ritualistic behaviour often find it difficult to stop once they are engaged in the behaviour, even though they may become increasingly anxious the longer the behaviour continues. There are people who frequently experience a build-up of negative emotion and physiological arousal which they find uncomfortable, yet they may be unable to stop the build-up once it has started.

Working effectively with triggers to reduce problematic behaviour requires:

- a clear understanding of the nature of the triggering problem;
- a clear understanding of the methods by which change might be effected.

The various methods which can be used to alter inappropriate trigger–action sequences and the circumstances in which these methods could effectively be used are described in the paragraphs which follow.

TRIGGER ELIMINATION

There may be clearly identifiable stimuli which consistently trigger a person's inappropriate behaviour. The stimuli may be associated with high emotional arousal and the need to terminate the situation. They may be associated with positive gains and the desire to access these. If consistent triggers can be identified then it may be possible to simply eliminate them. Thus, caregivers might be told that they should not . . . shout at a person, . . . remove a person's favourite comforter, . . . make a person take a shower if he prefers a bath, . . . enter the person's space without warning, . . . rearrange the furniture in a person's bedroom.

Clearly identifiable triggers could be removed from the person's physical environment, provided that their presence was felt to be unnecessary to the person's quality of life or to the quality of life of others. Thus if the presence of other people's bags triggered the stealing of money and other items from the bags, the bags could be kept out of sight. If the presence of electrical sockets triggered the insertion of fingers into them, then the socket holes could be covered over using safety sockets.

Trigger elimination is thus one option for resolving a trigger–action problem. It is applicable only if the trigger can easily be eliminated from the environment in which the person spends his life and if elimination of the trigger does not impair the quality of the person's life.

GRADED EXPOSURE

There may be an identifiable stimulus which consistently triggers an action that may be withdrawal or it may be approach. A stimulus may trigger escape or avoidance behaviour because the person finds the stimulus aversive. Problems arise because the stimulus cannot be permanently eliminated from the person's world and the person is regularly exposed to it. The stimulus causes anxiety or stress. Commonly encountered situations include being confronted by a phobic stimulus (for example, a dog, a spider, water) or finding oneself in a stressful situation (for example, the furniture has been rearranged, the familiar route has been altered, a bath has to be taken).

A stimulus may trigger approach behaviour because the person wants access to the stimulus but such access is inappropriate (for example, it may be potentially harmful for the person or damaging to the environment). Problems arise because the stimulus cannot be permanently eliminated from the person's world. For example, a person may consistently pull books and ornaments off shelves or tear pictures from walls.

In the situations described above it may be possible to find a way of altering the trigger–action sequence using a process called graded exposure. The principles are outlined below.

1. The level at which the trigger can be presented without the response (escape, approach) occurring is established. This becomes the baseline level. For example, a person who suffers from a dog phobia may feel comfortable looking at a picture of a dog or even watching a film about dogs. A person who dislikes baths may feel comfortable standing in an empty bath to wash his feet. A person who dislikes demands placed on him may accept a request to help himself to a sandwich from the table. A person who pulls items off the bookcase might tolerate a single small item placed in a corner on the top shelf.
2. The desired level of exposure to the trigger (for example, to stroke a dog, to tolerate a full bookcase, to have a bath) is established.
3. Using the baseline level as a starting point a hierarchy is drawn up of situations which take the individual closer and closer to the desired level. Below is an example of how a hierarchy might be constructed for a person suffering from an irrational fear of dogs. The steps of the hierarchy are small enough to create only a minimal change in the person's motivational state (to escape).
   (a) Look at picture of dog.
   (b) Look at video of dog.
   (c) Look through window at small dog on a lead, sitting with owner at far end of garden.

(d) Look through window at small dog on a lead standing with owner at far end of garden.

(e) Look through window at small dog on a lead walking with owner at far end of garden.

(f) Look through window at small dog on a lead sitting with owner half-way up garden.

(g) Look through window at small dog on a lead walking with owner half-way up the garden.

(h) Look through window at small dog on a lead walking with owner quarter-way up the garden.

(i) Look through window at small dog on a lead sitting other side of window.

(j) Look through window at small dog on a lead walking other side of window.

(k) Stand in garden watching small dog walking on lead at other end of garden.

(l) Stand in garden watching small dog on lead getting progressively closer.

(m) Touch dog.

(n) Start again with different dog.

4. Work starts at the easiest level and proceeds systematically through the hierarchy. The individual is exposed to the first stimulus in the hierarchy on a regular sessional basis until he can tolerate it without experiencing a desire to act (escape, approach). Exposure then starts to the stimulus which is the next item on the hierarchy. Several sessions of exposure may be required to any one stimulus before anxiety reduces.

Exposure to aversive stimuli

When working to help the individual tolerate an aversive stimulus, the length of exposure to the stimulus during a session is determined by the speed at which the person's anxiety decreases. Thus a session ends once the level of anxiety has subsided (at least to some extent). If anxiety does not reduce within an acceptable time-limit, then this suggests that the steps of the hierarchy are too large. Further exposure should not occur until the steps have been made smaller. Where possible, exposure to the aversive stimulus is carried out while the individual is made to feel as relaxed and comfortable as possible. The individual is reinforced for tolerating and remaining in the situation.

Exposure to desired stimulus

When working to help the individual tolerate the presence of a desired stimulus without the need to 'approach', the length of exposure is largely determined by the person's tolerance of its presence. If the person makes no approach to the stimulus, it can be left in view. However, when the person shows signs of approach and his attention cannot be diverted to other things, the stimulus should be discreetly removed. The principles of graded exposure can be applied to a wide range of situations where an identified stimulus triggers behavioural problems but the stimulus cannot be realistically removed from the person's world.

DISCRIMINATION TRAINING OF SITUATIONS
APPROPRIATE FOR THE BEHAVIOUR

A behaviour may be considered to be inappropriate because it occurs across too many situations, rather than because it is inappropriate in and of itself. Thus, a person may continually pick up and spin any object that comes to hand and as a result may pose a hazard within any environment in which he finds himself. A person may have a habit of tearing all paper (books, newspapers, wallpaper) which he encounters. A person may tear all items of clothing which he finds. Much obsessional behaviour is problematic not because of the behaviour itself (for example, asking questions, lining objects up, talking about topics of particular interest) but because of the extensiveness of the behaviour.

In situations like those described above steps can be taken to help the individual to discriminate the conditions under which the behaviour is appropriate and the conditions under which it is inappropriate and thereby limit the extent of the behaviour so that it becomes acceptable. Thus steps can be taken to help the individual to discriminate:

- the **items** which can be used for the behaviour in question (for example, appropriate objects to spin or tear);
- the **frequency** with which the behaviour can occur (for example, the number of times a question can be repeated);
- the **places** in which a behaviour can occur (for example, the places in which objects can be lined up);
- the **times** at which the behaviour can occur (for example, specific times of day when conversations about the person's 'special interest' can be held with carers).

A graded approach to change should be used if the person is likely to experience anxiety when the triggers for his behaviour are abruptly reduced. Thus times, places, frequency, items could be reduced gradually. As the person masters the small discrimination, another trigger is removed and the discrimination is made gradually larger. The steps involved in teaching the person to discriminate the appropriate triggers for his behaviour include the following.

1. Providing clear discriminable cues or reminders to help the person differentiate 'appropriate' and 'inappropriate' situations. Thus, using the above examples, the person who tears all forms of paper could be helped to discriminate appropriate and inappropriate things to tear by the presence of large coloured stickers on items considered to be 'appropriate' for tearing. The person who spins all objects in his environment could be provided with a clearly discriminable set of 'spinning objects' for his use. The person who continually repeats questions could be told he will only be given the answer a certain number of times. The person who lines objects up in all environments could be directed to his own room or the garden whenever he starts to line objects up. The person who obsessively engages in conversations about a topic of 'special interest' could be allocated a fixed number of times in the day when others would be available to be involved in these conversations.
2. Having established the cues for discrimination (for example, visual, verbal) the next step is to teach the person to use these cues to discriminate the situations where his behaviour is appropriate. This is done using planned prompts (Chapter 6, STEP 7) and reinforcement (Chapter 6, STEP 10), as for skill-teaching.

GENERALIZATION OF APPROPRIATE BEHAVIOUR

The situation may exist where an appropriate trigger–action sequence has been established, but the number of triggers for the behaviour are too few. The person has failed to generalize the action to other appropriate triggers. One common example of this phenomenon is when the individual will behave appropriately in the presence of maybe one or two caregivers, but in the presence of other carers finds it hard to control his own behaviour or emotions. Another common example is when the appropriate behaviour occurs in one setting but not in another. For example, a person will use the toilet and stay dry at home but will not use the toilet in any other place, such as school or college or the day-centre, and will consequently wet himself when in these settings. These are typical examples of how behaviour has failed to generalize across people and across places. The aim of intervention in such situations is to find ways of getting the person to generalize his positive behaviour, such that his action can be triggered by a wider range of appropriate stimuli.

Strategies for generalization include the following.

1. Introducing key stimuli which are associated with the successful triggering of the appropriate action (for example, a key worker, a piece of equipment, an item of clothing) into situations where

existing stimuli fail to trigger the action. The key trigger is then paired with a preselected stimulus until this new stimulus also becomes a trigger for appropriate action. For example, if a person will only use the toilet at home, a key trigger (for example, an identical toilet seat or an identical toilet-roll holder or even an identical wallpaper) could be introduced to other toilets (for example, in the day-centre or school) to aid the generalization process.

2. Introducing new stimuli into the situation where appropriate behaviour already occurs and pairing them with an existing successful trigger until they, too, become triggers for the appropriate behaviour. Thus, in the situation where a person behaves appropriately with only one or two specific individuals, generalization of appropriate behaviour would be effected by the following.

   (a) Pairing 'new' people with those who are already triggers for appropriate behaviour.

   (b) The 'new' person initially shadows the 'trigger' person as he carries out day to day activities with the individual, remaining in the background without becoming personally involved.

   (c) Provided that appropriate behaviour continues to occur in the presence of both the new person and the trigger person, the new person gradually moves closer to the trigger person until instructions and requests can be given jointly by the two carers. This may take several sessions.

   (d) Once the individual's appropriate behaviour can be reliably triggered by the joint efforts of the new person and the trigger person, the trigger person starts to fade out by gradually stepping back and allowing the new person to take over working with the individual. This may take several sessions.

   (e) The trigger person continues to phase out until his presence is no longer needed in order to trigger appropriate behaviour. The new person has now also become a trigger for appropriate behaviour.

   (f) The process is repeated with a second new person and then a third etc., until generalization occurs spontaneously.

BEHAVIOUR TERMINATION

A behaviour may be difficult to terminate once the person has engaged upon it: there may be no effective triggers for stopping the behaviour. Actions which typically fall into this category are certain obsessional and ritualistic behaviours. Once the person starts the behaviour (washing, dressing and undressing, or other elaborate rituals) it becomes difficult for him to stop. Sudden interruptions or demands to stop often result in an agitated outburst.

In such situations, there may be two issues to consider. The first involves setting a time-limit for the behaviour (the trigger for terminating the behaviour is the expiry of the time-limit). The second involves the addition of triggers to help the individual bring the behaviour to a close at the end of that time-limit. This may be particularly relevant if a person finds it difficult to be told abruptly that he should stop.

Placing a time-limit on a problematic behaviour

A time-limit may be useful in situations where the behaviour has started to take up very large amounts of time (for example, taking several hours to dress or wash). This situation often occurs in the context of the lowering of a person's mood state. The behaviour is unhelpful for the person inasmuch as he appears to become increasingly anxious the longer he continues with the behaviour. Where such a situation arises, setting a clear and reasonable time-limit on the behaviour and informing the person of the time-limit may be helpful. As in many trigger-level interventions, a graded approach may be more helpful than a sudden or large decrease in the time-limit.

Helping a person wind up a problematic behaviour

Problems may arise at the moment when a person is asked to bring his behaviour to a close. He may find it difficult to abruptly terminate his actions. Useful triggers to aid in such situations are ones that give the person a warning of the time remaining to wind up the behaviour. Such a warning reduces the level of anxiety associated with having a bring the behaviour to a close. Triggers which may prove useful include the following.

1. Informing the person that he has a fixed amount of time (for example, 10 minutes) to bring the behaviour to a close. Reminding him at least twice about the amount of time remaining (for example, after 5 minutes, after 8 minutes and again after 9 minutes). Informing him when the time-limit has been reached and/or using a timer to sound when the time-limit has been reached.
2. When the time-limit has been reached, rather than insisting that the behaviour ends immediately, giving the person time to end the behaviour himself by counting him out. The person is informed about the count, which is given aloud. For example, the person is told that on the count of 'five' the behaviour will have to stop. A slow count to 'five' follows and the person is informed that the time-limit has been reached.
3. When the time-limit has been reached, informing the person that

the behaviour needs to end but telling him that he can return to the behaviour later (this promise must be kept). The person learns that the behaviour must simply be adjourned, rather than terminated. Knowledge of this fact can reduce the anxiety which may be associated with ending the behaviour.

In all cases described above, the warning must be followed by the person being given the stated time to finish the behaviour. If, at first, he does not manage to wind the behaviour up himself at the end of the time-limit, he can be prompted to do so.

DIFFUSION OF HIGH AROUSAL

Where a person experiences a steady build-up of agitation or a strong negative emotion, the aim is to reduce the intensity of emotion being experienced in order to pre-empt overload and thereby avoid the likelihood of a person losing control of his behaviour. Working to avoid emotional overload by directly reducing the level of emotional arousal experienced is called diffusion. The active use of diffusion strategies with people experiencing increasing levels of emotional arousal considerably reduces the likelihood of behavioural outbursts occurring.

Diffusion strategies can be used at any time to try to reduce the level of a person's increasing arousal and agitation, although clearly the earlier that diffusion is implemented during the build-up phase the easier it will be to reduce arousal. The nearer the person gets to the tolerance limit of his arousal the harder it becomes to successfully reduce his agitation. The successful timing of diffusion is helped by a knowledge of recent events which might be contributing to emotional arousal and by detailed observation of the individual which enables the observer to gauge the level of emotional arousal being experienced and avoid the predicted behavioural outburst.

Diffusion strategies need to be adapted to each individual. In general, however, the following steps should be followed.

1. Remove any triggers which may add to the negative emotion or arousal. This requires reducing all immediate environmental pressures, which include ongoing demands and the level of background stimulation, in particular, the level of noise, heat and crowding. Often, it helps to take the person out of the immediate environment into a quieter place.
2. Actively work to reduce agitation and arousal (once immediate pressures have been reduced) using one of the following strategies.
   (a) Distract the individual with a non-pressured, pleasant activity (for example, a cup of tea, going for a walk, doing something constructive).

(b) Directly help the individual to reduce arousal through a calming activity (for example, muscular relaxation, a soothing bath, listening to music).

(c) Help the individual to 'get it out of his system' through a vigorous physical activity (for example, running, cycling, swimming, a brisk walk).

(d) Get the person to talk about what is causing him to be agitated.

Different approaches will be helpful for different people. It is important to find out what most helps each individual. Whichever strategy is adopted, a caring and sympathetic attitude should be adopted towards the person. Once the person has calmed enough it is then possible to try to help the person to resolve the problem.

SUMMARY

By focusing attention on the things which trigger disturbed or problematic behaviour and implementing change at this level a lot can be achieved in terms of reducing the level of problematic behaviour and helping the person overcome certain coping difficulties. There are various ways in which problematic behaviours can be tackled at the level of triggers. Detailed steps for setting up interventions based on the principles which have been described are set out below.

PROCEDURES FOR DEVELOPING INTERVENTION STRATEGIES TO REDUCE PROBLEMATIC BEHAVIOUR BY FOCUSING ON TRIGGERS

Step 1	Decide on the nature of the trigger–action problem and the intervention strategy to be used

1. If identifiable and consistent triggers have been found in relation to the problematic behaviour, then the nature of the triggering problem needs to be established. The various examples described in the previous section can be used as a guide for this analysis.

2. Having established the exact nature of the triggering problem it is then necessary to consider intervention options. The various types of triggering problems and associated interventions options are summarized in Table 5.1.

3. Once the options for intervention have been considered, further consideration should be given to the feasibility of the intervention, given its possible requirement for consistency and given its possible resource implications. The advantages and disadvantages of working

Table 5.1 Intervention options for problems associated with the triggering of behaviour

Triggering problem	Intervention option
Trigger associated with approach or escape behaviour; trigger can be eliminated	Eliminate trigger
Behaviour under control of too many triggers; behaviour has over-generalized	Limit the number of triggers controlling the behaviour (discrimination training)
Appropriate behaviour under control of too few triggers; behaviour has failed to generalize	Increase the number of triggers controlling the behaviour (generalization training)
Trigger associated with approach or escape behaviour; trigger cannot be permanently eliminated	Remove trigger and reintroduce (graded exposure)
Behaviour once started cannot easily stop; no effective trigger for stopping the behaviour	Provide new trigger to facilitate termination of behaviour (behaviour termination)
Arousal/negative emotion once started, continues to build	Remove triggers which might further increase arousal; add new triggers to decrease arousal (diffusion)

with triggers rather than working more directly with the results of the behaviour (Chapters 8 and 10) or working to teach the person greater self-control over the behaviour (Chapter 9) should also be considered at this stage. Consideration will take into account the individual himself, the resources available and the other available options for change.

Step 2   Set long-term objectives

Having decided to work directly with the trigger to reduce the problematic behaviour, the next step is to translate the intervention plan into a clearly stated long-term goal. The reader should refer to Chapter 3 (STEP 1) to help him plan realistic long-term goals. The long-term goal should be stated in clear objective terms using the format shown below.

Who	John
Will do what	will look at a dog without screaming or trying to run away
Under what conditions	when he encounters one in the street.
Who	Mary
Will do what	will allow five different members of staff to help her with eating her meal
Under what conditions	in the dining room each evening.

The long-term goal should be small enough that it can be achieved within 6–9 months.

Step 3   Set short-term objectives

The majority of interventions which focus directly on triggers are based upon a graded approach to change for their success – a gradual extension of triggers, a gradual reintroduction of a trigger, a gradual reduction of triggers. A graded approach requires that each stage is successfully completed before the person progresses to the next stage. The size of each step needs to be small enough for the person to experience only a minimal increase in anxiety or arousal when it is first introduced. It should be small enough to have only a minimum effect on behaviour: changes which are too large or too rapid are likely to increase inappropriate behaviour and/or emotional arousal and thereby hamper progress.

Long-term goals therefore need to be broken down into more immediately achievable ones, which become the short-term objectives. Again, the reader should refer to Chapter 3 to help him plan realistic short-term objectives. Short-term objectives are achieved when the carefully thought out criterion for success has been reached (for example, for three successive sessions).

Short-term objectives should be stated using the format described in Chapter 3 (STEP 4). Thus, the first short-term objective for the person experiencing the dog phobia might be as follows.

Who	John
Will do what	will stand at the window without screaming or trying to leave the room

Under what conditions	while a dog held on a leash lies on the grass at the other end of the garden
With how much help	with constant verbal encouragement from the person with him
To what degree of success	for five consecutive sessions.

The first short-term goal for a person who remains calm and co-operative in the presence of only one or two carers might be as follows.

Who	Mary
Will do what	will bang her head no more than four times
Under what condition	while June helps her to dress in her bedroom in the morning and Vera stands quietly by the door
With how much help	with frequent reminders to stay calm
To what degree of success	on three consecutive mornings.

Step 4 Plan the setting for the intervention

Some interventions may be implemented across all settings and situations (for example, trigger removal, behaviour termination, discrimination training). Others may be carried out on a sessional basis (for example, graded exposure, generalization training, discrimination training). If a sessional approach is logically possible, then the early stages of the intervention should be implemented on a sessional basis. This will make the task easier for the person and minimize anxiety.

Step 5 Plan triggers

This requires consideration of three factors.

1. Timing of the trigger. For example, when the person starts to touch the windows, when the person shows signs of agitation, when obsessional washing has continued for 1 minute, when the person is calm.

2. Method of presenting the trigger.
   (a) The trigger may be a verbal instruction (for example, directing the person to the appropriate place for engaging in the behaviour, telling the person that you will count to 'five').
   (b) The trigger may be a visual cue (for example, a timer, a sticker, specific items, the 'phobic' object).
3. Prompt to ensure that the appropriate action occurs. Prompts may be verbal reminders or instructions or they may be physical guidance (for example, to interrupt the action, to redirect from the inappropriate action, to redirect onto the appropriate action).

The reader should refer to Chapter 6 (STEP 7) for a fuller account of planning prompts for appropriate behaviour.

Step ⟩ 6 ⟨   Plan how to reinforce appropriate behaviour

The individual needs to know that he is succeeding and reinforcement may help motivate him to work harder to succeed. Appropriate reinforcement should be planned in advance (the strengths list will provide information about appropriate reinforcers for the individual). The reader should refer to Chapter 6 (STEP 10) for a full account of the planning of reinforcers for appropriate behaviour.

Step ⟩ 7 ⟨   Plan record of progress

In trigger-level interventions, one important set of measures are those which relate to the trigger itself.

- How frequently does diffusion successfully avert an outburst?
- How frequently can the behaviour be successfully diverted from an inappropriate trigger to an appropriate one?
- How frequently can a person bring his behaviour to a close without becoming aggressive or anxious?
- What level of the trigger can be tolerated without problematic behaviour occurring?

Such measures can be accompanied by a more general measure of the frequency of the problematic behaviour. The reader should refer to Chapter 11 (STEPS 2, 3 and 4) which details the steps for setting up accurate and manageable recording procedures.

Step 8   Plan review date

Whether the programme is simple or complex, it needs to be reviewed regularly to ensure that change is occurring in the direction desired. During the early stages of a programme of change, reviews may need to occur quite frequently. The programme procedures may need to be adjusted or amended, recording procedures may need to be refined. Thus the initial review should occur within 1–2 weeks of the start of the intervention. As the programme becomes more established and changes to the programme need to occur less frequently, so the reviews can occur less frequently. It should be a general rule, nevertheless, that as long as behaviour change is being worked towards, review of the programme needs to be a regular occurrence, certainly no less frequently than at 2-monthly intervals.

Step 9   Write the action plan or programme

Having worked out each aspect of the intervention strategy, the next step is to write down the details as a clear action plan or programme. A written programme may need to include the following details, depending on the level of complexity of the programme.

1. Long-term objective.
2. Short-term goals.
3. Time and place of session, people involved, any special materials needed for the session.
4. Procedures for implementing the programme, which should include:
   (a) appropriate timing of trigger;
   (b) method of presenting the trigger to the person;
   (c) prompt strategy to be used to ensure appropriate response to trigger;
   (d) any other accompanying instructions.
5. Reinforcement for appropriate behaviour.
6. The recording procedure: a recording form should be prepared and accompany the programme itself.
7. The date of review.

Figures 5.2 and 5.3 show illustrative programmes of trigger-level interventions which have been drawn up from the needs list in Chapter 2 (Figure 2.6): Figure 5.2 is an example of the use of diffusion and Figure 5.3 shows a programme based on the technique of graded exposure.

INTERVENTION PLAN	
Name *LARRY*	**Date of Programme** *3RD MARCH*

Need *LARRY NEEDS TO. LOSE CONTROL' LESS OFTEN*

Long-term Goal

LARRY WILL HAVE A MAJOR OUTBURST OF AGGRESSION NOT MORE THAN ONCE A MONTH

Short-term Objective

STAFF WILL USE DIFFUSION TECHNIQUES AS SOON AS LARRY SHOWS SIGNS OF AGRESSION

Place *HOME AND DAY-CENTRE*	**People Involved** *ALL STAFF*

Special Materials

BOX WITH OLD NEWSPAPERS. TAPE RECORDER AND LARRY'S RELAXATION TAPE

Procedure

ACTIVITIES WHICH LARRY FINDS RELAXING *TEARING PAPER INTO STRIPS. LISTENING TO MUSIC.*

TIMING OF TRIGGERS *WHEN LARRY SHOWS SIGNS OF AGITATION (SWEATING, AIMLESS WALKING FROM ROOM TO ROOM, 'BOUNCING' ON THE SPOT WHEN HE STANDS, SHREIKING).*

1. AS SOON AS LARRY SHOWS SIGNS OF AGITATION SAY 'COME ON LARRY, LET'S GO SOMEWHERE QUIET. YOU'RE LOOKING VERY TENSE'. DIRECT HIM TO HIS BEDROOM/RELAXATION ROOM AT THE DAY-CENTRE.
2. SHOW HIM THE BOX OF OLD NEWSPAPERS AND ASK IF HE WOULD LIKE TO TEAR SOME PAPER. PUT THE RELAXATION TAPE ON.
3. IF LARRY DOES NOT SHOW AN INTEREST, SIT DOWN YOURSELF ON A BEANBAG, TAKE THE BOX AND SLOWLY START TO TEAR A PIECE OF NEWSPAPER INTO STRIPS. ENCOURAGE LARRY TO SEE WHAT YOU'RE DOING AND ASK HIM EVERY FEW MINUTES IF HE WANTS TO HAVE A GO. USE A QUIET VOICE.
4. IF LARRY STARTS TO TEAR PAPER, SAY QUIETLY 'THAT'S GOOD, IT WILL HELP YOU TO CALM DOWN'. AS LARRY STARTS TO CALM DOWN, GIVE HIM PRAISE AND FEEDBACK FROM TIME TO TIME. 'THAT'S GOOD, LARRY, YOU'RE GETTING CALMER. YOU'RE DOING WELL'.
5. LET LARRY CONTINUE FOR AS LONG AS HE NEEDS TO. IF HE APPEARS TO BE CALMING HIMSELF, YOU CAN LEAVE HIM TO CONTINUE ALONE BUT CHECK ON HIM EVERY 5 MINUTES.

Recording Procedure	**Review Date**
COMPLETE THE ATTACHED RECORDING SHEET	*5TH MAY*

Figure 5.2 Example of trigger-level intervention using the technique of diffusion.

INTERVENTION PLAN	
Name *LARRY*	**Date of Programme** *7TH SEPTEMBER*

Need *TO TOLERATE PEOPLE BEING NEXT TO HIM*

Long-term Goal

LARRY WILL SIT NEXT TO PEOPLE FOR UP TO 15 MINUTES WITHOUT SCREAMING

Short-term Objective

LARRY WILL SIT AT A DISTANCE OF 3 FEET FROM A CARER WHILST ENGAGING IN A 1-TO-1 TABLE TOP ACTIVITY WITH NO MORE THAN THREE INSTANCES OF SCREAMING DURING FIVE CONSECUTIVE SESSIONS.

Time and Place of Session *1 X 15 MINUTE DAILY SESSION (IN DINING ROOM)*

People Involved *ALL STAFF*

Materials *ANY TABLE TOP ACTIVITY WHICH LARRY ENJOYS*

Instructions

1.   LET LARRY CHOOSE WHICH ACTIVITY HE WANTS TO DO. LET HIM GET SETTLED WITH IT AT THE TABLE.
2.   BRING A CHAIR ALONGSIDE LARRY'S AT A DISTANCE OF 3 FEET (2 ARMS' LENGTH) AND SIT QUIETLY DOING SOME PAPER WORK. RESPOND TO ANY INITIATIONS FROM LARRY. DON'T PUT ANY PRESSURE ON HIM.

Response to Appropriate Behaviour

AT THE END OF THE SESSION THANK LARRY FOR HAVING LET YOU SIT WITH HIM

Response to Inappropriate Behaviour

IF LARRY SCREAMS ASK ONCE WHAT THE MATTER IS BUT DO NOT MOVE AWAY. DIRECT HIM BACK TO THE ACTIVITY AND CONTINUE WITH YOUR OWN PAPERWORK.

Recording Procedure

RECORD NUMBER OF TIMES HE SCREAMS DURING SESSION (RECORDING SHEET ATTACHED)

Review Date

OCTOBER 8TH (BUT AS SOON AS CRITERION FOR SUCCESS HAS BEEN ACHIEVED, MOVE CHAIR 3 INCHES NEARER TO LARRY).

Figure 5.3 Example of trigger-level intervention using the technique of graded exposure.

Step 10   Establish baseline

Baseline measures are necessary in order for an objective evaluation of progress to be made. Baseline measures should be carried out under the same circumstance as the measures which will be used subsequently to measure progress (STEP 7). The reader should refer to Chapter 11 (STEP 6) for a fuller discussion of the setting-up of baseline recordings.

Step 11   Implement, review and move on

Objective and accurate information must be used to assess whether targets have been achieved. This is obtained from records of progress which have been summarized into graphical form for ease of analysis (Chapter 11, STEPS 8 and 9).

When working to change behaviour using small steps it is essential that programmes are continually adapted as each short-term objective is achieved according to the criteria which have been set in advance. Thus the next step in the change process (for example, graded reintroduction of trigger) must be introduced as soon as the previous objective is achieved. When arbitrary S.T.A.R. factors have been incorporated into the procedure in order to facilitate change (for example, prompts and reinforcers), then these eventually need to be faded out, just as they do in skill-teaching programmes (Chapter 6). This is all part of the process of moving on and each step needs to be carefully planned and monitored until new behaviour patterns have become well established.

SUMMARY

Working directly with triggers to reduce the occurrence of problematic or disturbed behaviour is an important level at which efforts of change can be directed. Such interventions are frequently aimed at helping an individual overcome personal fears and anxieties which might be contributing to the occurrence of problematic behaviours. Interventions at the trigger level range from the very simple to the very complex: their potential for change is considerable. For some problems they represent an alternative approach to more traditional approaches which rely on the manipulation of results for appropriate and inappropriate behaviour. For other types of problems, particularly fears, obsessions and rituals, they are frequently the intervention of choice.

ALTERING TRIGGERS ASSOCIATED
WITH PROBLEMATIC BEHAVIOURS

SUMMARY OF STEPS

⤳1⤶

Decide on the nature of the trigger – action problem
and the intervention strategy to be used

⤳2⤶

Set long-term goal

⤳3⤶

Set short-term objectives

⤳4⤶

Plan setting

⤳5⤶

Plan triggers for appropriate action

⤳6⤶

Plan reinforcement for appropriate behaviour

⤳7⤶

Plan record of progress

⤳8⤶

Plan review date

⤳9⤶

Write the action plan or programme

⤳10⤶

Record baseline measure

⤳11⤶

Implement review and move on

Teaching new skills

The occurrence of problematic behaviour is likely to be closely linked to deficits in key skill areas. Very often, behaviour which is perceived by others as problematic or inappropriate, is directed towards achieving important results and a person may lack more appropriate skills for achieving those results. Sometimes a person may want to control his own behaviour but may lack the relevant skills which would enable him to do so. Sometimes, a lack of specific skills may lead to failure in important areas of everyday life: failure may lead to frustration and anger; it may lead to the person avoiding those situations in which he fails. When working to help people overcome coping and behavioural difficulties it is essential, therefore, to look closely at the person's skills and to consider the person's behavioural difficulties in relation to these.

If a long-term solution to a problem is to be achieved, if a person's longer-term vulnerability to developing new problems is to be reduced, then he must, where relevant, be helped to acquire appropriate skills. If the individual already possesses the key skills needed to help reduce his problematic behaviour then ways need to be found to encourage the person to use these skills rather than rely on behaviour which others find unacceptable. Ways of encouraging people to use their appropriate skills are discussed in Chapter 7. The present chapter focuses on methods of teaching new skills to the individual.

TEACHING RELEVANT ALTERNATIVE SKILLS – GENERAL PRINCIPLES

DECIDING WHICH SKILLS ARE RELEVANT TO THE REDUCTION OF THE PROBLEMATIC BEHAVIOUR

The assessment will have highlighted the results which the individual achieves or seeks by the use of behaviour which is considered to be

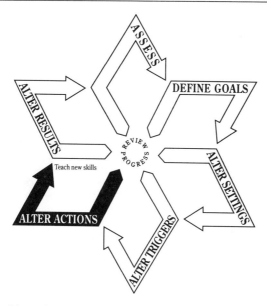

Figure 6.1 Teaching alternative skills.

problematic or inappropriate. It will also have highlighted any consistent triggers or setting conditions which might be associated with
the behaviour. This assessment information is used to pinpoint the
person's needs in relation to skill-learning. Some key skill areas are
described below.

1. Skills which are functionally equivalent to the inappropriate behaviour. If the problematic behaviour achieves specific and clear
   results for the individual, then the person may need to learn a more
   appropriate skill for achieving the same result. Examples of functionally equivalent skills are shown in Table 6.1.
2. Skills which are physically incompatible with the inappropriate
   behaviour. In situations where a behaviour occurs at a very high
   frequency and/or is dangerous (for example, self-injury or the eating
   of inedible items) it may be relevant for the person to learn a
   behaviour which is physically incompatible with the problematic
   behaviour. Examples of physically incompatible skills are shown in
   Table 6.2.
3. Skills which are functionally incompatible with the inappropriate
   behaviour. Functionally incompatible skills are those skills which
   enable a person to achieve a different outcome from a situation and
   thereby avoid the need for problematic behaviour. Examples of
   functionally incompatible skills are shown in Table 6.3.

Table 6.1 Examples of skills which are functionally equivalent to problematic behaviours

Inappropriate behaviour	Result achieved	Functionally equivalent skill
Biting	People move away	Pushing person gently on arm
Screaming	Get taken out of room	Opening door and leaving room
Face slapping	Demands stop	Saying 'No'
Throwing chairs	Attention from carer	Nudging people on arm
Hitting carers	Activity is provided	Saying 'I'm bored'
Playing with saliva	Sensory stimulation	Playing with water
Following staff	Occupation	Using a computer or playing a keyboard

Table 6.2 Examples of skills which are physically incompatible with problematic behaviours

Problematic behaviour	Physically incompatible skill
Persistent face slapping	Walking with hands in pockets, sitting on hands, sitting with arms folded
Persistently on the go	Sitting in one place
Persistent sucking of fingers	Holding 'feely object' in hand
Shouting	Whispering
Being rude to people	Being polite to people
Demanding attention	Being alone
Picking items off ground and eating them	Throwing picked-up items in bin
Physical tension	Muscular relaxation

Table 6.3 Examples of skills which are functionally incompatible with the problematic behaviour

Problematic behaviour	Aggression towards peers
Function of problematic behaviour	To disrupt aversive situation (being in a group)
Function of incompatible skill	To enable person to enjoy group situations
Functionally incompatible skill	To initiate conversations
Problematic behaviour	Hitting
Function of problematic behaviour	To terminate aversive situation (waiting)
Function of incompatible skill	To reduce aversiveness of waiting
Functionally incompatible skill	To be able to wait one's turn in a queue
Problematic behaviour	Temper tantrums during shopping trips
Function of problematic behaviour	To express anger at all money having been spent
Function of incompatible skill	To enable person to remain calm during shopping trips
Functionally incompatible skill	Budgeting of money

4. Skills which increase personal control. These are the skills which enable a person to direct his own actions and control his emotions. They include skills of self-monitoring, self-evaluation, self-cueing, self-reinforcement and arousal management. These skills are discussed fully in Chapter 9 and will therefore not be considered in any detail in the context of the present chapter.

SETTING CLEAR TEACHING GOALS

Efficiency is essential for effective teaching. Efficiency starts by translating learning needs into realistic long-term goals. Teaching occurs using a graded approach in order to simplify learning. Thus long-term goals must be broken down further into short-term teaching objectives, modest enough to achieve success within a short space of time. This may require a further assessment to establish how much of the skill can already be performed. From this a task analysis is performed to obtain a series of teaching steps, which will take the person from his current level of skill to the long-term goal. The reader should refer to Chapter 3 for a detailed account of the principles and procedures for establishing long-term and short-term goals for teaching.

DEVISING TEACHING PLANS

New skills can be learned in many ways. For example, they can be learned by watching others; or they can be learned by trial and error; they can be learned through experimentation; they can be learned through the formal and informal teaching efforts of others. On the whole, however, people with severe learning difficulties, by the very nature of their disability, find it difficult to make progress without active and structured help from those around them. This may require a lot of planning on the part of the person carrying out the teaching but such planning saves time in the long run and makes it far more likely that the individual will learn the key skills needed to help overcome his coping difficulties and to reduce the use of inappropriate behaviour.

When teaching a person a new skill attention needs to paid to every aspect of the teaching situation. In particular, attention needs to be paid to the settings for teaching, to the triggers which need to be provided to help him perform new skills and to the results which need to occur in order to inform the person about his performance and to motivate him to persist with learning.

Settings for skill teaching

Settings are those aspects of the environment or of the person which influence the person's motivations. They are an important source of influence upon learning and need to be taken into account when planning a teaching programme so that optimal conditions for learning can be created. Where natural settings do not provide the optimal conditions for learning (for example, when environments are too noisy or distracting, when a person is too tired or when there is not enough time available at times when teaching might naturally occur) then arbitrary settings may need to be provided. This may be particularly important during the earliest stages of learning a new skill. Arbitrary settings are those settings which have been deliberately set up in order to make learning easier. They might include a special teaching environment, special teaching times and specific people to carry out the teaching.

Triggers and skill teaching

Triggers are those stimuli which set off behaviour in a given situation at a given time. During skill teaching, triggers must be constructed which will ensure the performance of new behaviour. In this way the person gets a chance to learn. Such triggers are called prompts and they are withdrawn as the person becomes more proficient at performing the skill. Eventually the individual's skills come under the control of natural triggers.

Results and skill teaching

Results are critical factors in learning. When teaching people new skills, results need to be planned both for correct performance of the new skill and for errors. Reinforcers are the results that occur when a skill is performed correctly during learning: they serve both to inform the learner that what was done was correct and to encourage him to keep practising. In everyday life, successful use of a skill can be followed by a natural reinforcer (for example, a natural reinforcer for greeting another person is for that person to respond and engage in a conversation; the natural reinforcer for turning on the tape recorder may be a favourite piece of music playing). Natural reinforcers are the most effective way of sustaining skills. However, during early stages of learning, they may not provide a powerful enough incentive for the learner to persist with learning. There may, in addition, be a long delay between performance of the skill and the result (as between working and going out in the evening, getting dressed and having breakfast). When this occurs, arbitrary or additional reinforcers may have an important role to play.

The correction of errors is a second important result in skill teaching and must be done in a way which encourages rather than discourages performance. Correction is usually provided through the use of extra prompts which enable the learner to succeed without feeling that he has failed.

USING PRECISION TEACHING

Precision teaching is a very structured approach to teaching, where the teacher remains in control over all aspects of the teaching situation – its timing, its content, the help which is offered, the reinforcement which is given, the correction which is provided when success is not forth-coming and the amount of practice which is undertaken for each part of the skill. Errors are minimized, at least in the early stages of learning, by presenting tasks in a way that maximizes the probability of success and minimizes the probability of failure.

The setting for precision teaching

Precision teaching is often started in artificial or arbitrary settings in order to create optimal learning conditions. Thus the teacher is able to control such factors as noise, distraction, time available for the session, etc. As the learner becomes more proficient teaching is gradually extended into the environments where the skill is eventually to be used. This facilitates generalization of the skill.

The use of triggers in precision teaching

During precision teaching arbitrary triggers (prompts) are carefully planned in order to provide exactly the right amount of help the learner needs to succeed. The prompts are kept constant across teaching sessions. As the learner achieves mastery, the prompts are gradually reduced and faded in a planned and systematic way. Consistent trig-gers are also used to gain and maintain the learner's attention during teaching.

The use of results in precision teaching

In precision teaching, results are planned both for correct performance of a new skill and for errors. Arbitrary results, in the form of rewards, are often used to strengthen the learner's motivation to learn. These results are carefully selected in advance of the teaching programme. They are delivered systematically and consistently – initially for each correct performance of the skill – then they are gradually faded out until they can be delivered on an occasional basis only. Fading of the rein-forcers is, as with all aspects of precision teaching, carried out systematically (for example, reinforcement for two correct performances, then for three correct responses, then varied randomly every two or three correct responses, etc.).

Correction is also provided in a planned and systematic manner. When an error occurs, the response is corrected usually by increasing the level of the prompt. Thus prompts are progressively increased until correct performance occurs. Corrected performance is not reinforced.

Repeated practice and precision teaching

During precision teaching, skills are consolidated through regular, if not daily, practice. Within each daily practice session there may be several teaching trials so that the learning task is repeated several times over. Short daily 'sessions' with several 'trials per session' is the model frequently used for precision teaching.

Generalization and precision teaching

The distinction between natural and arbitrary settings, between natural and arbitrary triggers, between natural and arbitrary results is very important in relation to the teaching of new skills. 'Natural' refers to the settings and triggers that operate in the real world to tell the individual when a particular skill is appropriate. It refers also to the results that maintain the performance of that skill in the real world. 'Arbitrary' refers to the special settings, triggers and results that are often introduced into the teaching situation in order to ensure that learning occurs. These 'arbitrary' events do not occur in the normal course of events in the real world. Thus, in the natural environment a person may experience boredom, boredom triggers an approach to the caregiver who asks, 'What do you want?' The response 'Walk' (delivered verbally or using signing) may result in a walk, if the person is lucky. Alternatively it may result in the person being told that this activity is not possible at this moment in time.

The example given above shows how natural settings, triggers and results are the context for maintaining the skill of signalling 'Walk'. During learning through precision-teaching techniques, this skill might be taught in an arbitrary setting (for example, in a one-to-one teaching session each morning in a classroom at the day-centre). The response 'Walk' might be taught, using pictures or photographs and the prompt 'Show me the sign for . . .'. Additional prompts in the form of a demonstration or physical help may be used to trigger the response itself. The correct response might be rewarded with a lot of praise, in addition to a walk at the end of the session.

This way of teaching, though effective, introduces a lot of arbitrary events which may not be present in the real world under natural circumstances. For the person who has serious learning disabilities this is likely to mean that, although learning will occur, the skill will only be used when the arbitrary factors are present (for example, only in the classroom at the day-centre and only in response to the trigger 'What is the sign for . . .'). The skill will not therefore become functional in everyday life. The learner will have difficulty in generalizing from the arbitrary situation in which teaching occurred to the natural situation in which everyday practice is required. Teaching efforts are wasted if skills taught do not generalize to the learner's everyday world.

Precision teaching, therefore, requires the building of bridges from arbitrary to natural events. This is done using a process called graded change, which involves changing one thing at a time and changing each item in a series of small steps. This means meticulous planning, maximum consistency and careful monitoring. Thus, having taught the learner to sign 'Walk' to the appropriate picture, the teaching session must now be transferred to the natural setting. The teacher may now need to watch for signs of boredom and then ask the learner, 'What do you want?' She might then show him his coat and ask, 'Would you like to go for a walk?'. She might continue to use physical prompts or a demonstration to help the learner make the appropriate sign, and use praise and the walk as the reward for success. As the learner continues to progress, prompts and other triggers (showing of the coat, asking 'Would you like to go for a walk?') would be systematically faded out. Praise, too, would be gradually faded out.

The notion of graded change is central to precision teaching. It is a process by which the learner is 'moved on' from performing skills under arbitrary conditions to those situations in which the skills need to be performed in everyday life. This is achieved by frequently moving the learner on, using a series of short-term objectives, towards more independent and generalized usage of a skill. Thus arbitrary settings, triggers and results are systematically and gradually faded out as learning progresses.

USING INCIDENTAL TEACHING

Incidental teaching differs from precision teaching in that it aims to use more naturalistic methods for teaching. The learner has greater control during incidental teaching than during precision teaching in so far as it is the learner who initiates 'teaching' by requesting or initiating an event or object. This event or object is then used as the material around which teaching occurs and access to the event or object is the reinforcer for participating in the teaching session.

Incidental teaching appears on the surface to be less structured and rigid than precision teaching in that the amount of help offered to the learner varies from session to session. Correction for errors also is varied. Access to the reinforcer is automatic, whether or not performance is 'correct'. Despite being a more naturalistic teaching method and one which appears less structured, incidental teaching nevertheless requires as much planning and structure as precision teaching in order for it to be maximally effective.

The settings for incidental teaching

Incidental teaching occurs around situations and activities in which the learner has expressed an interest. Teaching can be conducted in natural settings which have been selected because they contain objects/ activities which the person is likely to want or enjoy and which are likely to motivate him. Thus, if the person enjoys going for walks then incidental-teaching procedures could be used to teach a number of skills around this activity. Examples include dressing (putting coat and outdoor shoes on), extending a signing vocabulary (signs for walk, shops, park, swings, road, cars, trees, people etc., etc., etc.!), road-crossing skills, and so on. Alternatively, natural settings could be deliberately enriched with items which are likely to be selected or requested by the person. For example, if a person enjoys the telephone, then a telephone could be made available and could be the material used for teaching skills such as fine motor control (pressing the various buttons), number recognition, saying 'Hello', introducing oneself by one's name, and so on.

Using triggers in incidental teaching

Two types of triggers are relevant here. First, the triggers for the teaching itself – in other words, the cues which are provided for the teacher, to let her know that the time is right for teaching. In incidental teaching, the cue for teaching comes from the learner himself. Only when he expresses an interest in an object or activity is teaching conducted. The teaching has been planned in advance and is relevant to the object of interest. The object is made available and is readily visible. For example, if the activity of going for a walk was to be used as the context for teaching a person to sign 'Walk' then the person's coat and outdoor shoes might be left lying around in a visible and easily accessible place. Teaching the person to sign 'Walk' would only occur if the person approached the coats or the door or gave some other indication that this was the activity he wanted.

The second important use of triggers in incidental teaching relates to the use of prompts. Since the person conducting the teaching is not in control of the timing of the teaching and teaching occurs in the natural environment where the timing may not always be convenient, the prompts used to help the learner are varied, depending on the time available for teaching. Thus, if the teacher is busy with other things at the moment when an interest is expressed by the learner, then a high level of prompt may be used in order to shorten the teaching. If there is time available, then the minimum prompt required may be used, thus requiring greater effort from the learner. Using the earlier example of teaching a person to signal that he wants to go for a walk, if the person carrying out the teaching was pressed for time, she might simply demonstrate the sign for walk and then immediately take the person out. If more time was available she would demonstrate the sign for 'Walk', wait for the learner to respond and help him as necessary, before taking him out for a walk.

Using results in incidental teaching

During incidental teaching the result for correct performance is access to the object/activity in which the learner has expressed an interest and which triggered the teaching session. Correction for errors may be varied, again according to the circumstances and the time available. Regardless of whether correct performance occurs, the learner has automatic access to the selected object or activity which triggered the teaching session. Thus, having demonstrated and not gained the appropriate response from the learner and the learner having resisted a further physical prompt to help him make the appropriate sign for 'Walk', the person carrying out the teaching would simply proceed with taking the learner out for a walk.

Generalization and incidental teaching

Incidental teaching is conducted in the natural environment, and triggers and correction procedures are varied and random. Reinforcers are in a sense 'natural' in that they are objects and activities occurring in the natural environment and in which the learner has expressed a specific interest. For these reasons, generalization of skills taught using incidental teaching procedures occurs naturally and automatically. A graded and systematic approach to generalization, as is necessary in precision teaching, is not usually required.

SUMMARY

Providing people with appropriate alternative skills is an essential component of a therapeutic package. If long-term solutions are to be achieved for a person's behavioural and adjustment difficulties, then this will probably require the learning of important new skills. Such learning may take some time and so an efficient approach to teaching is needed. This means careful consideration of the skills which are important to learn and the methods by which they can be taught. Two structured approaches to skill teaching have been presented here. In practice, the two approaches are frequently used in combination, depending on the skill being taught, the degree to which the person has already acquired parts of the skills and the resources available for teaching. When planning a skill-teaching programme, it is necessary to select the best approach or combination of approaches for the teaching in question. Specific procedures for planning and writing skill-teaching programmes are detailed in the second part of this chapter.

PROCEDURES FOR TEACHING RELEVANT NEW SKILLS

Step 1   Translate learning need into realistic long-term goals

The needs list (Chapter 2) will have identified important learning needs which must first be translated into clear long-term goals (Chapter 3, STEP 1) which are felt to be achievable within a 6–12-month period. Such goals are stated using the format shown below.

Who	Larry
Will do what	will sign 'Go away'
Under what circumstances	when he does not want people to sit next to him
With how much help	with verbal reminders only.

Step 2   Set short-term teaching objectives

Long-term goals need to be broken down into a series of small steps which take the person from his current level of skill to the long-term goal. The selection of the first and subsequent steps will depend on the following.

1. The current level of the skill.
2. The method selected for teaching the steps (backward or forward chaining, shaping, part-task or whole-task teaching). The reader should refer to Chapter 3 (STEPS 2 and 3) for a fuller account.

3. The context for teaching (natural or contrived setting). If the things and activities which a person enjoys (these will have been identified in the strengths list) can be used as the context (materials or activities) for teaching the skill, then teaching should be planned around these.

Once the methods have been selected by which to teach the steps and the context for teaching decided upon, a short-term objective can be stated. It should be small enough to be achievable within 3–6 weeks. It should be stated using the format illustrated below.

Who	Larry
Will do what	will sign 'Go away'
With how much help	with a full physical prompt
Under what circumstances	during the first hour after lunch (at day-centre)
To what degree of success	five times during each session.

Step 3   Plan the place where teaching is to occur

Natural settings

Ideally teaching should be carried out in the most naturalistic setting, i.e. in the place where the skill is to be finally practised. Thus social skills should be learned ideally at the point of contact with relevant others, communication skills should be learned as communications needs arise and self-occupation skills should be learned in places where they might eventually be practised.

Enriched natural settings

For incidental teaching, natural settings may be deliberately enriched with stimuli which the person is known to find reinforcing and in which he is likely to show an interest. These stimuli will become the focus for teaching once an interest in them is expressed.

Arbitrary settings which are of themselves reinforcing

Teaching may be deliberately constructed around an activity which the person finds enjoyable. For example, communication skills might be taught during a favourite activity, such as cooking, and social skills might be taught during a favourite activity, such as swimming.

Arbitrary settings which provide control over teaching

Natural settings may sometimes unnecessarily restrict the number of teaching occasions that can occur. There may also be too many distractions in such settings, thus preventing the person from focusing his attention. In such cases it may become necessary to create a special arbitrary teaching environment, at least for the initial teaching session, which will cut down the number of distractions and enable more concentrated practice of the skill. If special environments need to be created, then it may be helpful to bring into those arbitrary settings a number of natural setting factors, i.e. materials or people or even furniture which will help the person associate performance of the skill with the places where the skills are destined for. The greater the number of 'natural' setting factors that can be incorporated into teaching, the greater the likelihood that skills will generalize after learning has occurred.

Step 4 — Plan the times for teaching

Any time: learner signals interest in activity (incidental teaching)

If an incidental-teaching approach is being used, teaching times may occur throughout the course of the day, whenever the learner expresses an interest in an activity or item which has been identified as the stimulus for teaching. The stimulus is made available at all times and the teacher merely waits for the learner to initiate the teaching session.

Teacher selects time of teaching session: learner signals interest in activity (incidental teaching)

The stimulus which will be used for teaching and which the learner is expected to express interest in is made available during specific periods of the day or during particular sessions. This provides the teacher with greater control over the timing of teaching. Teaching occurs when the person expresses an interest in the activity. Thus, teaching times are controlled only inasmuch as the person carrying out the teaching selects when to make the activities/items available to the person.

Teacher selects teaching time (precision teaching)

The amount of time and help which is needed by the learner to benefit from the teaching and the amount of structure that this requires, will dictate whether a predetermined teaching time needs to be put aside. If teaching is very specific and highly structured, then the timing of teaching sessions is unlikely to be left to the learner, but is likely to be selected by the person carrying out the teaching. Selection of teaching time should be guided by the following.

1. If possible the times selected should be times when the person is most likely to be receptive to teaching. For example, if there are particular times of the day when a person is more relaxed and able to focus attention, then it would be wise to capitalize on this and use some of this time for teaching.
2. The reinforcer which is being used as part of the teaching plan may have a bearing on the selection of the most appropriate teaching times. Specific reinforcers may vary during the day as to how powerful they are. For example, if the person is learning how to make a cup of tea, it would be best to carry out teaching when the person is likely to be thirsty rather than just after he has already had a drink. If a self-occupation skill is being taught, the student's motivation to learn may be higher if the teaching time selected is one when there would normally be a relatively low level of stimulation and occupation going on around him than if he were to be removed from an activity which he greatly enjoys.
3. If there are particular times of the day when problematic behaviour is more likely to occur then skill teaching should be avoided at such times. For example, if the person is always very restless following a period of unstructured activity, then it is important not to try to teach at this time a skill that requires him to sit down and to give his concentrated attention.

Step ⟩ 5 ⟨ Plan who is to conduct the teaching

Teaching conducted by a variety of people

During incidental teaching, where skills are taught in the natural environment and where the timing of teaching depends on the person initiating the teaching by expressing an interest in a particular stimulus or activity, then the person conducting the teaching may be the person on hand when the person expresses his interest. If skills being taught are ultimately to be practised with a wide range of people (for example, social or communication skills), then teaching sessions should, if possible, be carried out by a variety of individuals so that the person learns as early as possible to associate usage of the skill with a wide range of people.

Teaching conducted by specific individuals

During early stages of precision teaching, the number of people conducting the teaching may need to be more limited and more carefully selected. Selection may depend on a number of factors. It may be that the learner responds well to only a few people in his environment. It may be that there are only a few people who are able to work through the difficult behaviour which the person shows. If this is the case then it may be important to have just these people carry out the initial teaching, to get the person started on the learning process.

Step ⟩ 6 ⟨   Plan trigger for teaching

Learner initiates teaching

If an incidental-teaching approach is being used, the trigger for the teaching session will be the learner expressing an interest in the activity or object which has been preselected as the focus for teaching.

Teacher initiates teaching

When the teaching session is initiated by the teacher, it may be necessary to plan a consistent way of focusing the learner's attention on the task. On the whole, such triggering should not be left to chance but a trigger, once selected, should be used in a consistent manner and repeated during each session in order that the person may learn more quickly what is expected of him. There are a number of ways which can be used to gain the learner's attention.

1. Materials: drawing the person's attention to the materials which are being used during teaching.
2. Reinforcers: if an arbitrary reinforcer is being used, then allowing the person to see and sample at the start of the teaching session the reinforcer which is to be used for correct performance during the session may help gain and maintain his attention.
3. Verbal instructions: simple and clear instructions such as 'look', 'listen', 'ready' can, if used consistently, come to signal the start of each teaching trial. If a person does not respond to verbal cues, then physical prompts, such as gently directing the learner's face towards

the instructor or task, can be another effective means of focusing attention to the task.

Step 7   Plan how to prompt the learner

Select appropriate prompt

Prompts can be provided in a number of ways.

1. Instructions: explaining to the person in words or gestures what should actually be done.
2. Demonstration: showing the person how to perform the task.
3. Physical guidance: physically helping the person by guiding his limbs to carry out the task. (In teaching the person to operate a cassette player, the teacher might hold a hand over the student's hand so that the correct buttons are located and pressed.)
4. Special equipment: providing the person with specially adapted materials to simplify learning (for example, using a specially adapted cassette player with extra large touch pads over the operating buttons).
5. Visual clues: using visual signals to indicate directly what to do (for example, putting different coloured strips on the start, rewind and forward wind buttons of the cassette player).

These ways are not mutually exclusive and often will be provided in combination. For example, in the initial stages of teaching the person to operate the cassette player, the equipment could be specially adapted, with colour-coded keys. Teaching itself might be conducted using verbal instructions plus demonstration with physical guidance, if necessary, to ensure correct performance.

When planning which prompts to use, thought needs to be given to the type of prompt that most suits the individual person. Demonstrating a task to a person who rarely looks in the direction of the person conducting the teaching or who does not show evidence of imitative skills is unlikely to be useful. Explaining in sentences what should be done can only be helpful if the person has some understanding of language. Physical guidance may lead to physical resistance from some learners.

Select appropriate level of prompt

As well as planning whether to use prompts and, if so, what type, it is also necessary to plan the level of help needed. If too much help is given, the person may come to depend entirely on prompting and learn nothing about the task itself. If too little help is given, the person may make too many errors and fail to learn altogether or learn inappropriate behaviour.

Prompts can be broken down into a series of steps in the same way as the tasks themselves can (Chapter 3). As an example, a physical prompt used to help the person insert a tape into the cassette player can be broken down into the following steps.

1. Holding hand over learner's hand and guiding the cassette into the slot.
2. Holding hand over learner's hand and guiding until 1 inch from the slot (person completes task unaided).
3. Guidance until 3 inches from slot.
4. Supporting learner on forearm and guiding arm to slot.
5. As for (4) but removing guidance 1 inch from slot.
6. As for (4) but removing guidance 6 inches from slot.
7. Supporting learner at elbow and guiding arm to slot.
8. As for (7) but removing guidance 6 inches from slot.
9. Person lifts and inserts tape into slot independently.

When determining the level of prompt to be used, it is important to use the **minimum** amount of prompting needed to ensure correct performance of the skill. In this way the person performs the task correctly but with as much active personal contribution as possible.

During teaching sessions which are entirely controlled by the person conducting the teaching, it is possible to be very consistent about the type and level of prompt being used. Indeed precision teaching is based upon very systematic and consistent use of prompts at a pre-selected level. If teaching is being conducted on an incidental basis, then there may not always be time to provide help in such a consistent way. Whenever teaching conditions permit, the minimum prompts should be used and correction should be systematically delivered. However, if teaching conditions do not permit this, then a greater amount of help may be provided in order to speed up completion of the teaching trial.

Step 8   Decide on number of teaching trials per session

Learning is bound to be faster if more teaching trials are provided: in other words, if the learner practises the task more often during each session. This may not always be possible or logical. For example, if the learner signs appropriately for 'Walk', when it has been demonstrated to him, then it would not be logical to ask him to practise the sign several more times before going out for a walk. However, it would be logical, if the learner was practising giving the right money in shops for goods purchased, to have him shop in three or four shops during a single shopping trip in order to increase practice of the skill. When more than a single learning trial is planned for a teaching session, then the number of trials to be presented during the session should be decided upon in advance.

Step 9   Plan how to correct errors

The careful planning of how to correct errors ensures that the learner does not feel he has failed in the task. It is a way of ensuring that he is given just enough extra help to enable him to succeed, before he becomes frustrated and gives up. Sometimes a single correction procedure will be used. Sometimes a graded series of prompts are planned so that the person is offered progressively more help until success occurs.

Select appropriate correction procedure

1. Demonstration: the person conducting the teaching demonstrates the correct response and then encourages the learner to try again. For example, if the person learning to rewind the audio cassette presses fast forward instead of rewind, the teacher simply demonstrates the correct response and offers the learner another chance to press the correct button.
2. Extra help: if a person cannot imitate, or if the task is difficult to demonstrate, then an alternative way of reminding is to take the person through the task with enough extra help to ensure success. For example, if a person fails to load the cassette into the tape recorder, the person teaching this skill to him might provide physical guidance to his hand to ensure success.
3. Interruption: if the person persists with the incorrect response and persistence is not felt to be helping him to learn (for example, persisting in trying to insert a tape back to front into the video player) then the response can simply be interrupted and the whole task restarted.

The word 'No' should be avoided when correcting errors during skill-learning. 'No' is a powerful word used to make a person stop what he is doing. It is often associated, through learning experience, with something unpleasant happening if the person does not stop. It may, therefore, trigger general 'freezing', anxiety or avoidance which may include aggression. None of these behaviours are useful in a learning situation!

In precision teaching, the correction procedure is used consistently throughout the teaching programme. When using an incidental-teaching approach, correction procedures are varied according to the time available to the person conducting the teaching. If time permits, a graded series of planned prompts will be used. If time is limited, maximum help may immediately be offered to ensure success. If time is very limited, the person will not be asked to perform the skill at all. The reinforcer, which was the stimulus which prompted the teaching trial, will simply be given to the person.

Plan the timing of the correction procedure

1. If the person seems not to know how to proceed then correction should occur quite quickly after an error has been made (within a few seconds, if necessary).
2. If the person tries to correct his own error then up to a minute might be given before giving extra help.
3. If the person persists with the incorrect response then correction should occur more quickly, within 10 seconds.
4. If the learner is making no response at all, then a fixed number of seconds, between 5 and 20, should be allowed before correction.

Step 10   Plan how to reinforce correct performance

Select appropriate reinforcer

Natural reinforcer

It is important always to consider the natural reinforcer for the skill in question and to use this whenever possible. For example, the natural reinforcer for a greeting response, such as 'Hello', would be a reciprocal greeting and perhaps a smile. The natural reinforcer for requesting an object would be the object itself. The natural reinforcer for having a bath would be a feeling of freshness and, perhaps, the pleasant smell of soap or talcum powder. Whenever possible the natural reinforcer should be used. (Natural reinforcers available in natural environments and combined with student-initiated teaching, based upon expressed interest in obtaining this natural reinforcer, are the conditions for incidental teaching.)

Arbitrary reinforcer

If the natural reinforcer cannot be delivered immediately (for example, the natural reinforcer for planting seeds would be the sight of flowers blooming in that place several weeks or months later), or if it is unlikely to be immediately meaningful for the person (for example, sharing things with other people), then it may be necessary to select an arbitrary reinforcer which can be given immediately and which is powerful enough to act as a source of encouragement. The person's strengths list will provide information on such effective reinforcers.

Plan how to use the reinforcer

1. A reinforcer will have its greatest strengthening effect on the be-haviour which immediately precedes it in time. It is therefore best for a reinforcer to **immediately** follow correct performance.
2. If reinforcement is to be used not just to strengthen motivation but also to make clearer to the learner what is expected, then it should follow only when the task has been performed correctly (corrected performance does not constitute 'correct').
3. If using a precision-teaching approach the reinforcer should follow the action on every occasion that the skill is performed correctly, during the early stages of teaching. As learning progresses, rein-forcement is systematically reduced until it can be delivered on a random and infrequent basis (for example, it might initially be re-duced to every second correct response, then to every third correct response, etc.) and then moved onto a random schedule (some-times after two, sometimes after four, sometimes after three correct responses, etc.).
4. During incidental teaching, reinforcement (which is the stimulus or activity which triggered the teaching trial) is always given, regard-less of whether the task was performed correctly or incorrectly.

Step 11 Plan record of progress

Having an objective record of progress enables those involved in the teaching to judge whether the teaching strategy is leading to improve-ments in the learner's level of competence.

Decide what to record

The simplest way of judging progress is to measure whether a person carried out a skill correctly or not. This is a two-way Yes/No system of measurement.

Did the person:

- insert the cassette player and press the start button?
- share his sweets with those around him?
- ask for help when in difficulty?

Progress is evident if the number of times that the answer is 'yes' increases. While this is a simple measure it is relatively insensitive to progress, particularly if teaching is being conducted using a graded series of prompts and correction. In this case, a more sensitive way to monitor progress is to record whether or not the person needed extra help to perform the skill and how much help was needed.

Did the person insert the cassette and press 'start' on the cassette player:

- without help?
- with verbal reminders?
- with physical guidance?
- not at all?

Did the person offer his sweets:

- spontaneously?
- with reminders?
- following a demonstration?
- not at all?

The more detailed the measure, the more sensitive it will be to changes, but the more complex and time consuming it will be to carry out.

Plan when to record

During skill teaching, recording should ideally be carried out at the same time as the teaching, particularly if a sensitive measure of performance, as that described above, is needed. If recording is left to the end of a teaching session, or if there is any time delay between the teaching and the recording, then the likelihood of recording errors increases.

Recording should ideally be carried out on every teaching occasion (continuous recording). However, if this is not practical then recording on selected occasions (sample recording) is the alternative option. The reader should refer to Chapter 11 for a detailed account of methods of recording and monitoring of progress. Regardless of whether a continuous or a sampling method is chosen, the recording should always be carried out during the teaching itself.

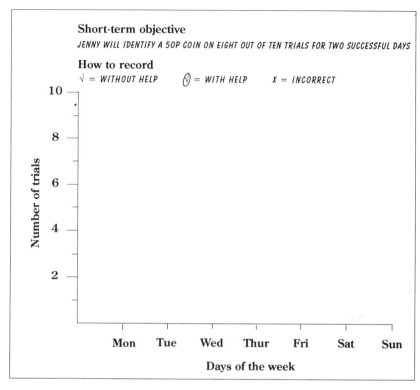

Figure 6.2 Example of a simple recording chart for recording the level of skill performance during teaching.

Prepare recording chart

A recording chart should be prepared in advance in order to make the recording more efficient. It should be designed in such a way that the learner's performance over time can be seen. Figure 6.2 provides an example of a simple recording chart. The horizontal line of the chart is divided up into sections of time (days of the week, sessions of teaching). The vertical line of the chart is divided up to allow for the recording of each teaching trial during the session (the number of trials per session will have been decided in advance).

Different ways of drawing up recording charts and different types of symbols which can be used to represent the person's level of performance, so that each possible outcome is represented by a different symbol, are illustrated in Figure 6.3. A key should be drawn on the chart to show how the recording is to be carried out.

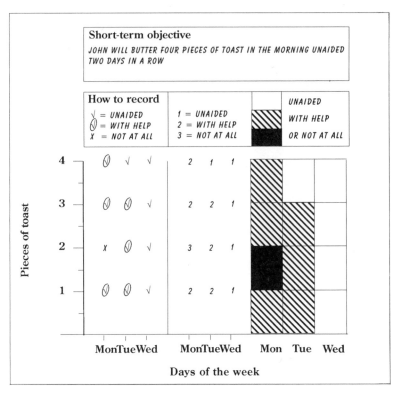

Figure 6.3 Example of how to complete a chart to record level of skill performance during teaching.

Step ⟨12⟩   Plan to consolidate learning

When planning teaching programmes that involve the use of arbitrary settings, triggers or results, it is important also to plan ways of helping the person consolidate learning. Three common ways of doing this are as follows.

1. Informing other people about the broad aim of the teaching programme and asking them to do their best to encourage the same sort of skill. While a person might be involved at a day facility in a systematic programme to take turns with other service users in a board game, relatives and friends might be asked more generally to do things with him that involve turn-taking.
2. Introducing the same concepts less formally with different materials. A person might be working on a systematic programme to learn

how to make choices between two items, but others who come into contact with the person may be asked to introduce choices in as many day-to-day situations as possible (informal or incidental teaching).

3. Introducing the same skills on different occasions. A person might be learning during specific sessions how to ask for items by name. If these same items are available at other times of the day, then the requirement to ask could be introduced into these other occasions (informal or incidental teaching).

Such practice in skill usage is important for consolidating new learning and should be built into a teaching plan. It helps to prevent learning becoming too specific and facilitates generalization of the new skill.

Step 13 Plan review date

A date must be specified on which the teaching plan will be reviewed in order to judge whether it should be continued or adapted. Such a date should occur within 4 weeks of the start of the programme and be part of a regular ongoing process of programme review.

Step 14 Write the teaching plan

Having decided upon each aspect of the skill-teaching plan, the next step is to write down the details in the form of a written programme. The written skill-teaching programme should include the following details.

1. Long-term goal.
2. Short-term objectives.
3. Time and place of session.
4. People to be involved.
5. Special materials.
6. Number of teaching trials per session.
7. Procedures which include:
   (a) method of gaining the student's attention, if appropriate;
   (b) instructions to be given to the learner;
   (c) type and level of prompt to be used to help person complete the task.
8. Reinforcement for correct performance.
9. Correction strategy.

10. Consolidation strategy.
11. Recording procedure and recording chart.
12. Date of review.

An example of a skill-teaching programme, which has been derived from the needs listed in Chapter 2, Figure 2.6, is illustrated in Figure 6.4. It illustrates the use of an incidental-teaching procedure to teach a functionally equivalent skill.

Step 15   Implement programme

The effectiveness of a well-planned teaching programme will depend, to a large extent, on how well it is implemented. From a practical point of view, a few simple rules should help increase the likelihood of success and provide encouragement to continue.

Prepare the session fully before engaging the person

The learner should never be kept waiting while the person who is to conduct the teaching prepares the teaching session or interrupts the session to collect forgotten materials. This is likely to discourage the learner and he may then be less eager to co-operate with teaching. All teaching materials and recording forms should be ready in advance and programme details should be fully understood. If several people are to be involved in the teaching, it is useful to run through the programme together at an early stage, using modelling and role play, to ensure details are understood by all those who will be involved with teaching.

Finish sessions on a note of success

To increase the likelihood that the learner and the person conducting the teaching will enjoy the teaching experience, it is important that teaching sessions always end with success. This will always be the case in programmes based on incidental-teaching procedures. During precision teaching ensuring that the session ends on success may sometimes mean allowing the person a final attempt which is over-prompted, or decreasing the level of demand for the final trial, in order to ensure success. Finishing on a note of failure can be discouraging for the person and decreases willingness to co-operate during subsequent sessions.

Name *LARRY*	**Date** *JUNE 10TH*

Long-term Goal

LARRY WILL GENTLY PUSH PEOPLE ON THE ARM WHENEVER HE WANTS THEM TO MOVE AWAY

Short-term Goal

LARRY WILL PUSH PEOPLE ON THE ARM WITH VERBAL PROMPTS FROM HIS CARERS WHENEVER

HE WANTS THEM TO MOVE AWAY ON FIVE OUT OF SIX ATTEMPTS ON FIVE CONSECUTIVE DAYS

People Involved

ALL CARE STAFF ON EVENING SHIFT

Time and Place *LOUNGE, AFTER TEA*	**Trials per Session** *6*

Procedure

WHEN LARRY HAS BEEN SEATED WATCHING TV FOR ABOUT 5 MINUTES GO AND SIT

YOURSELF NEXT TO HIM ON THE SOFA / ARM OF ARMCHAIR

ACKNOWLEDGE HIM BRIEFLY BUT DO NOT ENGAGE HIM IN ANY LENGTHY CONVERSATION

Response to Appropriate Behaviour

IF LARRY PUSHES YOUR ARM SAY "YOU WANT ME TO MOVE AWAY LARRY? OK".

STAND UP AND MOVE TO ANOTHER SEAT

Response to Inappropriate Behaviour

IF LARRY STARTS TO SCREAM, TURN TO HIM AND SAY "LARRY, IF YOU WANT ME TO MOVE

AWAY, THEN LET ME KNOW PROPERLY".

IF LARRY HAS NOT MADE THE APPROPRIATE RESPONSE AFTER 5 SECONDS, REPEAT THE

QUESTION, THEN IMMEDIATELY TAKE HIS ARM AND USE A PHYSICAL PROMPT TO HELP HIM

PUSH YOU GENTLY ON THE SHOULDER, SAYING "YOU WANT ME TO MOVE AWAY LARRY? OK".

STAND UP AND MOVE AWAY

Recording Procedure

FOR EACH OF THE SIX TRIALS, RECORD ON SHEET ATTACHED

I   =   *IF LARRY RESPONDED SPONTANEOUSLY*

II   =   *IF LARRY RESPONDED FOLLOWING A VERBAL REMINDER*

III =   *IF LARRY RESPONDED FOLLOWING A PHYSICAL PROMPT*

Date of Review *JULY 10TH*

Figure 6.4 Example of skill-teaching programme using incidental teaching of functionally equivalent skills.

Step 16   Review and move on

As each short-term objective is achieved, a decision needs to be made about how to extend the teaching. The teaching of a new skill may have involved teaching the skill one bit at a time, through a series of small teaching objectives. These short-term objectives will have been largely planned at the start of teaching following the task analysis, and a decision will have been made about the organization of teaching (part-task or whole-task teaching, backward or forward chaining, shaping). Each part of the task may have required the use of arbitrary triggers in the form of prompts. Each type of prompt may itself have been graded along a number of levels. The principle of graded change now must be used to move the person forward towards skill mastery. This means:

- reducing the level of prompting at each stage of learning (if several kinds of prompt are being used, then these also need to be reduced in a systematic and gradual fashion);
- increasing the proportion of the task which the person is required to complete;
- fading out the use of arbitrary reinforcers;
- fading in natural setting factors.

An example of a skill-teaching programme, which has been derived from the needs listed in Chapter 2, Figure 2.6, is illustrated in Figure 6.4. It illustrates the use of an incidental-teaching procedure to teach a functionally equivalent skill.
must do to obtain reinforcement is given below. In this example, a part-task, backward-chaining procedure has been used.

Long-term goal
Mary will let people know what she wants by leading them to an object and pointing to it.

Short-term objectives
1. When asked what she wants, Mary will move her arm in the direction of the object with physical guidance from wrist.
2. As (1) with physical guidance from elbow.
3. As (1) with light touch to elbow.
4. As (1) with no help.
5. When asked what she wants, Mary will move her arm in the direction of the object, index finger pointed with physical help to point finger.

6. As (5) with reminder (demonstration) to point.
7. With adult 5 feet from object, Mary will take hold of adult's arm and lead to object with physical prompt, then point to what she wants as in (6).
8. As (7) with no help.
9. As (8) with adult 8 feet from object.
10. As (8) with different adults present.
11. As (8) with adults outside room.

SUMMARY

Teaching alternative skills is an essential component of the therapeutic package. By definition, people with serious learning disabilities find new learning difficult and thus teaching them new skills takes time. Teaching can be made more efficient by careful planning of the methods and content of teaching plans. A graded approach enhances motivation because failure is minimized. A graded approach has implications for record keeping and close monitoring of progress so that the person can be 'moved on' towards long-term goals as soon as he is ready. Having mastered new skills, it cannot be assumed that these will automatically be used in situations where they are likely to directly reduce the incidence of inappropriate behaviour occurring. This is the subject which is addressed in Chapter 7.

In this chapter, the general principles of selecting important skills for the reduction of problematic behaviour have been described and the principles of teaching such skills have been outlined. Steps have been described which, if systematically followed, can help the reader move from the assessment stage described in Chapter 2 and the planning of specific teaching goals described in Chapter 3 to planning, writing and implementing programmes which will achieve these goals in the area of skill acquisition.

TEACHING ALTERNATE SKILLS

SUMMARY OF STEPS

1

Translate learning need into realistic long-term goal

2

Set short-term teaching objectives

3

Plan the place where teaching is to occur

4

Plan the times for teaching

5

Plan who is to conduct the teaching

6

Plan trigger for teaching

7

Plan how to prompt the learner

8

Decide on number of teaching trials per session

9

Plan how to correct errors

10

Plan how to reinforce correct performance

11

Plan record of progress

12

Plan to consolidate learning

13

Plan review date

14

Write teaching plan

15

Implement programme

16

Review and move on

Encouraging appropriate alternatives

7

Once a relevant new skill has been taught there is no guarantee that this skill will automatically replace the problematic or inappropriate behaviour or that it will be used in a way which prevents the problematic behaviour occurring. Teaching a new skill is one thing; getting the person to use it appropriately, in a way that directly impacts upon the problematic behaviour is another. It is this issue which the present chapter addresses. In particular it is concerned with how to replace inappropriate behaviour with skills which serve the same function as or which are directly incompatible with the problematic behaviour.

REPLACING PROBLEMATIC BEHAVIOUR WITH APPROPRIATE SKILLS – GENERAL PRINCIPLES

UNDERSTANDING WHY APPROPRIATE SKILLS ARE NOT PRACTISED

A person may have a number of useful skills which could be used to achieve important results; for example, to occupy his leisure time, to communicate his needs, to join in group activities, to do things independently. He may have been taught specific skills, following an assessment of his problematic behaviour – skills which he could use to achieve the same result as the result achieved by the problematic behaviour or which he could use as a direct alternative to the behaviour. Yet these available skills may be practised infrequently or not at all. The inappropriate behaviour continues to be used. There may be important reasons why this is so.

Lack of opportunity

Opportunities to practise appropriate specific skills may be unavailable. For example, an individual may be able to prepare some food items for

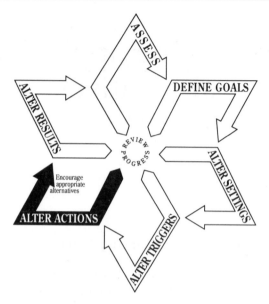

Figure 7.1 Encouraging alternative skills.

cooking or be able to wash up but these skills will not be practised if he is not allowed into the kitchen. Even if allowed into the kitchen he may appear unable to cook if the cooker is electric and he has been taught to use gas. A person may know how to stop himself from head banging by keeping his hands in his pockets but will not do so if he wears clothes without pockets. A person may know how to communicate 'No' but may not do so if sufficient time is not made available for him to communicate his need.

Restricted access (to places or materials or time) is one way in which opportunities to practise skills are denied. Another way is when other people do for the individual what he is capable of doing for himself. Making choices or decisions for a person rules out the possibility of that person being able to show that he can choose between activities or communicate that he does or does not want something. If a person's hand is always held when out in the street it will not be possible for that person to demonstrate independent ability in the use of road skills.

Lack of triggering

An individual's true competence may be hidden because the skill is still dependent on a certain amount of prompting (triggering) and the right prompt may be absent from the environment. For example, if a person has learned that he can only operate the music system if someone else gives permission, then if no one gives this permission he may appear unable to perform the skill. A person may know how to relax but not know the appropriate natural trigger (tension) which should elicit this skill, just the arbitrary trigger (being told to relax). Thus in the absence of the arbitrary trigger, he will never show this skill.

Lack of positive results

A skill may have been learned but not be used if, in practice, the skill does not achieve meaningful results for the person – in other words, if the skill is not reinforced. A person may be able to ask for a drink but will not do so very often if, whenever he asks, he is told to wait until it is 'time'. A person may be able to occupy himself with a constructive activity for several minutes but will not do so if he is ignored or left alone every time he engages in this activity. A person may be able to indicate that he does not want to do something but will not do so if, every time he uses this appropriate form of communication, his wishes are ignored and he is forced to do the activity.

Differential reinforcement of the problematic behaviour

It has been suggested earlier in this book that behavioural problems can be regarded as meaningful and skilled actions, which achieve important results for the individual. Illustrated above is the all too common situation where appropriate skills are used infrequently because they achieve only weak or occasional results. If, in the person's experience, inappropriate actions that serve the same purpose as appropriate skills achieve stronger or more frequent results than does an appropriate behaviour, then this illustrates the important process of differential reinforcement.

When a person has a number of possible actions which can be used in a situation and each action is associated with a different probability of reinforcement, then he will tend to act in a way that gets the best 'return' – he will spend more time on that behaviour with the greater likelihood of reinforcement. For example a person may find that when he screams and scratches himself, a caregiver will often sit with him and comfort him. However, when he tries to sit with the caregiver at other times, using a more appropriate approach, he is often sent away. By this process of differential reinforcement the frequency of screaming and scratching will increase and the frequency of approaching people will decrease.

To take another example, sitting quietly at table, waiting for food may mean that a person gets served last and has cold food. In contrast, throwing cutlery across the room and kicking other people at the table is likely to result in a faster service and warmer food for that same individual. If this consistently happens then the process of differential reinforcement is occurring. This means that there will be a likelihood of an increasing frequency of 'disruptive' behaviour at meal times and a decreasing frequency of appropriate behaviour.

To give one final example, a person may find that if he pushes someone's hand to stop a demand or request being made, the person may often persist with the demand. However, biting or scratching the person results more reliably in a withdrawal response. This again is an example of differential reinforcement. Biting and scratching is likely to increase while the more appropriate form of communication is likely to decrease because it achieves nothing for the person.

Such comparisons of 'returns' do not necessarily take place at the conscious level. The individual does not need to be aware of the differential probability of 'returns' for different behaviour nor does he need to make conscious judgements about which behaviour to use. His behaviour changes through the direct experience over time of different results being achieved for different actions.

The concept of differential reinforcement illustrates why behaviour that is regarded as inappropriate may persist even though the individual has learned other more acceptable ways of achieving the same results or alternative skills which could be used in place of the problematic behaviour. It stresses the importance of not only teaching relevant skills but also of making sure that such skills achieve meaningful results a lot more frequently than does the inappropriate behaviour.

REPLACING PROBLEMATIC BEHAVIOUR WITH MORE APPROPRIATE SKILLS

Opportunity provision

Ensuring that the environment provides appropriate opportunities for the individual to show the skills that he has is an obvious but not always carefully considered intervention. For example, a problematic behaviour that serves a self-stimulatory function might be counteracted if materials that the individual is known to use appropriately are available at times when boredom is likely to occur. A behaviour that serves the purpose of getting out of anxiety-provoking situations and into quiet and solitude may be counteracted if the individual has ready access to such a place (both in terms of the place being available and access being permitted).

Triggering appropriate skills

Giving the person time

People with learning difficulties may need time to take on board in-coming information and time to organize their own responses. Hurry-ing things along may be overwhelming and precipitate inappropriate behaviour as a 'fall back' position for getting a message across. One tactic, therefore, is to use pauses in order to give the individual time to respond appropriately. For example, giving the individual time to pick up paper and crayons before moving to physical prompting, waiting while the individual tries to communicate the message that is important to him before stepping in to anticipate the message or end the inter-action. Giving the person extra time may not only help him organize his thoughts and actions better, it may also help direct his attention to triggers which exist within the natural environment for appropriate skills.

Providing reminders and directing the person's attention to natural triggers

A second trigger tactic is direct prompting of the appropriate action in the situation and teaching the person what the natural trigger for the behaviour should be. This needs skilled reading of early warning signs of difficulties and stepping in to direct the person towards using his appropriate behaviour. For example, seeing an individual signing behind the back of another (and therefore about to be frustrated) will be diverted by prompting the person to attract the other's attention and then signing again. Seeing a person showing signs of emotional build-up then encouraging him to go to the quiet area that he some-times uses spontaneously will trigger constructive coping. Labelling the emotion (you're tense) just before encouraging the person to go to the quiet area will direct his attention to the appropriate natural trigger. If an individual starts to show signs of boredom, then drawing his attention to interesting materials that he can use to occupy his time may head off the outburst of inappropriate behaviour. Consistently labelling his emotional state (you look bored) before directing him to the alternative activity will draw his attention to the appropriate triggers for his behaviour. In this way skilled triggering may enable the individual to make better use of the skills that he has by teaching him when use of the skills is appropriate.

Reinforcement of appropriate alternative skills

Having created the opportunities for and triggered the behaviours to occur at the appropriate time (i.e. when the inappropriate behaviour would naturally occur), it is important to ensure that the appropriate behaviour is immediately and frequently followed by powerful reinforcement. Where functionally equivalent skills are being reinforced (i.e. skills which achieve the same results as the inappropriate action), the reinforcer is the natural reinforcer which is access to the thing the person wants. If an incompatible skill is being encouraged, then arbitrary reinforcement may need to be used, because the person may achieve no initial reinforcement from performing the skill (for example, sharing a packet of sweets with his peers).

Differential reinforcement of appropriate alternative skills

If the looked-for skills are well established but are used infrequently because they do not achieve meaningful results, and if, in addition, inappropriate actions dominate because they achieve better results, then reversing this situation will mean encouraging use of appropriate skills **and** discouraging inappropriate behaviours. This is achieved by:

- ensuring that appropriate behaviour is reinforced;
- ensuring that the inappropriate behaviour is not followed by positive results.

SUMMARY

There are many reasons why people fail to use their appropriate skills and persist with inappropriate behaviour. Once these reasons have been identified, appropriate remedial action can be taken to alter the situation. Procedures for helping the person to replace his inappropriate behaviour with appropriate alternative skills, which are functionally equivalent to or incompatible with the problematic behaviour, are detailed below.

PROCEDURES FOR REPLACING THE PROBLEMATIC BEHAVIOUR WITH MORE APPROPRIATE SKILLS

As with all aspects of teaching, getting the person to start to use his new skill in place of his inappropriate behaviour requires planning and consistent effort.

Step ⟩ **1** ⟨   **Identify need**

Following the assessment of the problematic behaviour, needs may have been identified in relation to the building of skills which are functionally equivalent to or physically incompatible with the problematic behaviour. Indeed, these skills may have been already taught as a first step in this process (Chapter 6). Examples of such needs might be: John needs to keep his hands down in order to prevent face slapping; Susan needs to use gesture rather than screaming to indicate 'Go away'.

Step 2   Translate need into long-term goals

Having identified the relevant needs and established that the relevant skill is present, each need must now be translated into a long-term goal. The goal, as with all long-term goals, should be one which can be achieved over a 6–9-month period. The goal should be stated in the following form.

Who	John
Will do what	will keep his hands in his pockets
Under what circumstances	when out for a 1-hour walk
To what degree of success	and show no more than 15 instances of face slapping during any walk.

Who	Susan
Will do what	will indicate using gesture that she wants people to go away
Under what circumstances	across all her environments
To what degree of success	and have no more than 10 instances of hair pulling each day.

Step 3   Identify short-term objectives

Since the skill in question has already been learned by the individual, the task now is about getting the person to use the skill appropriately. Short-term objectives are, therefore, likely to relate to specific situations where the skill is to be consolidated, and the level of help which will be provided to elicit the skill at the appropriate time. Short-term objectives are precise statements about the aim of the immediate intervention. They follow the format described in Chapter 3.

Who	John
Will do what	will keep hands in pockets
Under what conditions	during a 5-minute walk
With how much help	with constant reminders from carers
To what degree of success	until there are no more than five face slaps during four consecutive walks.

Who	Susan
Will do what	will gently push people's hand away
Under what circumstances	during one-to-one sessions at the day-centre
With how much help	with verbal and physical prompts
To what degree of success	until there is no more than one episode of hair pulling during a total of 3 days.

Step ⊰ **4** ⊱ **Consolidate setting in which the skill needs to occur**

Having defined the short-term objective and identified the situation in which the skill is to be encouraged, the next step is to organize the environment in order to maximize the likelihood of the skill being performed appropriately.

Ensure opportunities are available for practising the skill

The first thing to plan is that opportunities exist for the practice of the desired skill. If the individual is to be encouraged to keep his hands in his pockets rather than to slap his face, then the clothes that he wears should be fitted with large, easily accessible pockets. If a child is to be encouraged to use appropriate play skills rather than inappropriate ways of being stimulated then he will need easy access to relevant materials at times when he is most likely to get bored. If a person who uses inappropriate behaviour to gain the attention of his carers needs to use more appropriate social interaction skills, then it may be necessary to structure the environment so that time is made available for carers to be around just to respond to any positive initiations. If a person is to push people's hands away rather than scream, then it may be necessary to structure the environment so that people regularly attempt to engage the individual in an activity.

Ensure that the triggering of skills can be effected

The situations in which materials are made available need to be ones where prompts can be provided in order to teach the person to use appropriate alternative skills. It may be that prompts can be provided at all times of the day (whenever the person appears bored) and this is quite manageable given resources available. It may be, however, that a physically incompatible skill is being encouraged for a high-frequency behaviour (for example, keeping hands in pockets instead of face slapping) and the resources are not available to provide prompts whenever face slapping occurs. In such cases, it should be considered whether, during the early stages, the intervention programme should occur during fixed and predetermined sessions, when resources can be made available to consistently provide the required help. If a sessional basis is being used, then the materials should only be available during these sessions (put on clothes with deep pockets just before session is to begin). This will help the person to associate the presence of the materials with the required behaviour.

Create awareness

All those who are working with the individual should be made aware of the meaning of the problematic behaviour and the skills that the individual now possesses for achieving the same results or for achieving results which are incompatible with the behaviour. For example, people need to be aware that the inappropriate behaviour is a means of rejecting a demand and that the individual can signal 'No' by pushing people's hands away. They need to be aware that the inappropriate behaviour is a way of relieving boredom and that the individual knows how to engage in certain activities which he finds interesting and which prevent boredom.

All those working with the individual should, additionally, be made aware of any early warning signs that the inappropriate behaviour is imminent – warning signs of the person being bored, of feeling neglected, of feeling anxious or angry. This will enable people to step in at an early stage and direct the behaviour down more constructive tracks.

Step ⧓ 5 ⧓ Plan triggers

Select appropriate class of trigger

Additional triggers may need to be introduced if the opportunities created do not by themselves significantly increase the use of the appropriate alternative skills or if there is a wish to speed up the process of initial change by stimulating highly frequent usage of the alternative skill. The types of triggers which can be used have been described earlier (Chapter 6, STEP 7) when discussing the prompts available for the teaching of new skills. Getting people to use their skills may require the same kinds of prompts – suggestion, demonstration, physical guidance, visual cues.

Decide the timing of the trigger

1. Functionally equivalent skills. In this situation the timing of the triggers may be critical. The trigger needs to be timed in such a way as to pre-empt performance of the inappropriate action and build a new link between a natural trigger and a reinforcer. For example, if a person throws equipment in order to gain a carer's attention when an activity is finished and he wants something else to do, then the carer needs to watch carefully for signs that the activity is finishing and prompt a more appropriate way of communicating that he needs something else to do.
2. Physically incompatible skills. In these situations such precise timing is not required. For example, using one's hands constructively rather than slapping one's face, may require frequent enough reminders or guidance to pre-empt face slapping but without the need for the trigger to be synchronized very specifically with the situation. Helping someone to avoid boredom may require materials to be available and noticed, plus regular reminders to use them, but not require intervention as soon as the person stops being 'busy'.

Step ⟩ **6** ⟨ **Plan how to reinforce the use of appropriate alternative skills**

Reinforcing functionally equivalent skills

The aim here is to ensure that the reinforcement currently achieved for the problematic behaviour is now achieved by the appropriate alternative skill – a direct switch of reinforcement from the inappropriate to the appropriate behaviour. If throwing a dinner plate gets fast access to pudding then the combined intervention of watching for the first course being finished (awareness), prompting the person to push the plate to one side (triggering) and the immediate arrival of pudding (reinforcement) will maximize the likelihood of pushing the plate aside as opposed to throwing it. If physical aggression at unstructured times is a means of getting an exciting response from staff, then ensuring that activities are always available (opportunity provision), reminding the person about appropriate activities at these times (triggering) and an 'over the top' social response when these appropriate actions occur (reinforcement) will strengthen the likelihood of the person using these skills more often.

During the early stages of the programme, reinforcement must occur each time the appropriate behaviour is performed. For example, if an individual is being encouraged to say 'No' appropriately as opposed to biting others, then any use of the appropriate communication should be followed by the withdrawal of whatever is being offered or requested.

Reinforcing incompatible skills

In this situation the use of a more appropriate alternative skill may not necessarily provide adequate incentive for the individual to 'do the right thing'. In such cases the use of additional reinforcers, at least as a temporary measure, may need to be considered in order to make reinforcement of the appropriate skills more attractive than use of the inappropriate behaviour.

A person who occupies himself by picking up and eating rubbish may have lost the inclination to use his skills at craft work and domestic chores. Thus, additional social and material reinforcement for the in-compatible activity may increase its attractiveness and start to reinstate it as a way of organizing time so as not to get bored. If an individual is being encouraged to keep his hands in his pockets as an action incompatible with head slapping, then the likelihood of him using this alternative response may be increased if there are things of interest to the individual in his pockets (for example, 'feely' objects, small items of material reinforcement, noise makers). The selection of an 'arbitrary' reinforcer depends of course upon the individual's reinforcer pre-ferences. The person's strengths list will provide information about important reinforcers, things that the individual is known to work hard for. The effectiveness of the arbitrary reinforcer can be enhanced in two ways.

1. If it follows very soon after the target appropriate response.
2. If it occurs very frequently in the early stages so that appropriate behaviour is very likely to 'succeed'. Reinforcement for incompatible skills should, if possible, be more frequent than reinforcement which is currently being received from the inappropriate behaviour. For example, if eating inedible objects occurs up to ten times in a half-hour period, the reinforcer for the person using appropriate self-occupation or domestic skills would need to occur far more often – between 15 and 20 times in a half-hour period. The reader

should refer to Chapter 8 (STEP 4) for more information about planning the frequency of reinforcement for such a situation.

Step ⟩ 7 ⟨   Plan a response to the inappropriate behaviour

The aim of the work described in this chapter is to ensure that appropriate behaviour occurs more often and with greater success than the behaviour that has been identified as problematic. This means, on the one hand, ensuring that the appropriate behaviour, when it does occur, achieves powerful reinforcement and, on the other hand, ensuring that the inappropriate behaviour, if it occurs, does not achieve reinforcement. Chapter 10 provides a full discussion of techniques for responding to occurrences of problematic behaviour and the reader should refer to that chapter for a detailed account of how to plan this part of the intervention.

Step ⟩ 8 ⟨   Plan record of progress

The record of progress needs to take account of two measures.

1. The frequency of the behaviour regarded as problematic.
2. The usage of the appropriate alternative behaviour.

It is likely that while specific skills are being built up there will be some delay before this leads to change in frequency of the target behaviour. Thus, just monitoring the target behaviour might underestimate overall success. For this reason it is better that measures be taken of both the alternative skill(s) and the problematic behaviour.

Having decided upon what behaviour is to be recorded, the reader should refer to Chapter 11 for a detailed account of how to set up an objective and efficient monitoring system to record the selected behaviour.

Step ⟩ 9 ⟨   Obtain baseline

Before starting the intervention a baseline measure should be obtained. This provides a marker against which progress can be measured. If sampling techniques are being used, then the conditions under which baseline recordings are carried out should be identical with the conditions under which subsequent recording is carried out (for example, time of day, day of week, activities in progress), once an intervention programme has started. Chapter 11 (STEP 6) provides more information of the setting-up of baseline measures.

Step 10   Plan review date

The review date should initially be set between 2 and 4 weeks following the start of the intervention. This ensures that, if problems arise with the implementation of the intervention, they can be ironed out quite quickly. Subsequently, reviews should occur every 4–8 weeks.

Step 11   Write programme

Having planned all aspects of the intervention aimed at encouraging an appropriate skill or set of skills in place of inappropriate or problematic behaviour, details of the plan should be written in the form of a programme. The programme should contain the following details.

1. Long-term goal.
2. Short-term objectives.
3. Setting in which intervention is to take place.
4. Details about materials to be provided or made available.
5. Procedures for implementing the programme, which should include:
   (a) instructions to the person about what he should do in response to the stimuli which normally trigger the inappropriate behaviour;
   (b) details of early signs which will let people know that the behaviour is about to occur;
   (c) prompt strategy to be used to encourage the person to use the appropriate behaviour in response to the trigger.
6. Response to the appropriate behaviour when it occurs.
7. Response to the inappropriate behaviour.
8. Recording procedure and recording chart.
9. Review date.

An example of a written programme, which teaches and encourages the use of a functionally equivalent skill, is shown in Figure 6.4. An

Name *LARRY*	Date *NOVEMBER 17TH*

Long-term Goal

LARRY WILL WAIT FOR UP TO 2 MINUTES WITHOUT SCREAMING AFTER HE HAS REQUESTED SOMETHING TO EAT

Short-term Goal

LARRY WILL WAIT FOR 10 SECONDS WITHOUT SCREAMING AFTER HE HAS REQUESTED A BISCUIT FOR FOUR OUT OF FOUR TRIALS ON TWO CONSECUTIVE DAYS

People Involved   *MARY, JANE AND PHIL*

Time and Place   *LATE EVENING IN THE DINING ROOM*

Special Materials	**Trials per Session**
A COLOURING BOOK OR JIGSAW PUZZLE (LARRY TO CHOOSE). *FIVE SMALL BISCUITS HIDDEN IN A BAG.* *WATCH WITH A SECOND HAND ON IT.*	*4*

Procedure

1. INVITE LARRY TO COME AND DO SOME DRAWING OR HIS PUZZLE WITH YOU IN THE DINING ROOM. MAKE SURE IT'S QUIET IN THERE AT THE TIME.

2. ONCE HE HAS SETTLED WITH THE ACTIVITY, TAKE OUT ONE SMALL BISCUIT FROM THE BAG AND HOLD IT IN YOUR HAND.

3. WHEN LARRY REQUESTS THE BISCUIT, TELL HIM OF COURSE HE CAN HAVE IT BUT IN A MOMENT WHEN HE HAS DONE JUST A BIT OF THE ACTIVITY. START TIMING.

4. KEEP PROMPTING HIM VERBALLY TO DO JUST A LITTLE MORE (PLACE ANOTHER PIECE OF THE PUZZLE OR COLOUR IN ANOTHER AREA OF THE PICTURE).

Response to Appropriate Behaviour

AS SOON AS 10 SECONDS ARE UP AND LARRY HASN'T SCREAMED, LET HIM HAVE THE BISCUIT. WAIT A COUPLE OF MINUTES AND REPEAT FROM (2).

Response to Inappropriate Behaviour

IF LARRY STARTS TO SCREAM, PUT THE BISCUIT BACK INTO THE BAG SAYING HE CAN'T HAVE IT WHILE HE'S SCREAMING.
ENCOURAGE HIM TO GET BACK TO THE ACTIVITY.
WHEN LARRY HAS STARTED THE ACTIVITY AGAIN START THE PROGRAMME AGAIN FROM (3).

Recording   *NUMBER OF BISCUITS WHICH LARRY MANAGED TO ACHIEVE DURING THE SESSION*

Date of Review   *DECEMBER 14TH*

Figure 7.2 Example of a written programme which encourages use of a physically incompatible skill.

example of a programme which encourages use of a physically incompatible skill is shown in Figure 7.2. The programme has been drawn up from the needs list in Figure 2.6 (Chapter 2).

Step ⟩ **12** ⟨   **Implement, review and move on**

Progress is judged by change in skill usage or in the problematic behaviour over time, particularly by comparison of baseline measures with measures taken after programme implementation. Objective records of progress should be used in the review process. To simplify analysis of progress, data should be summarized in the form of graphs or other visual displays. These are discussed fully in Chapter 10.

As soon as the short-term objective is achieved, the next step towards achieving the long-term objective should be planned and written. As the alternative positive skills build up then the frequency of reinforcement can be gradually reduced so that it becomes more intermittent, like the frequency which occurs in the natural environment. Likewise, if arbitrary reinforcers are being used, these will need to be gradually faded until appropriate actions are maintained by more natural results. The key emphasis here is on the gradual reduction in overall frequency and predictability of reinforcement rather than sudden changes as soon as the positive actions have built up.

SUMMARY

There are a number of possible reasons why people fail to use important and appropriate skills which they have learned and, instead, continue to use behaviour which others find problematic or inappropriate. For one thing, there may be no opportunity to use their more appropriate skills. For another, the person may not have learned to respond with these skills to appropriate cues in the environment. Rather, he remains dependent upon prompts from carers or on specific materials with which the skill has been taught. Another reason why appropriate skills are not used may be through learning and the experience of differential reinforcement. Differential reinforcement occurs when some behaviour receives positive and looked-for outcomes for the individual while others do not. Once the reason for failure to use the skill has been established, then specific programmes can be set up to help and encourage the person to use his appropriate skills.

ENCOURAGING APPROPRIATE ALTERNATIVES

SUMMARY OF STEPS

1
Identify need

2
Translate need into long-term goal

3
Identify short-term objectives

4
Consolidate setting in which the skill needs to occur

5
Plan triggers

6
Plan how to reinforce the use of appropriate alternative skills

---
7
Plan a response to the inappropriate behaviour

8
Plan record of progress

9
Obtain baseline

10
Plan review date

11
Write programme

12
Implement, review and move on

Encouraging absence of the problematic behaviour

8

Certain problematic behaviour can, in some ways, be thought of as like any other human 'bad habit' – effective in the short term, but troublesome in the long term. While it is important to take away the need for the 'habit' (Chapter 5), to learn other ways of achieving important results (Chapter 6) and to experience the positive benefits of using more appropriate actions (Chapter 7) rather than inappropriate behaviour, there is also an inportant place in the therapeutic package for direct encouragement to give up the habit – the provision of powerful incentives for 'giving up'.

ENCOURAGING ABSENCE OF THE PROBLEMATIC BEHAVIOUR – GENERAL PRINCIPLES

UNDERSTANDING WHY 'HABITS' ARE NOT 'BROKEN'

The concept of differential reinforcement described in Chapter 7 illustrates why behaviour that is regarded as inappropriate may persist even though the individual has other more acceptable ways of achieving important results. The person will have learned through experience that the use of behaviour which others may consider to be problematic is more likely to secure for him the things that he wants than is behaviour which is socially appropriate. It is more difficult for others to ignore a behaviour which directly challenges them than it is to ignore a behaviour which does not. In any case, the outcome for certain problematic behaviour may be better than that achieved by other more socially acceptable behaviour. It may, for example, be much more fun to annoy someone than to sit around with a jigsaw puzzle! It reinforces the importance of not only teaching relevant skills (Chapter 6) but also of making sure that such skills achieve meaningful results and that these results are more attractive than those achieved by inappropriate be-

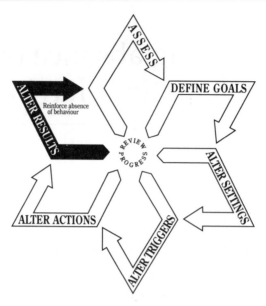

Figure 8.1 Encouraging absence of the problematic behaviour.

haviour (Chapter 7). Unfortunately, it is the case that 'old habits die hard'. Establishing new skills may take time. Remembering to use these new skills, which may be less intrinsically reinforcing, in place of other less appropriate but well established behaviour may prove difficult.

UNDERSTANDING THE PRINCIPLES OF DIFFERENTIAL
REINFORCEMENT FOR 'GIVING UP THE HABIT'

In many fields of human behavioural change (for example, smoking, dieting, alcohol use, offensive language), use is made of the principle of differential reinforcement to help people give up undesirable habits. In addition to helping the person develop alternative activities, which may be functionally equivalent to problematic behaviour (chewing nicotine gum or using a nicotine patch instead of smoking, exercising instead of not eating) or incompatible with the behaviour (drinking soft drinks instead of alcohol), a special incentive is also given for the person managing not to show the behaviour for a predetermined period of time (for not having a cigarette for a whole day) or for showing the behaviour progressively less often over time (smoking fewer cigarettes each day, taking fewer drinks, making fewer cutting remarks).

The same principles can be used to help reduce or stop other problematic behaviour. There are two strategies: differential reinforcement of other behaviour and differential reinforcement of lower rates of behaviour. These strategies are best used alongside programmes which teach and reinforce the use of equivalent or incompatible skills (Chapters 6 and 7). When used without the person also being offered help to develop strategies for not showing the behaviour, the person is essentially left to find his own strategies to help him to 'give up the habit'. He may or may not be successful.

Differential reinforcement of other behaviour

Differential reinforcement of other behaviour (DRO) involves providing the person with powerful reinforcement for completing predetermined periods of time without the target behaviour being shown. During these periods the person can do anything just as long as the target behaviour does not occur. If the target behaviour occurs during the predetermined time interval, reinforcement is forfeited. For example, a person who hits out at others several times during the evening might be reinforced for each hour that he manages not to hit out at others. At the end of each hour he is given feedback about his behaviour during the previous hour and reinforced if no hitting has occurred. If he has hit out during the hour he is told that no reinforcement is due and the reason is explained. A fresh opportunity to earn reinforcement occurs during the next and each subsequent hour.

Differential reinforcement of lower rates of behaviour

Differential reinforcement of lower rates of behaviour (DRL) involves setting a maximum target frequency for the problematic behaviour. If the frequency is not exceeded during a given time period then the individual is reinforced. If the frequency is exceeded during the time interval then the person is not reinforced. For example, a person who swears at an approximate rate of 20 times an hour might be reinforced for managing to swear not more than 15 times an hour throughout the evening. If he swears more then 15 times, he is informed that no reinforcement is due. Opportunity to earn reinforcement occurs again during the next and subsequent hours.

SETTING UP PROGRAMMES OF DIFFERENTIAL REINFORCEMENT

Level of understanding and active involvement required

Programmes based on DRO and DRL work on the basis of clear rules being set in advance about what is expected – the length of time during which the behaviour should not be shown; the maximum frequency of behaviour permissible. They do not require the person to have advanced concepts of time or number or even a clear understanding of the rules of the programme, at least in the case of DRO. Progress is dependent upon direct experience of the programme in operation – the experience of the reinforcement contingencies. It is not clear whether programmes based upon the reinforcement of lower rates of behaviour require that the person understands the rules. The absence of such awareness, however, should not rule out a DRL approach. In this situation a 'try it and see' approach should be used – in other words, running the programme and monitoring whether in practice it leads to behavioural change.

If a person is able to understand the principles of a programme of differential reinforcement, such awareness must be used to engage the individual more actively in the programme. At the very least, the programme needs to be fully explained (pictures and charts can be used to help the person understand the rules). The individual should, if possible, be actively involved in monitoring his own behaviour (Chapter 9), particularly the recording of successful intervals. More complex social motivations can then be engaged, stressing the value of the achievement of 'giving up' the problematic behaviour. Where appropriate, a 'contract' approach could be used so that the details are planned and agreed in conjunction with the person himself and written up as a simple 'contract' spelling out the rules of the programme.

Deciding how many behaviours to include

A programme based on DRL works best if it is kept simple. This means working on one target behaviour at a time. If a DRO programme is being planned for an individual who shows a number of problematic behaviours then the decision is less simple: all, some or only one can be included in the criterion for reinforcement. It is very much a decision for those planning the programme. The advantages and disadvantages have to be weighed up. On the one hand it is vital that the individual experiences high frequencies of reinforcement and the inclusion of multiple behaviours might make this difficult. On the other hand if only one or two behaviours are included then there is a risk that the programme will actually reinforce the other problematic behaviours. One way to overcome this problem is to start simple, including only one or two target behaviours. As these behaviours start to reduce, then more behaviours can be added into the 'contract'.

Establishing the basis of reinforcement

Programmes of differential reinforcement are based upon the delivery of reinforcement for the absence/reduction of problematic behaviour.

They are dependent for their success upon the appropriate selection of the basis for reinforcement – the setting of the time intervals for DRO, the setting of maximum target frequencies for DRL. Appropriate time intervals and target frequencies have to be set in a way that enables the individual to achieve reinforcement more often than he fails to achieve reinforcement.

Differential reinforcement of other behaviour (DRO)

The initial interval set for reinforcement depends upon the average time between occurrences of the target behaviour. Thus some initial measurement of the frequency of the behaviour is needed before a programme is set up. As a general principle, the initial interval (at the start of the programme) is set at approximately half the length of the average interval measured during the baseline period. For example, if a behaviour occurs, on average, 12 times in a 12-hour period, this in turn means an average of once during a 60-minute period. Thus the initial interval for reinforcement would be set at 30 minutes. If a behaviour occurs, on average, 15 times during a 60-minute period, this in turn means an average of once every 4 minutes: the initial interval should then be 2 minutes. If a behaviour occurs, on average, ten times a minute, this in turn means an average of once every 6 seconds and the initial reinforcement interval should, therefore, be 3 seconds. Setting the initial reinforcement interval at half the average frequency ensures that the individual has a very good chance of 'success' during the early stages of the programme.

Differential reinforcement of lower rates of behaviour (DRL)

The initial maximum frequency set depends upon the frequency of the behaviour. As with DRO, a baseline measurement is needed before a programme is set up. As a general rule, the first target is set at or around the highest frequency measured during the baseline period: if the frequency of the behaviour has been shown to range from 10 times a day to 50 times a day, then the initial maximum frequency should be set at around 50 times a day. In other words, the person should earn reinforcement if the frequency of his behaviour does not exceed 50 times in a day. Setting the initial maximum target so high ensures, as with DRO, that the individual has a very good chance of experiencing 'success' during the early stages of the programme.

The experience of early success in programmes of differential reinforcement is critical. Early success gives the person the opportunity to experience the programme in operation – to learn the rules and to experience the positive outcomes which can be achieved. It also engages the person's motivation to participate actively in the programme, because he knows that success is not only possible but easily achievable.

Selecting appropriate reinforcers

Both differential reinforcement strategies require that the reinforcement used is strong and meaningful to the individual. This often means the use of arbitrary reinforcers which act as a reward for success. It is also important that the reinforcer used is distinctive to the programme because this increases the strength of the reinforcer. For example, if popcorn is used to reinforce periods of time without eating inedible objects, then it is helpful if popcorn is not available at other times. If a special activity is to be used to reinforce periods of time without aggression, then it is helpful if this activity is not generally available at other times.

The maximum duration of the reinforcer to be used needs to be proportionate to the reinforcement interval. Thus if the reinforcement interval is every 3 minutes, then the reinforcer needs to be one which can be 'consumed' within a few seconds. If the reinforcement interval is every hour, then the reinforcer needs to be one which can be 'consumed' within a few minutes. If the reinforcement interval is every week then the reinforcer can be one which takes several hours to 'consume'.

Using symbolic reinforcers

Symbolic reinforcers have no value or motivational significance in and of themselves. Their value lies in the fact that they can be exchanged for things that the person finds reinforcing: they 'buy' goods and services. Money is the commonest example of a symbolic reinforcer. In behavioural change programmes, commonly used symbols include check marks or stickers on a chart, poker chips or plastic rings.

Symbolic reinforcers can be used in any situation where arbitrary reinforcement forms part of a behavioural change programme. They are particularly useful in the following circumstances.

1. It is difficult to organize and deliver the key reinforcer without interfering seriously with other activities (for example, if the most effective reinforcer for an individual is an activity such as playing a game of cards or making a cup of tea).
2. The key reinforcer requires a considerable time to 'consume' and cannot be given on a brief and frequent basis. (A computer game, for example, may take time to set up and run through. Trying to terminate it every few minutes in order to refocus the person on

earning the next access time would destroy the value of this reinforcer and generate frustration and antagonism.)

3. The key reinforcer cannot be made immediately available (for example, going to the cinema, going on a boat trip).
4. It is not desirable to deliver the reinforcer on a frequent basis (for example, frequent use of sweets and caffeinated drink might be undesirable on both health grounds and from the point of view that the person will tire of the reinforcer so that it loses its effectiveness).

If any of the above circumstances apply, then symbolic reinforcers can be considered as a way of enabling the person to gain access to such reinforcers through the programme.

1. Symbolic reinforcers can be given immediately and then exchanged for primary reinforcers at convenient times. For example, if a programme requires reinforcement to be delivered every few minutes for the absence of unacceptable behaviour and if the selected reinforcer is 'rough and tumble' play with a favourite adult, then symbolic reinforcers such as tokens can be given at the end of each interval when the behaviour does not occur. Once the individual has earned a predetermined number of tokens, these can be exchanged for a session of rough and tumble play.
2. Symbolic reinforcers can, potentially, be exchanged for a wide range of reinforcers. Having earned a designated number of tokens the person could exchange these for one of a range of goods and activities. This enables a programme to incorporate shifts in the strength of any one particular reinforcing event.
3. Symbolic reinforcers can be used rather like money: the more that the person has earned, the more he is able to 'buy'. At exchange times the individual 'shops', choosing from a range of different reinforcers each of which has its own 'price'. The more favoured the reinforcer, the higher the price.

Responding to occurrences of the target problematic behaviour

A programme based on DRL will usually be set up with a visual representation of behaviour frequency (for example, using counters in a stack, stickers on a chart). Occurrences of the target behaviour are logged in such a way that the person can see clearly the number of remaining permissible occurrences. For example, a stack of counters can be prepared with one more counter than the maximum agreed frequency. Each time the target behaviour occurs, one counter is removed. If at least one counter remains on the stack at the end of the interval then reinforcement is given. If no counters remain, no reinforcement is given.

In programmes based on DRO there are two ways of responding to occurrences of the target behaviour within the time interval. One is to 'reset the clock' each time the problematic behaviour occurs. This means that when the behaviour occurs the interval is immediately terminated and as soon as the behaviour stops a new time interval is started. The person is informed of this as the clock is reset. This process continues and reinforcement is given whenever a whole interval is completed without the target behaviour occurring.

The second approach is 'lost interval'. The programme period is seen as divided into intervals which cannot be changed, for example, 12–1 p.m., 1–2 p.m., 2–3 p.m., 3–4 p.m., etc. If the target behaviour occurs during an interval, the clock stays running until the end of the interval, even though reinforcement for that period has been 'lost'. At the end of the interval the individual is informed that reinforcement was lost because of the occurrence of the behaviour. A new interval is then started. This process continues with reinforcement following only those intervals during which the target behaviour did not occur.

The 'lost' interval approach is probably the more common. It tends to be easier to administer because it enables time to be set aside in advance for delivery of reinforcement and provision of feedback to the individual. During the approach involving 'resetting' the clock, those administering the programme are not able to predict when time has to be set aside for reinforcement and feedback to be given. Thus it is more likely to interfere with daily routines.

Moving on

Both differential reinforcement strategies are initially set up in such a way as to make the achievement of reinforcement highly likely. As soon as the person understands how the programme operates and is consistently experiencing success, the principle of graded change must be used to start to bring the appropriate behaviour under the control of natural reinforcers. This means progressively extending the target for achievement and then gradually and systematically reducing the frequency and power of reinforcement. Abrupt withdrawal of reinforcement is likely to result in abrupt reversion to the old habit.

In programmes based on DRO, progress is made by the person successfully completing increasingly longer periods of time without the target behaviour occurring. Extending the time period is dependent upon the person reliably succeeding in not demonstrating the behaviour during the time interval. For example, a programme may have been set up to run every evening with an initial reinforcement interval of 1 hour, using a 'lost interval' procedure. Once the person was reliably managing not to show the behaviour during 4 out of 5 hours of the evening, the time period could be extended to $1\frac{1}{2}$ hours. He would now need to not show the behaviour for $1\frac{1}{2}$ hours in order to earn reinforcement. Again, once he was consistently managing to do this for, maybe, 3 out of 4 time intervals of the evening, the time could be extended again – this time to $2\frac{1}{2}$ hours. He would now need to go for $2\frac{1}{2}$ hours without showing the behaviour in order to earn reinforcement. Any occurrence of the behaviour during the time interval would result in the forfeiting of reinforcement. Finally, the time period could be extended again. This time the person might be required to manage the whole evening without the behaviour in order to earn reinforcement. At this stage the power of the reinforcement could start to be reduced, until a more naturalistic reinforcer (for example, being congratulated on having had a good day) was maintaining the behaviour.

In a programme based on DRL, progress is made by the target maximum frequency being systematically reduced. Thus, a person who initially was reinforced for swearing not more than 15 times in an hour throughout the evening might now be required to swear not more than ten times during an hour in order to be reinforced. Exceeding this number would result in the reinforcement being forfeited. Once the person was reliably earning reinforcement for most hours of the evening, the target would be shifted downward again – this time to not more than five times during each hour. Finally he would be required to manage each hour of the evening without swearing in order to earn reinforcement.

Keeping the work aimed towards long-term objectives

The success of progress based on DRO and DRL is dependent on the programmes being gradually extended and then faded out. This may take several months, or longer! Taking a long-term perspective in behavioural management is not easy to to. This will only happen if programmes are regularly reviewed, if short-term objectives are carefully formulated and if records of progress are used to guide decision making as to whether a programme needs to be modified or changed. Programmes that are not reviewed and that remain unchanged over long periods of time lose their sense of urgency. People can then become careless about their implementation and the effectiveness of the programme will be lost.

SUMMARY

Two techniques have been presented which seek to encourage the individual to decrease reliance on problematic behaviour by directly reinforcing their absence or reduction. These are differential reinforcement of other behaviour (DRO) and differential reinforcement of lower rates of behaviour (DRL). General principles have been discussed for the operation of programmes using these techniques. Procedures for planning the specific steps required for developing effective programmes are detailed below.

PROCEDURES FOR DEVELOPING PROGRAMMES WHICH REINFORCE ABSENCE OF THE PROBLEMATIC BEHAVIOUR

Step ⟨ 1 ⟩   Identify need

The statement of needs generated from the initial formulation of the problematic behaviour (Chapter 2) will carry at least one statement pertaining directly to the reduction or elimination of the problematic behaviour. For example, Russell needs to stop biting other people; Jenny needs to reduce the frequency of her swearing. It is these needs which may be directly targeted for programmes based on DRO and DRL.

Step ⟨ 2 ⟩   Set long-term goals

Chapter 3 discusses in detail how long-term goals are set. The long-term goal will be a realistic statement about the acceptable level of the behaviour once the programme of change has been achieved. It should be stated in precise terms using the following format.

Who	Russell
Will do what	will bite other people
To what degree of success	not more than once a month
Under what circumstances	in any situation.
Who	Jenny
Will do what	will swear at people
To what degree of success	not more than ten times a day
Under what circumstances	at the day-centre.

Step ⟨ **3** ⟩	**Differential reinforcement of other behaviour or differential reinforcement of lower rates of behaviour**

A decision must now be made about the type of approach to use: differential reinforcement of other behaviour (DRO) or differential reinforcement of a lower rates of the behaviour (DRL). There are no hard and fast rules upon which to base this decision. The decision may be based upon:

- what seems to be the most appropriate and logical approach given the nature of the problem;
- the likelihood of the person grasping the rules of the programme.

Step ⟨ **4** ⟩	**Plan basis of reinforcement**

1. The basis of reinforcement for DRO is a completed time interval without the occurrence of the target behaviour. The initial reinforcement interval is set at approximately half the length of the average interval measured during baseline. Figure 8.2 shows how to calculate the initial reinforcement interval.
2. The basis of reinforcement for DRL is the person not exceeding the predetermined frequency of behaviour during a given time interval. The time interval is any manageable chunk of time during which the programme will operate (for example, all day, all evening, 1 hour). The initial maximum permitted frequency during the time interval is approximately the highest frequency recorded during baseline for the predetermined chunk of time (for example, maximum recorded during baseline is 20 times a day or 50 times during an evening or seven times in an hour).

Step ⟨ **5** ⟩	**Decide length of initial sessions**

Programmes can run on a continuous (all day) basis or sessionally (during predetermined periods of time only). The duration of the programme should be determined by:

- practical consideration
- possibility of change.

From a practical point of view, a programme which runs all day should have a maximum of four or five reinforcement intervals: any more and consistency is likely to start to break down, unless people are

---

Calculating the reinforcement interval for a DRO programme

Step 1

Calculate the average frequency using the formula

$$\frac{\text{Total frequency recorded from all units (weeks, days, hours, sessions)}}{\text{Number of units}}$$

Step 2

Calculate the average interval between occurrences of the behaviour using the formula

$$\frac{\text{Number of subunits which make up the time unit}}{\text{Average frequency per unit}}$$

* Subunits = 7 days, 12 hours, 60 minutes, etc.

Step 3

Divide the average interval by 2 to obtain initial reinforcement interval

Example

A total of 336 hits were recorded over a 7 day period (12 hours each day)

Average frequency = $\dfrac{336}{7}$

= 48 (per 12 hr day)

= 4 per hour

Average interval between

occurrences   = $\dfrac{60}{4}$ (number of subunits in 1 hour)

= 15 minutes

Initial reinforcement interval

= $\dfrac{15}{2}$

= 7 1/2 minutes

Figure 8.2 Calculating the reinforcement interval for differential reinforcement of other behaviour (DRO) programmes.

allocated exclusively to running the programme. From a 'possibility of change' point of view, the person's ability to sustain positive behaviour is likely to depend on its current frequency. Graded change is the key to success. Thus, the higher the initial frequency, the shorter the overall duration of the initial sessions – this applies to both DRO and DRL programmes.

- A DRO programme aimed at reducing a behaviour which currently occurs approximately twice per day (once every 6 hours) can easily be operated using four reinforcement intervals over the whole day.
- A DRO programme aimed at reducing a behaviour which currently occurs approximately twice an hour (once every 30 minutes) and which requires using reinforcement intervals of 15 minutes could, from a practical and 'possibility of change' point of view, be operated for a maximum of $2-2\frac{1}{2}$ hours.
- A DRO programme aimed at reducing a behaviour which currently occurs approximately twice a minute (once every 30 seconds) and which requires using reinforcement intervals of 15 seconds could, from a practical point of view, run for up to 30 minutes. From a 'possibility of change' point of view several 3–5-minute sessions through the day might be more productive.
- A DRL programme aimed at reducing a behaviour currently occurring at a frequency of 100 over a 4-hour evening might be more effective if the evening was subdivided into four smaller chunks of time – say four 1-hour periods with a maximum frequency of 25 permitted during each hour. This increases the possible frequency of reinforcement and makes success feel more attainable (the person must 'try' for an hour in order to succeed rather than for 4 hours).

Step ⟩ 6 ⟨ Set short-term objectives

Having decided upon the basis of reinforcement and the length of the session, it is now possible and, indeed, essential to set the short-term objective. This is stated in clear behavioural terms, as described in Chapter 3 (STEP 4) using the following format.

Who	Jean
Will do what	will slap her face
To what degree of success	not more than five times
Under what circumstances	during a half-hour session
To what degree of success	for eight out of ten consecutive sessions.

Stating the 'degree of success' is important at this stage because it will ensure that the programme does not move on too quickly (before the criterion for moving on has been achieved) and that it does not continue for longer than is necessary.

Step 〉7〈 Plan settings

The time

If the programme is to run on a whole-time basis or if the programme is to run during a specific time of day because this is when particular problems occur (for example, during unstructured times, during the morning routine), then no arbitrary decisions need to be made. If, however, the programme is to run on a sessional basis because the frequency of the behaviour is too high to start on a whole-time basis then, at least initially, the session should be run during a time and activity when inappropriate behaviour is less likely to occur (the person's strengths list should provide information about this).

Opportunity for alternative skills

When planning the setting for DRO and DRL programmes, opportunities should be made available during the sessions for the person to practise equivalent or incompatible skills (Chapter 7, STEP 4) which he has been taught and encouraged to use. This may require ensuring that equipment or specific activities are available and accessible.

Step 〉8〈 Plan triggers

Triggers to signal reinforcement rules

If a sessional approach is used then discriminative cues should be planned which help the individual to recognize that new rules of reinforcement are in operation – in other words that the programme has started. Triggers include:

- visual cues, such as the presence of a timer to mark the reinforcement intervals;
- a brightly coloured chart to record the outcome of the session on an interval by interval basis;
- a distinctive container in which reinforcers are kept;

- a 'signature tune';
- a verbal explanation (perhaps accompanied by the visual or auditory cue).

The trigger must be presented when the programme starts and removed when it is no longer running. Getting out the timer or chart will signal that new rules of reinforcement apply and this will, hopefully, lead to behaviour adjusting to these new rules. Putting the timer away will signal a reversal to 'normal' rules of reinforcement.

Reminder to use appropriate alternative skills

If functionally equivalent or incompatible skills have been taught and encouraged then the person should be reminded periodically that these alternatives are available and attention drawn to any relevant materials (for example, materials for self-occupation).

Step ⟩ 9 ⟨ Plan results

Plan social reinforcement for use of appropriate alternative skills

When a DRO or DRL programme is combined with the encouragement of alternative skills (Chapter 7), then the individual must be praised for using these alternative skills appropriately. The programme must specify which specific skills to praise. Initially praise should be frequent, then reduce to a more intermittent basis.

Select reinforcement for successfully completing time interval

The reinforcer which the person attains by completing the predetermined time interval without showing the behaviour or without exceeding the maximum permitted number of occurrences of the behaviour should meet the following criteria.

1. The reinforcer should be powerful.
2. The reinforcer should be delivered immediately.
3. The duration of 'consumption' of the reinforcer should be proportionate to the time interval.
4. The person should not become satiated with the reinforcer (through too frequent access).

If the reinforcer meets the above criteria, it can be used directly, without any problems. If the reinforcer fails to meet criterion 4, then a selection of reinforcers can be used. The individual should choose from the selection or, if he lacks the skills to do this, reinforcers from the selection could be delivered on a random basis. If the reinforcer fails to meet criteria 1, 2 or 3, then the use of symbolic reinforcement should be considered.

Plan delivery of symbolic reinforcement

Option 1

1. The total number of symbolic reinforcers (tokens) needed for exchange to primary reinforcement is determined in advance (for example, three out of four tokens each evening). This is stated in the short-term objective.
2. Symbolic reinforcers (tokens) are given at the end of each successful time interval (for example, each hour).
3. Symbolic reinforcers are exchanged for the primary reinforcer at a time which has been specified in advance (for example, at the end of each evening) provided that the predetermined number of tokens have been achieved. The individual is involved in determining whether the correct number has been earned for exchange to occur.

Option 2

1. The total number of tokens which can be earned during the 'session' (week, day, evening, hour, etc.) is calculated.
2. A differential pricing is established for different reinforcers, the most powerful reinforcers costing most. For example, 10 tokens = trip to the cinema, 8 or 9 tokens = walk in park, 6 or 7 tokens = cup of tea with selected carer, 5 or 6 tokens = a can of a favourite drink, less than 5 tokens = no reinforcement.
3. At the prearranged time the person reviews the number of tokens and the reinforcement which has been earned.

Establish consequence of failing to successfully complete time interval

1. The interval runs its course. The person is informed at the end of the interval that reinforcement has been forfeited. A new interval is started.
2. The interval runs its course. The person is not informed that reinforcement has been forfeited. A new interval is started. This option should only be used if the person has a very severe level of learning difficulty and does not understand the rules of the programme.
3. As soon as inappropriate behaviour occurs, the person is informed

that the 'clock is to be reset' and a new interval is immediately begun.

Practical considerations determine selection of 1 or 2 over 3, whichever is the most manageable given staff resources and daily routines. If all options are equally manageable, then the 'reset time' interval should be selected.

In 1 and 2 above, a response may also need to be planned for occurrences of the problematic behaviour. The reader should refer to Chapter 10 for an account of the principles and procedures for planning a direct response to the problematic behaviour.

Step ⟩10⟨   Prepare supportive materials

DRO and DRL programmes may require a variety of supportive materials for their success. These materials must be prepared in advance of the programme.

1. Timers, with a signal which sounds loudly, can be used to signal the end of the reinforcement interval. Kitchen timers which have a loud 'tick' are useful because the sound of 'ticking' can be an additional source of information for the individual indicating that the programme is in operation.
2. If material reinforcers, in the form of activities or consumable goods, are to be used then these must be kept available.
3. Visual representation of behavioural occurrences: programmes based on DRL may require some visual display of the number of occurrences of the behaviour which are still permitted before reinforcement is lost. The maximum permissible can be represented as marbles in a jar, rings on a stack, etc., anything that is clearly visible and where individual items can be easily removed. The materials chosen must be prepared and made available.
4. Symbolic reinforcers come in the form of tokens, which can be anything from a plastic ring to a coloured sticker on a chart – anything small and portable that the person is likely to enjoy having. A supply of these should be purchased before the start of the programme.
5. Place to collect tokens – this could be a chart on a wall with velcro strips onto which tokens can be stuck, or it could be a purse or pouch in which tokens can be collected. The important thing is that tokens should not be lost or destroyed before they are exchanged.
6. If a token chart is being used, then a chart may need to be prepared which depicts

Figure 8.3 Example of a pictorial token chart which uses a differential pricing system.

(a) the number of tokens (pictorial or numerical depiction) required for reinforcement to be given;

(b) a representation (picture or word) of the reinforcer/s to be earned;

(c) a place on which to place the tokens (unless these are being kept on the person).

7. If the individual lacks numeracy or literacy skills then a visual representation of pricing will be needed. For example, plastic tokens could be collected in a narow jar, rings stacked up on a stick, stickers built across a chart. The price of reinforcers could be represented in the same way – the required numbers of tokens in a jar, rings on a stack, stickers across the chart, placed next to a picture of the actual reinforcer. Figure 8.3 illustrates an example of a simple pictorial token chart which carries a differential pricing system.

Step 11   Plan record of progress

The success of DRO and DRL programmes is measured by the frequency of reinforcement achieved during each session. DRO and DRL programmes automatically generate measures of target problem behaviours.

- A programme based on DRO provides a measure of the number of intervals for which reinforcement is not earned. This, in turn, provides an estimate of the frequency of problematic behaviour during the period of programme operation.
- A programme based on DRL requires the recording of each incident of problematic behaviour in order to determine whether or not reinforcement should be given. In theory it is only necessary to record up to the target level as, once the target is exceeded, reinforcement is omitted no matter how many more times the behaviour occurs. However, in practice it is easy to construct recording so that all incidents are noted.

DRO and DRL programmes should not be started without a baseline having been taken, as this baseline is used to set the basis for reinforcement (STEP 4).

A recording form should be drawn up to track performance over sessions. It should include the following.

1. Duration of the reinforcement interval.
2. Length of session.
3. Number of times reinforcement was earned during the session.
4. Number of occurrences of the target behaviour during the session.

Step 12   Plan review date

If the programme is quite complex then it will need to be reviewed soon after starting, within a few days, in order to ensure that there are no problems with its administration. Once running smoothly, it should continue to be reviewed regularly, initially at 2–4-week intervals.

Step 13   Write a programme

Whatever type of approach is being used there should be a written programme that includes the following details.

1. Long-term goal.
2. Short-term objectives.
3. People involved.
4. Time and place of sessions.
5. Special materials, which should include:
   (a) reinforcers;
   (b) recording charts;
   (c) items such as timers and devices for monitoring the frequency of behaviour;
   (d) stimuli which provide the cue to the start of the session.
6. Procedures, which should include:
   (a) details of how to introduce the session (if appropriate);
   (b) trigger tactics (prompts) for directing the person to use appropriate alternative skills.
7. Response to positive achievements, which should include:
   (a) feedback and informal social reinforcement for using positive alternative skills;
   (b) the criterion for reinforcement (absence of a problematic behaviour, problematic behaviour at or below a set target) and length of reinforcement interval;
   (c) details of the reinforcer to be used;
   (d) details of how the reinforcement is actually delivered.
8. Response to inappropriate behaviour.
9. Recording procedure and recording chart.
10. Review date.

An example of a programme based on DRO is shown in Figure 8.4: it has been derived from the needs list in Figure 2.6.

Name *LARRY*	Date *JULY 20TH*

Long-term Goal

LARRY WILL TRAVEL IN THE MINIBUS WITH FIVE OTHER PEOPLE ON BOARD WITHOUT SCREAMING AND RUSHING ABOUT

Short-term Goal

LARRY WILL TRAVEL IN THE MINIBUS WITH DRIVER AND TWO OTHER PEOPLE FOR A 15 MINUTE JOURNEY WITHOUT SCREAMING AND RUSHING ABOUT ON TWO OUT OF THREE CONSECUTIVE TRIPS

People Involved   *KEY WORKER PLUS TWO OTHER STAFF AND ONE RESIDENT*

Time and Place   *2 EVENINGS A WEEK TO LOCAL PARK*

Procedure

LET LARRY SIT ON THE DOUBLE SEAT ON HIS OWN AT THE BACK OF THE BUS.
MAKE SURE THERE IS A SMALL BOX WITH PAPER IN IT FOR HIM TO TEAR IF HE GETS ANXIOUS.
REMIND HIM THAT HE CAN TEAR SOME PAPER IF HE FEELS TENSE.

Response to Appropriate Behaviour

1. WHEN LARRY HAS REMAINED SEATED FOR 5 MINUTES WITHOUT ANY SCREAMING TELL HIM HOW WELL HE'S DOING AND HOW NICE IT IS TO SEE HIM CALM.
2. OFFER HIM AND EVERYONE ELSE A SWEET, SAYING IT IS BECAUSE LARRY HAS BEEN SO CALM.
3. REMIND LARRY THAT HE CAN TEAR SOME PAPER IF HE STARTS TO FEEL TENSE.
4. RESTART TIMING THE NEXT 5 MINUTES AS SOON AS YOU HAVE HANDED OUT THE SWEETS. GO BACK TO (1).

Response to Inappropriate Behaviour

IF LARRY STARTS TO SCREAM OR GETS UP FROM HIS SEAT STAND IN THE AISLE TO STOP HIM GETTING TO THE FRONT OR TO THE DOOR.
QUIETLY DIRECT HIM BACK TO HIS SEAT AND TELL HIM IT'S DANGEROUS TO WALK AROUND THE BUS.
TELL HIM THAT THE NOISE IS UPSETTING EVERYONE.
REMIND HIM THAT HIS BOX OF PAPER IS ON THE SEAT.
IF HE CONTINUES TO SCREAM AND RUSH ABOUT, STOP THE MINIBUS AND WAIT FOR LARRY TO SIT DOWN (SAFETY PRECAUTION).

Recording
1. NUMBER OF SWEETS ACHIEVED
2. NUMBER OF TIMES HE STOOD UP OR SCREAMED AND LENGTH OF EACH EPISODE

Date of Review   *AUGUST 10TH*

Figure 8.4 Example of a programme based on differential reinforcement of other behaviour (DRO).

Step **14**	Inform and teach the individual how the programme operates

Teach the rules of the programme

Before starting a programme of differential reinforcement, every effort should be made to explain to the individual the rules of the programme. For people with more limited verbal comprehension skills some other ways might be used to explain the programme.

Aim

> To earn three tokens in 30 minutes and to exchange them for a primary reinforcer (drink of cola).

- Pictures to show what will constitute success in terms of access to reinforcement and what will result in forfeit of reinforcement.
- Role-play sessions of the major elements of the programme, including showing all supportive materials and demonstrating how they are used in the programme.

Establish the basic value of symbolic reinforcers

Symbolic reinforcers have value only because the person understands that they can be exchanged for important goods and activities. For those with adequate verbal skills this understanding may be reached by explanation. For others a direct teaching approach will be need to teach symbol value and the rules of exchange. Basic symbol (token) appreciation might be taught as follows.

Steps

1. Give one token. Exchange immediately for a small drink of cola.
2. Give one token. Wait 10 seconds. Exchange for small drink of cola.
3. Give two tokens, one every 10 seconds. Exchange for small drink of cola.
4. Give three tokens, one every 10 seconds. Exchange for small drink of cola.
5. Give three tokens, one every 20 seconds. Exchange for small drink of cola.
6. Give three tokens, one every 30 seconds. Exchange for small drink of cola.

7. Give three tokens, one every minute. Exchange for small drink of cola.
8. Give three tokens, one every $1\frac{1}{2}$ minutes. Exchange for small drink of cola.
9. Give three tokens, one every 2 minutes. Exchange for small drink of cola.
10. Give three tokens, one every 4 minutes. Exchange for small drink of cola.
11. Give three tokens, one every 6 minutes. Exchange for small drink of cola.
12. Give three tokens, one every 10 minutes. Exchange for small drink of cola.

Step ⟩ **15** ⟨   **Implement, review and move on**

As short term-objectives are achieved, programmes need to be moved on. Moving on should occur in one of the following ways.

1. Extend the time during which the programme operates (if started on a sessional basis).
2. Extend the reinforcement interval (DRO), using small increments in time.
3. Decrease the permitted target frequency (DRL) using small reductions in frequency.
4. Increase the number of behaviours which are included in the programme.
5. Reduce strength of arbitrary reinforcers.

In all cases the key principle of graded change must be used: large and sudden changes are likely to lead to the loss of gains made. The programme may need to be rewritten each time it is 'moved on' and the new rules explained to the individual.

SUMMARY

Programmes based on differential reinforcement for the absence or reduced frequency of a problematic behaviour can be used as an adjunct to work which directly encourages the use of more specific behaviour in place of problematic behaviour. It is a way of increasing a person's motivation to 'give up the habit'. Such programmes are highly structured and require a great deal of planning and preparation. They depend for their success on firing the person's interest and enthusiasm very early on – by making it very easy for the person to succeed during the early stages of the programme. Thereafter, the programme must keep moving forward to provide new challenges for the person, as soon as he starts to make progress: this maintains his interest and motivation. The programmes should be gradually extended and arbitrary reinforcement systematically reduced until more naturalistic reinforcement maintains the person's motivation to behave appropriately. Abrupt withdrawal of reinforcement or abrupt cessation of the programme will, almost inevitably, result in the loss of any gains made.

ENCOURAGING ABSENCE
OF THE PROBLEMATIC BEHAVIOUR

SUMMARY OF STEPS

1

Identify need

2

Set long-term goal

3

DRO or DRL

4

Plan basis of reinforcement

5

Decide length of initial sessions

6

Set short-term objectives

7

Plan settings

8

Plan triggers

9

Plan results

10

Prepare supportive materials

11

Plan record of progress

12

Plan review date

13

Write programme

14

Inform and teach the individual how the programme operates

15

Implement, review and move on

Teaching and encouraging self-management

9

The emphasis of the book so far has been upon the kinds of work that other people can do so that people with learning difficulties are able to cope without the need to engage in behaviour regarded as problematic. The present chapter looks at ways in which people with learning difficulties can take a much more active role in managing their own actions. Teaching and encouraging self-management is important for a number of reasons.

1. From the perspective of normal development, human beings progress from being entirely dependent upon others for guidance and support to making more decisions for themselves, directing and managing their own actions. It is important to see this as a developmental transition also for people with learning difficulties. It should be stressed that the transition is not one from complete external control to that of complete self-management. Actions remain under a range of controlling variables – some coming entirely from the individual ('I don't hit people because I believe that hitting people is wrong'), some from the world that the individual lives in ('I don't hit people because hitting may get me into trouble'), some coming from internalizing the external controls ('I don't hit people because that behaviour is frowned upon by my society'). It is the balance between internal and external control that shifts over time. This normal developmental process, inevitably delayed in people with learning difficulties, may be thwarted altogether because of social attitudes leading to a self-fulfilling prophecy – if people with learning difficulties are regarded as inherently dependent, then there is no point in giving them the opportunity for self-management and therefore they will fail to acquire the necessary skills. This is one reason why it is important to take specific action to ensure that these normal transitions from external control to self-direction of behaviour are permitted to occur.

2. Modern culture lays great emphasis upon the value of the auton-
   omous individual. The person who is able to control and direct
   his own actions is held in high regard. If people with learning
   difficulties are to be perceived with value then learning self-
   management skills becomes important. Indeed, there is increasing
   concern among carers that certain techniques of behavioural change,
   which have been used with people who have learning difficulties,
   may be too reliant on external control. There is a growing move, for
   both adults and children, towards encouraging and enabling the
   individual to exert control over his own actions and over his own
   behavioural change process.
3. From a practical point of view the drive towards greater integration
   into the community of people with learning difficulties means that
   demands upon the individual to conform and to be more independent are greater than ever before. The complex and variable nature
   of community living places greater demands upon individuals to act
   appropriately in a wide range of situations. This means that they
   must take and act on a very wide range of decisions.

In this book so far, it has been people other than the individual
concerned (parents, teachers, professional carers, instructors) who
decide which skills to build up and which behaviour to decrease. It is
people other than the individual himself who provide triggers and
results for his appropriate actions. It is people other than the individual
himself who control settings, remove or alter the triggers and results
for behaviour judged as problematic. It is people other than the individual himself who monitor and evaluate his progress. This represents
a high level of external control. Such external control poses difficulties
for those involved in therapeutic intervention programmes. It can
create problems for the generalization of behavioural improvements to
new situations where the controlling agent is not present to manage
settings, triggers and results. This in turn creates heavy demand on
time and effort if gains are to spread across situations and over time.

For the person with learning difficulties who is the recipient of
external control programmes there are other difficulties. It may lead the
individual to view himself as incapable of independent action, thus
increasing his sense of dependency and blocking this area of personal
development. It may create frustration if he has developed personal
decision-making skills but is not given the opportunity to use them.
Frustration may contribute to the further creation of behaviour deemed
to be inappropriate. Finally, it may influence how others view him,
seeing him as by nature unable to take responsibility for his own
actions.

There are, therefore, many good reasons for involving people with

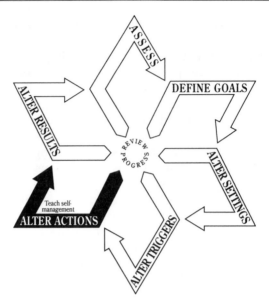

Figure 9.1 Encouraging self-management.

learning difficulties in the management of their own behaviour, for helping them to take greater responsibility for their actions and for reducing reliance upon external methods of behavioural change and control – in other words, for teaching and encouraging self-management.

SELF-MANAGEMENT – GENERAL PRINCIPLES

DEFINING SELF-MANAGEMENT

Self-management describes the situation where some of the key factors which influence how an individual behaves come from within the person or are in some other way under the direct control of the individual. The word 'some' is a reminder that self-and external control are not contradictory ideas. The influences over human behaviour in any situation are many and varied and may include factors over which the individual has direct control and those over which he has no control. The precise balance of external and internal control factors will depend upon both the situation and the level of development that the individual has reached. In general terms, two broad categories of self-management can be identified – self-direction of behaviour and independent problem solving.

Self-direction of behaviour

Self-direction of behaviour occurs when the individual implements specific procedures to ensure that certain specific behaviour occurs. He can structure settings (for example, arrange a time and place for studying which is likely to be distraction-free). He can manipulate cues which increase or decrease the likelihood of performing certain actions (for example, write out a time-table for what is to be studied). He can provide direct triggers for the starting and stopping of his behaviour (for example, set an alarm clock to signal the start of a study period, then reset it to signal the end of the study period). He can provide reinforcing results for desirable actions (for example, a refreshment break following completion of a time-tabled piece of study). He can monitor and evaluate his progress (for example, chart the proportion of study assignments completed in relation to the number planned). In this way the individual takes active steps to ensure that certain of his own behaviour occurs.

Independent problem solving

This is the way in which the individual tackles new situations and works out which behaviour is appropriate to the situation. It means defining the nature of the problem (for example, this is a crossword which means that key words need to be derived from the printed clues and fitted into the spaces available). He can then generate possible solutions (for example, words that could be related to the clue), consider the options (for example, check answers for 'plausibility' and fit in terms of number of letters), implement an action (for example, write in the answer). He will continue to monitor and evaluate progress (for example, number of clues answered, 'fit' between answers) and adjust behaviour in the light of this monitoring until the crossword is complete. This kind of self-management involves the use of a general strategy relevant to many problems plus specific knowledge about the particular situation.

THE DEVELOPMENT OF SELF-MANAGEMENT SKILLS

Not everything is known about how self-management skills are acquired in the course of normal development. However, at least four processes seem to be important.

The presence of reasoned external controls

The presence of external controls accompanied by an explanation about why such controls are present enables the individual to 'internalize' rules of social behaviour ('develop a conscience'). By this process behaviour remains acceptable even when external controls are absent. This may be particularly important for the development of self-management of behaviour which is socially desirable.

The opportunity to practise self-management

Like any other skill, self-management skills are acquired through practice. For example, a person may be given the opportunity to be 'trusted' to behave in a certain way or he may be set problems and encouraged to find the solution for himself.

Demonstration of self-management

Self-management may be acquired because the individual observes other people practising it. He sees others, who are important figures in his life, engaged in self-management of their actions, for example, following do-it-yourself manuals, writing reminders for themselves, working out problems, showing restraint.

Direct teaching of self-management

The individual may receive input which directly teaches him self-management – teaches him how to follow a set of directions for himself, encourages him to make plans for himself, prompts problem solving by carefully phrased questions. Self-management may be taught just like any other skill.

Although all the details are not understood it is clear that the environment has a key role to play in determining whether or not an individual develops self-management skills. It is also clear that independent problem solving is much more dependent upon the development of language skills (or other symbolic capacities) than is self-direction of behaviour. Research evidence would suggest that language may need to be somewhere between the 3- and 8-year level for the person to be able to use more strategic approaches to self-management.

Self-direction of behaviour (monitoring and evaluating one's actions, cueing and reinforcing one's own behaviour) is not so dependent upon higher levels of general and linguistic development. In principle it would seem more widely applicable for the people with whom this book is concerned. In practice there is considerable evidence that, with ingenuity, people with quite severe degrees of learning difficulty can be taught skills which support self-direction of behaviour. For these reasons the main focus of the chapter is upon the development of those skills.

SELF-RECORDING

Self-recording is the systematic collection of information about one's own actions. On an everyday basis people rarely keep a strict count of their behaviour. For example they may be unaware of how many times a day that they bite their finger nails, use the phrase 'you know', smile at colleagues. However, if an individual wishes to alter the frequency of an action then monitoring can be very helpful. For one thing, keeping a count of behaviour provides feedback about progress. For another, the act of recording behaviour can have a reactive effect on that behaviour so that the frequency changes.

Self-recording as a monitoring device

Self-recording of behaviour regarded as problematic can be useful as a monitoring device. The individual records his own behaviour before, during and after an intervention. For this function accuracy is clearly of major importance and the individual needs to be trained to discriminate and record all incidents of the behaviour in question.

Self-recording as a therapeutic tool

Reactivity is the term given to the situation when the act of recording one's behaviour directly affects the frequency or severity of that behaviour. It is a well recognized phenomenon. Reactivity makes self-recording a potentially powerful intervention in its own right. When used for this purpose, accuracy of recording is less important than the factors which influence the reactivity itself.

Reactivity is more likely if a person is motivated to change his behaviour. This in turn relates to the value that a behaviour has for the individual. If he considers the behaviour to be positive and desirable then self-recording is likely to increase that behaviour. For example, if a person considers it desirable to increase the amount of positive feedback which he gives to colleagues about their work, then the process of recording each time he give positive feedback to others is likely to increase the behaviour. If a person considers his behaviour to be undesirable and negative then self-recording is likely to decrease that behaviour. For example, if a person wishes to stop biting his finger nails, then the process of recording each time his fingers touch his mouth is likely to have a reducing effect on the behaviour. A neutral stance means little likelihood of reactivity either way.

The value a person assigns to a behaviour may reflect his own idiosyncratic judgment processes. The fact that others find the behaviour undesirable is no guarantee that the individual will also judge it in that way. Having said this, the environment can influence a person's judgments and reactivity. If there are clear goals for the individual to work towards, if he receives feedback about progress and reinforcement for increasing or decreasing target behaviour, then the reactive effects of self-recording are likely to be stimulated.

SELF-EVALUATION

Self-evaluation is a judgment about how well or badly one has performed, rather than a straightforward recording of what one has done. Accurate self-evaluation can act as a strong incentive for people to alter or to maintain their behaviour and is a constructive source of feedback which can give people direction for improving their performance. There are two components to self-evaluation.

1. A standard against which to measure one's performance.
2. A comparison of one's performance to the standard.

The standard can be set by others (for example, any form of physical aggression is unacceptable) or it can be set by the person himself (for example, 'Good means not hitting people unless I have been threatened or hit first'). Having a clear standard enables the person to make an accurate evaluation of his behaviour by comparing what he has actually done (self-monitoring) to the standard which has been set.

Self-evaluation is an important antecedent for self-reinforcement. In addition, because positive self-evaluation will have been frequently paired with reinforcement during the course of learning, it may take on reinforcing properties and become an important source of encouragement in and of itself. This raises important points about negative self-evaluation – the judgment that one has not done very well. It is important that people accept that they can make mistakes and get things wrong – it is human to be imperfect! Knowing what one has done wrong should provide a setting condition for trying to do better. If, however, negative self-evaluation is paired with punishment (for example, being scolded) it may take on aversive properties and become a source of emotional discomfort and active avoidance: the person will be unwilling to admit he has made mistakes. It is important to make sure that negative self-evaluation is not associated with aversion but that it is associated with reflection and plans to improve. This may require particularly careful handling with individuals who have a past history of punishment associations with negative self-evaluation or with those people who, for other reasons, become severely disturbed in the face of mistakes or failures.

SELF-CUEING

Arousal inhibition

Often, behaviour identified as problematic is preceded by an increase in emotionality just prior to the behaviour: the person becomes angry, anxious, embarrassed or excitable. While there are differences between these emotions they are all accompanied by increased activity in the nervous system and a level of discomfort that this automatically brings (for example, increases in heart rate and muscle tension). Taking action to check such increasing arousal reduces the level of discomfort and makes it easier to avoid becoming aggressive or acting in other unacceptable ways in order to get out of the situation which caused the increase in emotionality (the natural 'fight–flight' response).

Some of the things that may help decrease arousal, individually or in combination, are sitting down, taking slow deep breaths, counting slowly, clenching fists or squeezing an object and then letting go, eating something. If the individual can respond to increases in arousal by initiating one or more of these tactics then the likelihood of a 'fight–flight' response is reduced.

Alternative action triggering

Arousal inhibition provides, sometimes literally, a breathing space. In most situations it would be helpful if the individual could initiate an alternative, more acceptable way of dealing with the situation, of responding to the things that are triggering behaviour regarded as unacceptable, for example, communicating in another way what he does or does not want to happen, walking away from provocation. These 'alternative actions' may be triggered by memory or by the individual having some form of 'external' reminder, which can take the form of instructions or pictures on a small card that the individual carries around, or spoken instructions on a tape played through a personal stereo. These reminders enable the individual to act effectively without guidance from another person. They do not eliminate the trigger situation itself but they add-in some extra triggers which enable the individual to substitute independently an acceptable for an unacceptable action.

This kind of self-cueing is also relevant to skill-learning and skill-practice situations. An individual may master skills not by being taught the skills by someone else but by learning to follow a set of cues, such as a sequence of pictures illustrating the different steps of a skill, which guide him through the task without the help of another person. Self-cueing can be used in the same way to help a person remember what to do without having to rely on someone else to give reminders.

Common examples of this are the use of carefully sequenced written, spoken and/or picture materials such as do-it-yourself manuals, recipes, shopping lists, video/audio tape programmes.

SELF-REINFORCEMENT

Self-reinforcement is a process whereby the individual provides a positive outcome for his own appropriate actions. In the course of development most people learn to reinforce their own actions, thereby increasing the frequency of reinforcement that they receive and decreasing their reliance upon others to reinforce their actions. Self-reinforcement can be effected in two ways.

1. A person may praise or congratulate himself for something that he has done or achieved. This is positive self-talk.
2. A person can arrange for himself some external reward for his efforts or achievements. For example, a person on a diet may reward himself with new clothes when a target weight is achieved, a person may reward a period of hard work with a holiday. On a more immediate basis, a refreshment break may be used to reward completion of a study task or domestic chore.

People with learning difficulties often remain very dependent on reinforcement provided by other people. They may not be able to reinforce their own behaviour and thus the overall amount of reinforcement that they receive is likely to be less than that received by others. There can be many reasons for this but two are particularly important. For one thing, people with learning disabilities may not have free access to material reinforcers or activities and may only be able to gain access to these things through other people. For another thing, people with learning difficulties may never have learned to evaluate their own performance, to judge when they have done well and to comment positively to themselves following such evaluation.

USING SELF-DIRECTION SKILLS

Self-management is not an all-or-nothing process. Behaviour will usually be under the control of both external and internal forces. Self-direction skills can be used in a number of ways to help overcome behavioural difficulties and to teach new skills.

At a general level it is important to make every effort to involve the individual in planning his own therapeutic programme. This might involve selecting which skills need to be learned, identifying what behaviour is problematic, sorting out the details of a behavioural change programme (for example, selecting reinforcers). Involvement at these initial stages should be seen as part of the process of encouraging self-management. Individual self-direction skills may then be combined with predominantly external methods of behavioural control, such as those described in other chapters of this book. Alternatively, the individual can be taught to take control over various aspects of the work. For example, when teaching a person to cross the road, the effectiveness of the teaching might be enhanced by incorporating a self-evaluation component so that the individual learns to assess and judge his own performance. This introduces one element of self-direction into an otherwise externally controlled programme. Productivity in a work-skills programme might be enhanced by teaching self-monitoring of work output. When teaching a complex sequence of actions, such as cooking a meal or doing a job of work, independent functioning may be assisted by teaching the individual to use a sequence of pictorial cues or written instructions to trigger each new behaviour in the sequence. Self-management of a problem behaviour might be effected by teaching the person to discriminate and label the trigger for his behaviour, to provide himself with verbal instructions on what appropriate action to take in the situation and to praise himself for behaving in this way. In all these cases, self-direction programmes can be combined with some additional external control in the form of reminders, feedback and reinforcement for appropriate use of self-direction skills.

CORRESPONDENCE TRAINING

Specific self-direction techniques have been combined into 'packages' which have been used to tackle behaviour regarded as problematic. One such package is correspondence training: it combines external-control and self-control methods and has the potential for helping many of the people with whom this book is concerned.

Correspondence training is a way of getting a person to match his behaviour to his intentions. It involves teaching the person to make positive statements about how he will act in a specific problematic situation and then reinforcing him if he acts in a way which corresponds to the stated intention. Thus the intention statement comes to act as a trigger for appropriate actions, thereby bringing the behaviour under self-control. The intention needs to be set up in terms of specific actions. The method of stating the intention can be varied, according to the individual's abilities – verbal statements, picture sequences, role-play sequences are all options to consider. The elements in such a training programme include the following.

1. Teaching the individual to state in specific terms how he should behave in a given situation, identifying perhaps three or four key

behavioural components which constitute behaviour appropriate for that situation.
2. Immediately prior to the target situation, getting the individual to indicate accurately how he will behave in that situation.
3. Immediately following the situation, providing specific feedback to the individual about the correspondence between his stated intentions and his actual behaviour in the situation. The individual should be encouraged to self-evaluate as part of this stage, by providing feedback about his own actions.
4. Reinforcing the individual for accurate correspondence between the stated intention and actions taken. Again, getting the individual to make the decision for himself about whether reinforcement is merited and, if so, what reinforcement will be given, can be part of this step and build up self-reinforcement skills.

An example of the use of correspondence training is shown in Figure 9.2. Correspondence training offers an interesting approach to developing self-direction around behaviour whose occurrence is linked to specific situations.

EMOTIONAL MANAGEMENT

This set of procedures is a second example of a self-direction 'package'. It is designed to help a person manage high levels of emotional arousal which if not checked lead on to inappropriate actions. Anger and anxiety are two of the most important emotions associated with behavioural difficulties. There are four stages in the development of an emotional response.

1. An event occurs, often in the external environment (for example, something is said – a comment, request or denial).
2. The event is interpreted by the individual (for example, 'I don't understand', 'He's getting at me', 'That's unfair', 'That's a horrible noise'). The individual may or may not be consciously aware of the interpretation.
3. The body responds physiologically (for example, increase in muscle tension, increase in heart rate).
4. Action is taken (for example, shouting, hitting out, running away).

Emotional management aims to intervene at stages 2, 3 and 4, individually or in combination. It may target altering the interpretation, altering the physiological response and/or altering the action taken. More specifically it can include teaching a number of skills.

1. Recognizing increasing arousal.
2. Altering the interpretation of the event.

Case example of the use of correspondence training

Mark, whose problematic behaviour was aggression towards other children, was taught to behave appropriately, as opposed to aggressively, using correspondence training. In each situation where aggressive behaviour occurred a 'correspondence' procedure was adopted. The application of correspondence training to one such situation (the playground at school) is described below. The procedure was adapted to include self monitoring and self evaluation.

1. During a practice session in the morning Mark was told by his teacher "Today I want you to play nicely in the playground". The term 'playing nicely' was defined using four behavioural statements:

Playing nicely means staying near the bigger children.
Playing nicely means riding your bike in the track area only.
Playing nicely means playing with a ball.
Playing nicely means walking or running around the playground.

2. Mark was prompted to repeat the general intention to play nicely and to repeat the specific behavioural statements.

3. Just prior to playtime Mark was asked how he would behave during playtime and what he would be doing in the playground. He was prompted to repeat the statements he had learned earlier.

4. Periodically throughout playtime Mark was reminded of the intentions he had stated earlier.

5. Immediately after play he was given very specific feedback by his teacher about the correspondence between the way he actually behaved and his previously stated intention.
"You said you would play nicely in the playground and you did. You stayed with the bigger children, you played ball and rode your bike in the track area and you walked around on your own".

6. Mark was praised for acting in a way which corresponded with his stated intentions to be good.

7. The same procedure was repeated each day. As Mark learned the statements about what constituted 'playing nicely' the direct feedback about his behaviour began to be preceded by questions by his teacher to elicit self-monitoring and self-evaluation. "How did you behave in the playground during play? You said you would play nicely. How do you think you managed?"

8. Mark was praised for accurate self-evaluation (even if he had been aggressive) and received a special reward if his actions had corresponded with his stated intentions to play nicely.

9. As the programme developed, Mark was asked not only to evaluate his behaviour but also to judge whether the criteria for receiving a special reward had been met.

Figure 9.2 Example of the application of correspondence training.

3. Altering the physiological response by relaxation or distraction.
4. Identifying an alternative action to perform in the situation.

Not everyone will be able to master skills at every level. For example, altering interpretation does require more advanced capabilities. However, most people should be able to master some of the skills and this will help them to cope more effectively with stressful situations. Details about altering the physiological responses and altering interpretations are given below.

Altering the physiological response through relaxation skills

Anger and anxiety are often accompanied by increased levels of physiological activity, including muscular tension, before any obvious behavioural action is taken. Increased levels of physiological activity serve as a trigger for behaviour (for example, an aggressive outburst). One element of self-management is to counteract this physiological response in order to reduce the likelihood that the behaviour regarded as problematic will be triggered. Being able rapidly to induce a relaxation response is a way of effecting this and there are a number of approaches to relaxation training.

Progressive muscular relaxation is one approach. Progressive relaxation involves teaching the person to relax all the major muscles of his body progressively more and more quickly, until he is able to relax his whole body 'on cue'. The steps involved in learning progressive muscular relaxation are illustrated in Figure 9.3. Not everyone with severe learning and behavioural difficulties will be able to manage this particular form of relaxation training. However, if the principles are understood then a lot more people can be helped. Some of the key elements of relaxation training include:

- a means of inducing a relaxed state;
- regular practice over a long period of time;
- the association of a distinctive (and 'portable') cue with the relaxed state;
- a gradual shortening of the training sessions with increasing use of the cue (and less use of the full induction procedure) to trigger relaxation.

With these principles in mind a number of alternative approaches to relaxation become plausible.

1. There are other ways of inducing the relaxed state. Examples include: just relaxing muscles (no tension), breathing only, massage, aroma, music, rhythmic visual inputs.

PROGRESSIVE MUSCULAR RELAXATION	
Progressive muscular relaxation involves the following major muscle groups	
Muscle group	**Muscles involved**
Arms	Hands, biceps, forearm muscles
Face	Muscles around the forehead, eyes, nose, cheeks and jaw
Neck	Muscles at back of neck. Muscles at front of neck
Shoulder	Muscles around shoulder blades
Chest	Chest muscles
Stomach	Stomach muscles
Legs	Calf muscles, thigh muscles

Teaching Progressive Muscular Relaxation

1. Each separate muscle is identified for the person.

2. The person is taught to recognize the difference between a tensed and a relaxed muscle by practising tensing and then relaxing each muscle in turn (always in the same order).

3. Once the person has learned to recognize the difference between a tensed and a relaxed muscle muscle (usually after one or two practise sessions) tensing the muscles is omitted from training so that he now just relaxes each muscle in turn.

4. After a few sessions, muscles are grouped so that the person relaxes two or three muscles together (left arm, right arm, face, neck, chest, shoulders, stomach, left leg, right leg).

5. As sessions progress the person learns to relax more muscles together (both arms, face and neck, torso, legs) and the relaxation sequence gets shorter.

6. In the end the person is able to initiate the relaxed state quite quickly (usually within a minute).

7. During the training the person is also taught how to control breathing and use slow deep breaths as an aid to effective relaxation. He is encouraged to take a few slow deep breaths after he has relaxed each muscle or muscle group.

8. During training certain cue words are used ('calm and relaxed', 'relax', 'let go', 'go loose and floppy'). These cue words become associated with the relaxed state and eventually can be used on their own to trigger the relaxation response. This makes it possible to effect relaxation in real world situations when anger or anxiety are increasing.

Figure 9.3 The steps involved in learning progressive muscular relaxation.

2. There are other kinds of distinctive and 'portable' cues associated with the relaxed state, which could be used. These include: a picture, an aroma, taped sounds, a particular posture ('head down', 'eyes closed').

There are a large number of possible combinations, which could be individually tailored to the needs and abilities of the individual, thereby making it possible for a very large number of people with learning difficulties to learn how to alter their physiological responses when faced with a difficult situation.

Altering the interpretation of an event using cognitive reappraisal

Through observation and interviewing of the person concerned and those who live and work with that person it is often possible to identify situations which are very likely to trigger an anxiety or an anger response (for example, being shouted at, being ignored, being refused something, being unable to do a task). The strength of the emotional response is likely to be influenced by the individual's interpretation of the situation. Strong responses, which raise the likelihood of be-havioural difficulties, follow interpretations such as 'He's nasty', 'He hates me', 'He's got it in for me', 'People will think I'm stupid', 'Everyone is looking at me'. One way, therefore, of reducing the level of emotional response is to teach the person alternative, less 'provocative' ways of interpreting the situation. For example, the inter-pretation 'He's nasty' could be replaced with the interpretation 'He's too busy at the moment to talk to me', the interpretation 'He's got it in for me' could be replaced with the interpretation 'I'll be able to have it later', the interpretation 'People will think I'm stupid' could be replaced with the interpretation 'Everybody needs help sometimes', the interpretation 'Everyone is looking at me' could be replaced with the interpretation 'Most people are busy and not noticing me'. These alternative interpretations may reduce the level of emotional response by reducing the importance attached to the situation ('It doesn't really matter'), by helping the individual to reinterpret the intentions of others ('He didn't do it on purpose') and by enabling the person to change expectations about himself ('I don't always have to get things right').

This kind of work requires that the person concerned has well developed language skills. It is likely to require considerable practice, using role play initially and then transferring what has been learned into the real world situation. It is therefore not accessible to those with more severe degrees of disability.

Putting the elements of the 'emotional management' package together

There are a number of possible elements to an emotional management 'package'. The elements can be learned separately and then combined as a chain of responses to arousing situations. The full sequence would be as follows.

1. Recognize when one is becoming angry or anxious.
2. Label the emotion ('I feel cross').
3. Activate a relaxation response.
4. Reinterpret the situation.
5. Initiate a behaviour suitable for the situation (this of course depends very much upon the specifics of the situations that the individual has difficulty coping with).

Managing the full sequence is likely to require high levels of ability. However, elements in the sequence, particularly the use of relaxation to counteract high physiological arousal, may be accessible to people at all levels of ability. Relaxation skills may, in and of themselves, help the person cope with stressful situations without acting in ways that are regarded as problematic. The transition to full self-management is likely to be gradual with a lot of help needed by way of reminders or other prompts from external sources in the early stages of learning.

SUMMARY

The concept of self-direction includes a range of skills, which vary in their level of difficulty and in the approaches needed to teach them. Some of the skills will be achievable for a very large number of people with learning difficulties, others will be accessible only to those with better developed representational skills. Procedures for helping people to develop the skills of self-direction are detailed below.

PROCEDURES FOR HELPING PEOPLE DEVELOP SELF-DIRECTION SKILLS

Self-direction skills are taught using the same procedures as those described for skill teaching earlier in the book. Thus many of the considerations will be the same.

Step ⟩ **1** ⟨   **Identify the need**

The concepts of self-management and self-direction cover a wide range of skills. It is important, therefore, to identify which specific skills it is intended to teach the individual. At one level, the need for teaching some aspects of self-direction arises with every programme of behavioural change. At another level, specific self-direction packages may be identified as appropriate for certain individuals. The needs list may have identified a specific need for self-management: such a need was identified in the needs list in Figure 2.6, i.e. Larry needs an appropriate means of reducing his agitation.

Step ⟩ 2 ⟨   Translate need into long-term goal

Needs must be translated into realistic long-term goals, i.e. ones which are achievable within 6–12 months. Long-term goals should specify the level of external support that the individual will need at the end of training. For some the goal will be to use self-direction skills as and when required, without any prompts or reminders. For others, particularly those who have more severe levels of learning difficulty, more modest goals of using skills with help from those supporting them might be appropriate.

Long-term goals should be stated using the format shown below.

Who	John
Will do what	will monitor his involuntary vocal utterances
Under what circumstances	during individual sessions
With how much help	without prompting.

Who	Lisa
Will do what	will evaluate her own behaviour
Under what circumstance	at the day-centre
With how much help	with help from her instructor.

Step ⟩ 3 ⟨   Select appropriate teaching method

Precision teaching

Precision-teaching techniques are described in detail in Chapter 6. During precision teaching the teacher exerts a high level of control over the teaching situation, using whatever prompts are necessary to ensure that the target behaviour is performed without a mistake. This might involve physical prompts to mark each occurrence of a behaviour onto a recording chart, instructions to deliver or to collect reinforcement at the appropriate time, arbitrary reinforcement for producing a self-direction skill. Correction of error is likely to involve increasing the level of prompting provided (for example, moving from verbal to physical prompting).

Demonstration, practice and feedback

This is a less structured and controlled approach which involves the individual more actively in the teaching process. Teaching relies more heavily upon modelling techniques and involves the following.

1. Demonstration. For example, demonstrating to the person how to record or evaluate behaviour, how to provide cues and reinforcement for actions.
2. Role play is used so that the individual practises the techniques which have been demonstrated and the teacher provides feedback about the competence shown.
3. Once the techniques have been mastered during sessions using role play, the person is encouraged to practise the techniques in the natural environment as needs arise.
4. Feedback is provided about the appropriateness of behaviour and the use of self-direction skills. Such feedback must focus on specifics, for example, 'You were very good this morning. You didn't lose your temper at all. When X called you a name, you counted to ten, took some deep breaths and told him that he had no right to say that to you'.

Incidental teaching

Incidental teaching of self-direction skills uses the natural environment as the setting to teach the skills. The skill of self-evaluation might appropriately be taught using incidental teaching-techniques by taking advantage of natural situations as they arise during the course of each day as the context for teaching. Incidental teaching requires that prompts and reinforcement are carefully planned in advance of teaching and used whenever the situation permits. When the situation does not permit, for example, when time is limited, prompts may be increased to speed up the teaching on that occasion. Access to reinforcement is automatic. Chapter 6 describes incidental-teaching techniques in greater detail.

Step 〔4〕   Set short-term objectives

As in all skill teaching a graded approach should be used. This means breaking down self-direction skills into teachable steps and using part- or whole-task teaching methods. The skill of self-recording, for example, has two separate component skills: the skill of discriminating when the target behaviour occurs and the skill of recording the behaviour. These skills may need to be taught separately and then chained into a sequence. Chapter 3 describes in detail how to break tasks into steps and plan appropriate approaches to teaching. Once a decision has been made about the approach to teaching, a teaching objective should be established. The short-term teaching objective is one that can be achieved within 1–6 weeks. It should be clearly stated using the format shown below.

Who	John
Will do what	will mark on a card whenever he utters an involuntary vocalization
Under what circumstance	during one-to-one sessions at the day-centre
With how much help	with verbal reminders from his instructor
To what degree of success	for three consecutive sessions.

Again the reader should refer to Chapter 3 (STEP 4) for detailed information about the planning of short-term objectives.

Step 〔5〕   Plan settings for teaching

The settings for teaching include:

- the place and/or the activity
- the time
- the people involved.

Teaching may be carried out in a special environment or during time-limited sessions. Alternatively, the natural environment might be the most appropriate setting. Specific times and particular people may need to be involved, particularly during the early stages of learning.

Chapter 6 (STEPS 3, 4 and 5) provides specific instructions for the planning of appropriate settings for teaching.

Step 6   Plan triggers for teaching

Triggers for self-direction skills will need to be planned. Triggers are the prompts which need to be used in order to elicit appropriate behaviour. For example, physical prompting might be needed to teach use of wrist counters for self-recording. Demonstrations, careful questioning and pausing might be needed to teach techniques of self-evaluation. Procedures for planning appropriate triggers for skill-teaching are also detailed in Chapter 6 (STEPS 6 and 7).

Step 7   Select and prepare special materials for teaching

Special supportive materials may make self-direction accessible to people who lack skills such as the ability to count, the ability to write, the ability to speak or the ability to discriminate.

- Self-recording might be made possible for an individual who is unable to count or has difficulty using pencil and paper by providing him with a special wrist counter or stickers to place on a chart or marbles to take from one container to another or coloured beads to place onto a wrist band.
- Self-cueing could be effected with the use of visual aids. For example, a set of photographs or a sequence of instructions on a personal stereo may enable the individual to work his own way through a sequence of tasks.
- Self-evaluation should not be precluded because an individual has limited language skills. A photograph of the individual smiling could be used to represent a positive evaluation (I did well). A photograph of him frowning could be used to represent a negative evaluation.
- Self-reinforcement might be facilitated by the use of visual aids. Thus, the linking of self-reinforcement to the completion of a specific number of target behaviours could be given a visual representation, for example, taking reinforcement when the marble container is empty/full, taking reinforcement when the beads reach all the way round the wrist, taking reinforcement when the spaces on the chart have been filled.

- Discrimination of high emotional states might also be helped by the use of special materials. Devices are becoming available which might help individuals discriminate when they are getting emotionally upset or stressed. Examples include T-shirts which change colour when body temperature changes, cards to grip that change colour in relation to physiological changes, small portable heart-rate monitors.

Supportive materials can enable people with a very wide range of abilities to access self-management and self-direction and reduce their dependence upon others. These and any other materials which may be needed during teaching should be prepared in advance.

Step 8 Plan results

Results need to be arranged so that use of the target self-direction skill is reinforced and errors are corrected. In relation to self-recording, reinforcement should be given for accurate logging of behaviour even though the behaviour being logged may be an action regarded as inappropriate. Chapter 6 (STEPS 9 and 10) provides details of how to plan appropriate reinforcement and correction of errors during teaching.

Step 9 Plan record of progress

Systematic record keeping is an essential part of any programme of behavioural change. It is no less important for programmes aimed at teaching self-direction skills. The reader should refer to Chapter 6 (STEP 11) and to Chapter 11 for a full account of how to set up monitoring procedures to measure the person's progress during teaching.

Step 10 Plan to consolidate learning

Self-direction should, ideally, be exerted by the individual across all situations: the aim is to generalize the skills across as many situations as possible. In the long term, the person should self-cue whenever possible, rather than have carers cue his behaviour. He should evaluate his own actions and use positive self-talk to reinforce appropriate behaviour and achievements which occur in the course of each day.

Procedures for the consolidation of new learning are detailed in Chapter 6 (STEP 12).

Step ⟩11⟨ Plan review date

As with all change interventions, a date on which the teaching plan will be reviewed should be agreed in advance. The review date should occur not more than 4 weeks after the start of the programme. Thereafter, regular reviews should occur throughout the teaching programme.

Step ⟩12⟨ Write the teaching plan

Having planned all aspects of the teaching, the details need to be written as a formal programme, which should include the same details as those used for the teaching of other skills (Chapter 6, STEP 14).

Step ⟩13⟨ Take baseline

A baseline measure of performance allows an objective evaluation of progress to be made, following the implementation of a skill-teaching programme. Details of the procedures for setting up baseline recordings are presented in Chapter 11 (STEP 6).

Step ⟩14⟨ Implement, review and move on

Objective records of progress, in the form of graphs or charts (Chapter 11, STEP 9) are used to assess progress and to judge whether short-term objectives have been achieved. As each short-term objective is achieved, the principle of graded change must be used to move the person forward towards skill mastery. Chapter 6 (STEP 16) details the procedures for this part of the intervention plan.

SUMMARY

The growth of interest in self-management reflects three types of concern. One is the difficulty in effecting long-lasting and generalized change in some situations. The second is the recognition that in the course of human development there is a shift in the balance between external and self-control and that the acquisition of self-management starts early in development and becomes increasingly refined over time. There is not a sudden change where the individual moves abruptly from being entirely under external control to being entirely self-controlled. The process of change is a continuous process and should form part of any work which aids personal development. The third concern is more to do with social value. The underlying philosophy of many services is to enable people with learning difficulties to function in ways that a society values. If a society places high value on independent action and achievement then the demonstration of personal autonomy by people with learning difficulties will make it more likely that they will be seen in a positive light by other members of that society.

These psychological and philosophical pressures mean that self-management forms an ever more important dimension of work for people with learning difficulties. In this chapter some of the principles of self-management have been outlined and methods for teaching the relevant skills described. It is clear that aspects of self-management and self-direction are accessible at even very severe degrees of intellectual impairment. Other aspects are more heavily reliant on language and representational skills and may, therefore, only be accessible to those with a milder degree of intellectual impairment. Self-management techniques offer a potentially valuable addition to more traditional approaches. When planning work to overcome behaviour identified as problematic it is important always to look for a self-management component to the work, as an adjunct to more externally controlled programmes.

ENCOURAGING SELF MANAGEMENT

SUMMARY OF STEPS

1
Identify the need

2
Translate need into long-term goal

3
Select appropriate teaching method

4
Set short-term objectives

5
Plan settings for teaching

6
Plan triggers for teaching

7
Select and prepare special materials for teaching

8
Plan results

9
Plan record of progress

10
Plan to consolidate learning

11
Plan review date

12
Write the teaching plan

13
Take baseline

14
Implement, review and move on

Responding to
problematic behaviour
10

It has been stated many times in this book that behaviour which appears to others as problematic or inappropriate is meaningful and important for the individual concerned: it may be a way of expressing the person's needs and wants; it may be a source of stimulation or occupation; it may be an expression of the person's emotional state; it may be a means of exerting control over the world in which the person lives. The person may have no other way of achieving these very important outcomes. Thus, simply trying to discourage the use of such behaviour, without providing help in a number of other areas of personal functioning, may not only be unhelpful but it may also be unethical.

In previous chapters many types of interventions have been described: some aim to reduce problematic behaviour indirectly by altering the settings which increase the individual's vulnerability to act in ways others may consider to be inappropriate; others aim to reduce the need to use problematic behaviour by teaching and encouraging the person to use better ways of satisfying his motivations and needs. Interventions have also been described which aim to influence problematic behaviour more directly – at one level by directly encouraging and rewarding the absence of the behaviour and at another level by working with the stimuli which trigger the behaviour and trying to break or alter the trigger–action sequence or pattern.

Some of the interventions described are intended as longer-term measures to help the individual cope better with the pressures of his world. Their impact on the frequency and severity of a problematic behaviour is not expected to be immediate. Other interventions are intended to have a more immediate impact on the behaviour. This impact is achieved by providing powerful reinforcement for appropriate behaviour and by ensuring that any reinforcement achieved by the problematic behaviour is reduced to a minimum level. This is the

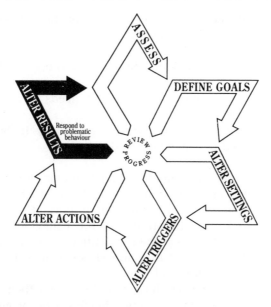

Figure 10.1 Responding to the problematic behaviour.

process of differential reinforcement. Either way – whether the interventions are long-term or short-term, direct or indirect – the problematic behaviour itself must be addressed and a response planned for its occurrence. It is this aspect of the therapeutic package which is the subject of the present chapter.

RESPONDING DIRECTLY TO PROBLEMATIC BEHAVIOUR – GENERAL PRINCIPLES

UNDERSTANDING THE INFLUENCE OF THE RESULTS OF BEHAVIOUR ON THE LEARNING PROCESS

Positive results and their influence on behaviour

When any behaviour occurs which has an immediate outcome for the person in terms of satisfying his wishes, relieving unpleasant emotional states or enhancing personal self-esteem, then learning takes place. The person may learn that:

- the behaviour is effective for achieving specific results under specific cirumstances;
- the behaviour is ineffective for achieving specific results under specific circumstances.

Over time and through further experience of the outcome of the behaviour, the person may also learn:

- the amount of the behaviour which needs to occur before the need or desire is met;
- the intensity with which the behaviour needs to occur before the need or desire is met;
- which of a range of behaviours is most likely to be effective in meeting the need or achieving the desire.

Whatever the origin of a problematic behaviour, for example, head punching because of pain or screaming because of frustration, the outcome for the individual over time is an important source of learning which influences further occurrence of the behaviour. Thus, if face slapping results in the sympathetic attention of a caregiver then the individual will have learned that face slapping may be one effective way of gaining sympathy and attention. If screaming results in the individual being given something that he wants then he will have learned that screaming may be one effective way of getting his immediate needs met.

If, over time, the person learns that the longer his behaviour continues the more likely it is to achieve the desired outcome (for example, screaming for 10 minutes rather than screaming for 10 seconds), then a more protracted form of the behaviour is likely to develop. If, over time, the person learns that his behaviour (for example, banging the table) achieves the desired outcome only inconsistently, whereas another behaviour (for example, throwing chairs) achieves the outcome more consistently, then the behaviour which achieves a more consistent outcome will eventually be selected over the less effective one. If, over time, the person learns that gentle face slapping tends to be ignored but hard face slapping gets an immediate response, then hard face slapping is likely to become the behaviour of choice. Such shaping of behaviour does not occur with the conscious awareness of either the person performing the behaviour or the person responding to the behaviour.

Neutral results and their influence on behaviour

If a behaviour achieves no positive outcome for the person (for example, needs are not met through screaming or face slapping), then such behaviour will not come to be used to achieve any particular outcome. It may quickly be dropped by the person. If, for some reason, a previously obtained outcome stops occurring, then eventually the use of the behaviour for this outcome will fade away.

Negative results and their influence on behaviour

If a behaviour achieves unpleasant or negative results for the individual (for example, the person is scolded for screaming, the caregiver withdraws her attention from the person because of aggression, the person misses the bus to the day-centre because he refuses to dress and has to stay home for the day) then, provided the outcome is not desired by the individual, further use of the behaviour in these situations may be discouraged. The possibility of the undesirable outcome recurring will deter the individual from using the behaviour again in similar circumstances. In other words, the greater the likelihood of the negative outcome occurring again, the greater the likelihood of the person not performing the behaviour. Consistent negative outcome for a behaviour, therefore, decreases the likelihood of the behaviour occurring again.

**Behaviour which is an expression of high emotional arousal –
a special case**

There appear to be certain circumstances where the consequences of a person's actions play a relatively small role in shaping or maintaining that behaviour. These are situations where a behaviour is an expression of a powerful emotion and, as such, may not be under the person's control. It occurs because the person can no longer contain his high level of arousal or emotion, not because he wishes to achieve any particular outcome. Often such an expression of uncontrollable emotion (anger or distress, for example) is manifested in the form of screaming, aggression, destructiveness to self or property. Sometimes the behaviour may result in the person experiencing relief from the intense emotion. Sometimes there may be little relief; instead there may be shame or guilt, yet the behaviour will recur. Experience of these consequences will have little impact upon the frequency of the behaviour.

THE NEED FOR PROVIDING CONSISTENT RESULTS FOR
PROBLEMATIC BEHAVIOUR

From a learning perspective, inconsistent experience of results, as described earlier, can have a marked influence on shaping a person's behaviour, making it more prolonged or intense; making the type of behaviour used to achieve a specific outcome more severe. Consistency is essential in order not to further strengthen the use of inappropriate behaviour during the course of everyday interactions.

Problematic behaviour can arouse strong emotions in carers, particularly if they feel that the behaviour is directed at them personally.

Strong emotional reactions of carers can sometimes lead them to respond to problematic behaviour in reactive and unhelpful ways – in order to 'teach the person a lesson'. The person who shows the problematic behaviour is, thus, in a vulnerable position. This is another reason why finding a consistent and planned response to a problematic behaviour is essential.

From a 'change' perspective, steps aimed at discouraging the behaviour must combine the use of a positive outcome to reward non-occurrence of the problematic behaviour (Chapters 7 and 8) with the planned non-occurrence of a positive outcome or the planned occurrence of a negative outcome for the behaviour. There needs to be a very high probability of these results occurring in order for them to exert a reducing influence on a behaviour: consistency is therefore essential.

There are three classes of response to problematic behaviour which need to be considered.

1. Responses which seek to maintain a positive therapeutic relationship.
2. Responses directed towards helping an individual to regain control over his behaviour when such control has been lost.
3. Responses aimed at discouraging the use of inappropriate behaviour.

MAINTAINING A POSITIVE APPROACH

When working with people who show problematic or inappropriate behaviour on a day-to-day basis, there should be a general policy among the care team that, in the absence of any other agreed strategies, a low-key, non-confrontational approach be adopted in the face of such behaviour, as follows.

1. Where possible, ignoring occurrences of a behaviour or, if this is not felt to be possible, responding in a calm non-confrontational manner by simply commenting very briefly and without obvious emotion on the inappropriateness of the behaviour and the reasons for it – then moving on to another topic.
2. Where appropriate, diverting the person onto a more appropriate or interesting activity, without referring to the behaviour itself.
3. Where necessary, calmly and without fuss interrupting a behaviour, and then diverting the person's attention onto some other activity or topic.

Interactions with the person around his inappropriate or challenging behaviour should be conducted in a calm manner which does not convey criticism or distaste or shock. As soon as the behaviour stops, a positive approach to the person should be adopted with no further reference to the behaviour. Such a general approach will ensure that the atmosphere remains at all times warm and non-critical and will also minimize the risk of the person getting a reaction to his behaviour which he might find socially reinforcing and which may start to shape his behaviour in inappropriate ways.

HELPING THE INDIVIDUAL TO REGAIN CONTROL OVER HIS BEHAVIOUR

When behavioural outbursts are the expression of a strong, uncontainable level of emotion or arousal (for example, fear, anger, anxiety, excitement), then the immediate response to the behaviour should be directed towards helping the individual to regain control over his behaviour and to recover from the emotional outburst. It should not aim to directly discourage similar behaviour in the future. A high level of emotional arousal which the person is unable to contain is, of itself, a highly aversive state for any individual to find himself in. Secondly, learning does not readily occur when a person is in such a highly aroused state. Thus, there are good reasons why the immediate response needs to be aimed at helping the individual to calm down rather than finding a way for the individual to learn the inappropriateness of the behaviour.

When a person loses control over his emotions and behaviour then the following actions should be taken.

- Make the situation safe for all concerned.
- Help the person regain control by reassuring the person, gently encouraging him to calm down and, if necessary, taking over control of the behaviour (perhaps by holding the person or taking him to a quiet room), all the time continuing to reassure him.
- Once the person has calmed, help him to become more comfortable.
- Give the person a little more time to completely recover from the outburst before asking him to do anything else.
- Do not discuss the incident with the person until he has fully regained his composure; then, if the individual is able and willing, try to find out what caused the upset and discuss with him how similar upsets might be handled in the future. If the person is unable to engage in such a discussion then show care and concern by spending a little time ensuring that he has fully regained his composure.

DISCOURAGING THE USE OF PROBLEMATIC BEHAVIOUR
THROUGH EXTINCTION

Extinction is an intervention which is based on ensuring that the positive results, which the person is accustomed to achieving through this behaviour, no longer occur. It is potentially a very effective way of discouraging the use of problematic behaviour. It requires, for its effectiveness, a good understanding of the results which the person seeks to achieve.

Extinction of social results

If the outcome that a person is seeking is a social one – people taking notice, being sympathetic, giving their undivided time, showing amusement, getting cross or upset, showing shock – then extinction requires that those at whom the behaviour is directed withhold this social response. This might require: not responding to an individual whose screaming occurs in order to attract attention; not reacting when an individual spits in order to see his victim's reaction; not flinching when an individual pinches in order to see a pained response; not leaving the table to clear up a meal which has been tipped onto the floor in the expectation of observing and enjoying the ensuing commotion; not laughing when the person takes food from others' plates; not appearing shocked when the person strips off his clothes in the middle of the lounge; giving attention to the person's victim rather than admonishing the person for his aggression. If it is not possible to withhold the specific outcome which is sought, or if a variety of social outcomes are sought, then it may be better to withhold any form of social response to the behaviour – in other words, acting as if the behaviour had not occurred or was not occurring.

Extinction of sensory results

If the behaviour has been assessed as achieving sensory results, then extinction will entail eliminating these results in some way. For example, if an individual spits in order to play with the saliva, immediately wiping away the saliva each time spitting occurs removes the desired results. If the person bangs his head against noisy surfaces in order to achieve an auditory outcome, then placing a cushion between the head and the noisy surface while the individual is banging his head against it will cut out the noise result. If a person urinates in order to experience the sensation of warm liquid trickling down his leg, then providing the person with stay-dry pads will eliminate this looked-for result.

Extinction of material results

Material results may also be involved in maintaining a problematic behaviour. If lying down and screaming in the middle of a super-market results in crisps or a can of fizzy drink being produced, then extinction will require the withholding of such an outcome when the behaviour occurs.

Extinction of escape

Not all the results achieved by problematic behaviour are positive gains. Equally powerful in maintaining a behaviour is an outcome which constitutes escape from a negative situation (for example, an unpleasant or difficult task, a frightening or stressful situation). In such cases extinction means preventing such escape when the behaviour occurs. For example, if a person bites his hand whenever he is asked to wash or dress in order to have someone to do these activities for him, then extinction requires insisting that the activities are carried out despite the hand biting. If a person screams when approached by a caregiver in order for the caregiver to withdraw, then extinction requires continuing with the interaction despite the screaming. Of course, such an intervention could only be undertaken if the situation from which the person was seeking to escape was not of itself un-reasonable and if other measures were also being taken to make the situation less aversive (Chapter 5).

DISCOURAGING THE USE OF PROBLEMATIC BEHAVIOUR THROUGH THE APPLICATION OF COST RESULTS

Cost results are those results which immediately follow a behaviour and thereby make it less likely that the behaviour will occur again: they are called punishers. The experience of cost results for inappropriate or unacceptable behaviour is a powerful factor in human learning. It is used in the human socialization process (for example, parents scolding their children) and is a method by which society sets and maintains its rules (for example, the enforcement of law). The use of cost results has been shown to be a powerful and effective therapeutic tool for the reduction of a variety of behavioural difficulties.

In recent years, however, the use of cost results in the behavioural change process has been the subject of much debate among those working with people who have learning difficulties. There are import-ant reasons why the appropriateness of using cost results has been questioned.

1. Historically, the costs which have been imposed on people with learning difficulties have tended to be extreme and devaluing (for

example, spraying water in a person's face, applying noxious tastes to the tongue following an occurrence of an unacceptable behaviour). The use of such costs has been justified by a conviction that the person would not understand more socially appropriate costs.

2. The imposition of costs has involved exerting a lot of control over a person, which reinforces in the person a sense of inferiority and powerlessness. More dangerously, such control can reinforce, in the person imposing the cost, a sense of superiority and power. Such a sense of power and control undermines the concepts of equality, respect and positive regard which are prerequisites for a therapeutic relationship.

3. The accepted widespread usage of costs to control and change the behaviour of people with learning difficulties has resulted, in the past, in the overuse and abuse of cost results by carers who perhaps did not understand the full implications of the therapeutic use of such techniques.

What role, then, do cost results have in the therapeutic package provided by those attempting to help people with behavioural difficulties to find more appropriate ways of coping with their world? Cost results, after all, enable people in all cultures and in every society to learn appropriate behaviour through the consequences of their actions; as such they form an essential part of the learning process. To deny people with learning difficulties the opportunity to learn from the negative consequences of their actions is to deny them access to a natural learning process. The use of costs, therefore, remains an important and powerful therapeutic tool but only when used in combination with the other more positive-based strategies described in this book. Used in isolation, the effects of cost procedures are short-lived and there is a tendency for the person to develop new, equally inappropriate, behaviour in place of the target behaviour.

If it is felt that the experience of consistent cost results will help the individual to reduce his problematic behaviour then it is essential, also, that the costs which are imposed meet the following criteria. Cost results must be:

- ethically acceptable
- socially valid
- individually meaningful.

It is, therefore, important to examine what is meant by these criteria.

The criterion of ethical acceptability

To meet the criterion of ethical acceptability, imposed costs must not:

- be excessive to the severity of the problem in question;
- inflict physical harm to an individual (for example, slapping the person or pulling his hair);
- inflict psychological harm to an individual (for example, by threatening or frightening the person in any way);
- devalue the individual by treating him in ways which undermine his worth as a human being (for example, making him sit in a corner of the room with his back to the group);
- deprive the individual of the things which are rightfully his (for example, his personal possessions) even for a short period of time;
- deprive the individual of things which are essential to his physical well-being (for example, food, drink, warmth).

The criterion of social validity

To meet the criterion of social validity, costs should be ones which might normally be incurred for behaviour considered to be socially inappropriate or unacceptable. This means that costs should be socially natural or logical. For example, failing to wash or bathe for several weeks might naturally result in others avoiding a person's company. Arriving home later than arranged might logically result in the family having finished dinner and the late-comer's meal being cold or dried out. Behaving in a rowdy manner in the cinema might logically result in a person being thrown out by the manager. Insulting or hurting somebody might naturally result in being given the cold shoulder by that person. Making a mess on the floor might logically result in being expected to clear the mess up. Consistently intimidating those with whom one spends one's day might logically result in being excluded from the setting in which the intimidation occurs.

Socially valid costs help provide meaningful and realistic social feedback to the individual about the appropriateness of his behaviour (for example, 'When I hurt people they don't want to be with me', 'When I don't wash people don't want to be near me'). Compare this to socially unnatural or illogical messages (for example, 'When I hurt people they lock me in a room by myself', 'When I don't wash people take away my favourite video'). These latter messages simply convey a message of control which others exert over the person's life and the consequent powerlessness of the individual concerned.

The criterion of meaningfulness

In order to be therapeutically effective, costs should be individually meaningful: they should clearly communicate to the person why his action is inappropriate (for example, 'That hurts', 'That's dangerous',

'That's upsetting', 'That frightens me') and they should be communicated in a way that is likely to discourage future performance of the behaviour. Thus, if a person enjoys solitude and generally shies away from human contact, then it would not be an individually meaningful cost for him to be left alone and avoided for being aggressive. It might be more meaningful to enter into his personal space and offer a lengthy explanation of the effects of the behaviour on others. If, on the other hand, a person enjoys individual attention from his caregivers, then spending a lot of time explaining to him why his aggressive behaviour was inappropriate every time it occurred would not be an individually meaningful cost result, rather it would be a positive outcome for that person's inappropriate action. It might be better to avoid his company for a short period of time following each occurrence of the behaviour. Cost results other than those which fulfil the criteria of ethical acceptability, social validity and meaningfulness to the individual are unlikely to be helpful to the individual and should, in the opinion of the authors, not be used.

HOW RESULTS AFFECT BEHAVIOUR

Adopting a positive approach

The adoption of a calm, non-confrontational approach (which merely comments on, interrupts or diverts the individual's behaviour) as the 'default' approach, i.e. the approach to use when no formal programme has been devised, will ensure a positive atmosphere, based on warmth, equality and positive regard. Such an atmosphere will provide an important setting condition for other constructive work. It may also prevent the inadvertent social shaping of inappropriate behaviour. By itself, it is not anticipated to have any marked reducing effect on the behaviour.

Managing loss of control

Helping a person when he loses control of his actions because of high levels of emotional and physiological arousal, is not intended to be a learnings situation for the person. The results which are applied in this situation are, quite simply, intended to make the situation safe and to restore calm. Showing the person kindness and understanding in such a situation is unlikely to result in an increase in the frequency of the behaviour!

Extinction

The extinction burst

It has been consistently demonstrated than when an expected outcome is withheld from the individual (extinction) there is always a sharp initial increase in the behaviour (its frequency and/or its severity) as he tries harder to gain results. This phase is called the 'extinction burst'. Typically the behaviour will reach a peak within a few weeks following the implementation of the programme and then gradually start to decrease. Extinction procedures are often abandoned because those implementing the programme are unaware that an extinction burst will occur and believe that the programme is failing as the behaviour starts to increase in frequency or severity. Another reason why extinction procedures are often abandoned is because, during the extinction burst, the frequency or intensity of the behaviour may increase to a level that it is no longer considered safe or tolerable. The result is that a social response eventually occurs, the person eventually escapes from the situation, the sensory outcome is eventually attained. In considering the appropriateness of an extinction procedure it is therefore essential to bear in mind the full implications of the extinction burst.

The baseline reinforcement frequency

The frequency with which a behaviour achieves looked-for results before the start of an extinction programme will influence the speed of progress. If the behaviour frequently achieves a positive outcome then the extinction programme is likely to start to be effective quite rapidly because the individual will quickly notice the lack of positive outcome. If, however, during the pre-intervention phase, the behaviour has achieved only an occasional positive outcome, then there is likely to be a much slower reduction in the frequency of the inappropriate behaviour because the individual will take a longer time to notice the change in the outcome for his behaviour.

Cost results

Unlike extinction, which usually results in an initial increase in behavioural frequency or severity, followed by a steady decline in frequency and severity, cost results tend to have a more immediate impact on behaviour. If the 'cost' is individually meaningful, then an immediate and steady decline in behavioural frequency and severity should be observed. Such a decline should start to occur within a few weeks of the programme being implemented.

SUMMARY

The first part of this chapter has provided an overview of the general principles involved in responding appropriately to problematic behaviour. The second part of the chapter details the specific steps required for constructing effective and ethically acceptable responses to problematic behaviour as part of a broader intervention strategy for change.

PROCEDURES FOR PLANNING A RESPONSE TO A PROBLEMATIC BEHAVIOUR

Step ⧑ **1** ⧒	**Identify positive intervention into which response to problematic behaviour is to be incorporated**

The first step in planning a response to a problematic behaviour, which is to be therapeutically helpful, is to identify the positive programme or strategy which is to run in parallel with it. A response to a behaviour which is an expression of an intolerable level of emotion is likely to be part of an intervention which has been developed to help diffuse a person's agitation (Chapter 5) or which encourages the use of arousal management skills (Chapter 8) or which seeks to construct less stressful environments for the person (Chapter 4) or which seeks to address personal issues which give rise to emotional disturbance (Chapter 4).

A response to a behaviour which currently achieves a positive outcome for an individual is likely to be carried out in conjunction with an intervention which teaches and encourages the use of specific alternative skills (Chapters 6 and 7) or which directly reinforces the absence or lower frequency of the behaviour (Chapter 9) and which provides settings which are rich in potential reinforcers for the person (Chapter 4). Extinction procedures or cost results should not be applied in isolation from other positive strategies.

Step ⧑ **2** ⧒	**Select response type**

As with each aspect of the intervention package, planning an appropriate and therapeutic response to the problematic behaviour requires an understanding of the function of the behaviour for the individual (Chapter 2). The assessment of the behaviour is used to guide the planning.

Circumstances: behaviour is an expression or release of high emotional arousal

If the behaviour occurs because the person can no longer contain a powerful emotion, such as anger or agitation, and it is a way of expressing or alleviating that emotion, then the appropriate response type will:

- seek to make the situation safe, if there is a danger that someone may get hurt in the process;
- seek to help the person to calm down as quickly as possible.

Circumstances: behaviour achieves a specific identifiable result

If a behaviour is considered to be inappropriate and the aim is to discourage its use, then one way is to ensure that the anticipated positive results are no longer achieved (extinction). Extinction can be used under the following circumstances.

1. There is a single clearly identifiable result which the person seeks from his behaviour (for example, the individual seeks to get a reaction from those around him or seeks to opt out of a difficult situation or derives sensory stimulation). If the behaviour achieves a number of results (for example, attention on some occasions and escape on others) then extinction would require different responses to different situations. This, in practice, is very complex and difficult to do because it requires that carers make instant judgments about the outcome which is being sought.
2. A way can be found which will stop the result occurring when the behaviour happens. This is perhaps easiest if the looked-for outcome is a social or material one. Extinction will mean simply not reacting to the individual's behaviour (social extinction) in the way that he wants or not reacting to it at all. It may simply mean withholding the material outcome which is sought. If the looked-for outcome is escape, then extinction will involve seeing the activity through to its conclusion, despite protestations from the individual. This may be very difficult in practice, particularly if the individual uses aggressive or self-injurious behaviour to achieve such an outcome. If the looked-for outcome is sensory stimulation, then it may prove difficult to block certain sensory outcomes (for example, the stimulation obtained from teeth grinding or squealing).
3. The predicted increase in the frequency or the severity of the behaviour (extinction burst) can be tolerated and managed safely. For some behaviour this may be possible to do, but for others it may not prove so easy. For example, if during social extinction a person's face slapping developed into headbutting of walls and started to

occur more frequently during the extinction burst, then it would be too dangerous to leave the person to continue and not respond to him. If, during escape extinction, a person's destructive behaviour developed into physically aggressive behaviour towards caregivers and peers, then it would be unethical for caregivers to continue allowing this behaviour to continue. Before embarking upon an extinction programme it is important to consider just how severe the behaviour might become during the extinction burst and to consider whether it would continue to be possible to prevent looked-for results occurring under those circumstances.

4. The looked-for results are likely to be prevented each time the behaviour occurs. With regard to sensory extinction, consistency would mean having adequate staffing resources to respond immediately to each occurrence of the behaviour (i.e. each time the person grinds his teeth, rocks, screams, sucks his fingers). The high level of supervision required for this might be impossible to achieve in many settings. With regard to social extinction, such consistency would require a firm commitment from everyone who comes into contact with the person not to provide the looked-for outcome. A behaviour may be regarded by some carers as so obnoxious (for example, spitting or smearing) that they may find it impossible not to react in the way the person finds reinforcing.

If the four criteria described above cannot be met, then extinction should not be attempted.

Circumstances: the function of the behaviour is unclear; the behaviour has many functions; extinction is not appropriate

When a behaviour is considered to be inappropriate and the aim is to discourage its use then cost results can be considered if the above circumstances apply. A cost result must be selected which is ethically acceptable, socially valid and individually meaningful. Thus, a person who disrupts group situations could be asked to leave the situation when disruptive behaviour begins. A person who is aggressive might be ignored for a period of time. A person who smears might be asked to clear up the mess that has been made. If a response cannot be found which is not only individually meaningful, but is also socially valid and ethically acceptable, then a cost should not be applied to the behaviour.

Circumstances: extinction is not appropriate; an appropriate cost cannot be found

In these circumstances, the 'default' low-key approach should be used: the response to the behaviour should be minimal and non-confrontational. At most, there will be a comment about its inappropriateness and a brief explanation of why it is inappropriate. The behaviour may be interrupted without fuss and the person redirected to a more appropriate activity or subject using a calm approach.

Step 3 Plan details for implementing selected response

Having decided on the response which will be given to the problematic behaviour, details must be worked out for the method of implementing the response.

Restoring safety and calm

Planning how to help a person to calm down may require detailed planning of the following.

1. The way a situation is to be made safe. Details should be included of who should be involved and who should do what (for example, first person on the scene ushers out everyone from the area, second person on the scene approaches the individual using a calm, reassuring tone).
2. How to reassure and calm the individual – what to say or do (for example, stand to the side, use particular words, touch arm lightly, etc.).
3. How to take control over the person's behaviour if this is necessary. For example, if the person is to be held, then details of how this should be done should be specified. If a person is to be directed to a safer environment, then such an environment (safe haven) should be prepared in advance and the person accustomed to spending time there, engaging in calming and relaxing activities. Details of how the person is to be escorted to the 'safe haven' should also be specified.
4. How to manage the situation once the person has calmed (for example, offering a drink, offering time alone).
5. Any further action which needs to be taken (for example, discussing the incident with the person).

Extinction and cost results

Responses will differ according to the specific situation but regardless of the response being planned, all details about its implementation must be decided upon at this stage, rather like a precision skills teaching programme. Details to be planned include:

- instructions for interrupting the behaviour (i.e. what is to be said and what is to be done), if appropriate;
- a brief explanation prior to the cost result, of why the behaviour is inappropriate (for example, 'That hurts', 'That's dangerous');
- instructions for implementing the cost or extinction procedure (i.e. what is to be said and what is to be done);
- instructions for responding if the person becomes unco-operative with the procedure (i.e. what is to be said and what is to be done).

In this way, maximum consistency will be obtained between carers and the likelihood of the response being implemented in a calm and objective way will be increased. When planning the implementation of cost procedures, the following rules should be observed.

1. Cost procedures must be implemented immediately, i.e. as soon as the problematic behaviour occurs.
2. Cost procedures must be implemented consistently, i.e. each time the problematic behaviour occurs.
3. If instructions have to be used, these should be brief and given once only.
4. Cost procedures should be as brief as possible, i.e. just long enough to be meaningful to the person. Having said that, the cost result should not be terminated until the behaviour to which they are applied has stopped. For example, if a person is to be ignored for a period of 30 seconds each time he screams, then if screaming is still occurring after 30 seconds has elapsed, the person should continue to be ignored until screaming stops and a further 3–4 seconds has elapsed. In the event that the duration of the cost response consistently extends beyond 5–10 minutes (because the behaviour has not stopped and this state of affairs has not improved within two weeks following implementation of the cost procedure, then the procedure should be abandoned and the 'default' low-key response adopted until a more appropriate cost can be found.

Step 4   Rehearse the response to the problematic behaviour

Although a good method of planning will ensure a good programme, it is unrealistic to expect all the fine details to be decided upon without trying out the programme first. There is nothing more discouraging for carers than to be asked to carry out a programme which is clearly impractical from the first time it is tried. If a programme states that a person should pick up anything he throws but the person is unco-operative, then the people trying to implement the programme may find themselves in an impossible situation if that person happens to be physically strong and heavy. Such situations can be avoided by trying out the programme first, using role play. Role-play rehearsals of a programme can be enhanced if video facilities are available to film and replay the programme. Such thorough preparation ensures a fully practicable programme, which will encourage those who have to implement it.

Step 5   Plan record of progress

Accurate monitoring of progress is essential, especially when costs or extinction are being used. Chapter 11 (STEPS 1–4) describes in detail how to set up monitoring procedures for the recording of problematic behaviour and the reader should refer to that chapter for guidance. An objective record of the person's progress will be needed to justify continued use of cost or extinction procedures: a recording chart should be prepared in advance (Chapter 11, STEP 5).

Step 6   Plan review date

As with all intervention programmes, a date for review must be specified at the time of planning and writing the programme. Time must be allowed for the programme to be implemented consistently: 3 or 4 weeks is a reasonable period for an initial review of this type of programme. Thereafter, the programme should be reviewed at least monthly.

Step 7   Write the behaviour-management strategy

The strategy which has been selected as a response to the problematic behaviour should be added to the programme, as discussed in previous chapters, under the heading 'Response to inappropriate behaviour'. It should include details of:

- the target behaviour;
- the method of interrupting the behaviour if appropriate, including exactly what is to be said and done;
- the response to the target behaviour, including exactly what is to be said and done, the exact duration of the response and the conditions for ending the response;

- the way of responding if the person fails to co-operate with the procedure, including exactly what is to be said and done;
- the details of recording procedures and a recording chart.

It is important that the planned response to the behaviour is not written as a separate 'programme' as this will undermine the importance of the other more positive aspects of the intervention.

Figure 8.4 illustrates a DRO programme which includes a planned response to a problematic behaviour: the response is based on the 'default' low-key approach. Figure 5.3 illustrates a trigger-level intervention based on graded exposure, which combines escape extinction as the planned response to the problematic behaviour. Figure 7.2 illustrates a programme which encourages the use of a physically incompatible skill: it incorporates material extinction as the planned response to the problematic behaviour.

Step ⟩ **8** ⟨   **Take a baseline measure**

The reader should refer to Chapter 11 (STEP 6) to help him plan the measurement of the baseline frequency of the behaviour, which is essential if the effectiveness of the strategy is to be accurately assessed. A programme should not be implemented until a baseline measure has been obtained.

Step ⟩ **9** ⟨   **Implement, review and move on**

Cost and extinction procedures tend to show fairly rapid effects on the behaviour which they follow. Extinction procedures should start to see the beginning of a decrease in the behaviour within 3–4 weeks of the start of the programme and following the extinction burst. Cost procedures should, if individually meaningful, start to see a decrease in the problematic behaviour within 1–2 weeks of the start of the programme, with no initial increase in the behaviour (as occurs when using extinction). Whatever the procedure selected, if there has been no positive effect on the person's behaviour within 2 months, the response must be reviewed and a more appropriate one found.

Records of progress should be summarized in the form of a graph or a chart (Chapter 11, STEPS 8 and 9) to facilitate an objective and accurate review of the person's progress.

Once the planned result starts to have a positive effect on the behaviour, the use of the result needs to be sustained until the problematic behaviour is occurring at a very low rate. By this time, it is hoped, the individual may have learned better ways of coping with his difficulties. When a decision is eventually made to remove the planned results from the overall programme, the behaviour should continue to be monitored for a time lest the problem behaviour recurs or starts to increase.

SUMMARY

An appropriate response to a problematic behaviour, based on the assessment of the function of the behaviour, is an important final consideration in the planning of the therapeutic package which is designed to help an individual overcome or cope with his behavioural difficulties. Failing to plan how to respond may leave carers floundering or reacting emotively and inconsistently. A prepared and rehearsed response will enable carers to act in a calm, sensitive and therapeutically useful manner. If a behaviour has hitherto achieved desired results for the person, then these results should, if possible, be prevented from occurring. If such prevention is not feasible then it may be necessary to add a cost result. The provision of a cost result to an individual should be carefully planned to ensure that the cost is individually meaningful. It must in addition be ethically justified and socially valid. If a response cannot be found which meets all of these criteria then a low-key non-confrontational approach to the behaviour should be continued. The planned response must be written into a more general programme of positive interventions and should not be separated from them. As with all major aspects of the therapeutic package, the effect of the intervention should be carefully monitored to ensure that progress is indeed occurring.

**RESPONDING
TO PROBLEMATIC BEHAVIOUR**

SUMMARY OF STEPS

1

Identify positive intervention into which
response to problematic behaviour is to be incorporated

2

Select response type

3

Plan details for implementing selected response

4

Rehearse the response to the problematic behaviour

5

Plan record of progress

6

Plan review date

7

Write the behaviour management strategy

8

Take a baseline measure

9

Implement, review and move on

Reviewing progress
11

The S.T.A.R. approach emphasizes the importance of accurate records and objective assessment of progress in all areas of work – in the teaching of new skills, the strengthening of skills already present, in the reduction of problematic behaviour, in monitoring the effects of setting-level interventions. Competent monitoring of progress is as much an ingredient of successful work as the programmes of intervention themselves. Previous chapters have detailed the steps needed to set up monitoring systems for environmental and personal setting changes, skill learning, skill usage and for problem-behaviour reduction. The present chapter describes in greater detail how to ensure accuracy in records kept and how to analyse these records using graphs and charts.

REVIEWING PROGRESS – GENERAL PRINCIPLES

The need for systematic record keeping has been stressed throughout this book but the records will be of little value unless they are presented in a way which is intelligible and which allows them to be analysed easily. Given the long-term perspective often needed, records may become copious and difficult to analyse unless they are condensed and summarized. A verbal or written summary of progress is cumbersome and difficult to interpret: the more information it contains, the harder it is to assess trends or to notice subtle changes. A far more useful and effective way to summarize information is in pictorial or graphical form.

Visual summaries, such as graphs and charts, are a very effective means of presenting information about behavioural change. There are a number of reasons for this.

1. They enable details of change over time to be grasped at a single glance.

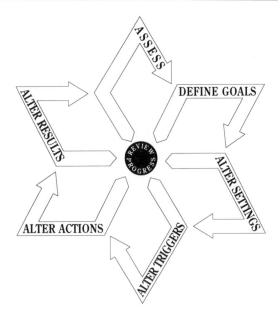

Figure 11.1 Reviewing progress.

2. They are a clearer, more economic means of conveying information than words or numbers.
3. They can be made interesting to look at and thus hold attention far better than written or verbal reports.
4. They can show relationships and trends which are not readily apparent from the examination of individual recording sheets, because a lot of information can be presented simultaneously.
5. They provide a concise and permanent record of progress which can be updated regularly without the need for summaries to be re-written each time a new piece of information is added.

In general, therefore, graphs and charts provide a more comprehensive and better balanced view of progress than could be derived from verbal or written presentations alone.

Visual summaries of progress are also important for other reasons: they can play a role in motivating those involved in programmes of behavioural change. Graphs and charts provide a visual display of achievement and progress which serve as a permanent reminder of work which is being undertaken. This is particularly so if the charts are displayed in a prominent place and are made colourful and attractive. Positive evidence of progress will motivate people to continue their efforts and provide them with ongoing positive feedback about their efforts.

ORGANIZING THE APPROPRIATE INFORMATION

If information is to be summarized accurately in a visual form it must be collected from the outset in an objective, concise and systematic fashion. Two contrasting methods of collecting information are shown in Figure 11.2. A comparison of these two methods shows that the descriptive record of behaviour will prove far more difficult to summarize accurately and objectively. Descriptive accounts of behaviour are useful in the initial stages when an assessment of a behaviour is being carried out. In these circumstances detailed accounts of settings, triggers and results, as described in Chapter 2, are essential. Such detailed assessment is required before any intervention plan is formulated and may need to be reinstituted if progress does not occur and further assessment is required. However, once intervention plans have been implemented such detailed records are no longer required. It now becomes more important to measure the specific behaviour which has been targeted for change in terms of its frequency, duration or the amount of help needed to perform it.

This means that recording should focus upon those aspects of behaviour that are easy to measure. Actions that can be seen, such as slapping one's face or throwing items of furniture, are easy to count. If not the behaviour, then the outcome of behaviour can provide an objective measure, for example, the amount of food eaten, injuries to staff, repair requisitions. Whether actions or their outcome are being measured, definitions must be precise if ambiguity for the observer is to be avoided. For example, the term 'mealtime behaviour' can encompass a variety of separate actions, such as sitting at table, holding a knife and fork, finger feeding, taking other people's food, tipping drinks. It would be very difficult to obtain accurate measures of a behaviour which was so poorly defined that the observer had no real idea of what to focus on and what to record. In order to obtain accurate records each relevant action needs to be defined separately. Alternatively, a single key behaviour might be identified (Figure 11.2). As another example, the term 'anxious' can mean different things to different people. One person might judge an individual to be anxious when he bites his finger nails, another when he paces about the room, another when he engages in a lot of ritualistic behaviour. Without a precise definition, objective and accurate records will not be obtained.

The information required is about actions or the outcome of actions. These can be measured in terms of some numerical value or score. Scores can he added or averaged and transferred to a visual summary in a way that verbal reports cannot. It is therefore important to plan recording systems carefully so that they provide objective measures which can be transformed into simple scores.

Date	Descriptive record of behaviour
5TH FEB	WAS VERY GOOD TODAY. ATE ALL HIS MEAL, SPAT ONLY ONCE AND DIDN'T SCREAM VERY MUCH. STOPPED FINGER FEEDING WHEN SHOUTED AT AND USED SPOON
6TH FEB	LUNCH AWFUL. TIPPED EVERYONE'S PLATES AND DRINKS. KICKED ANN SEVERAL TIMES AND DIDN'T WANT TO EAT. WAS SENT OUT
7TH FEB	SUPPER. ATE EVERYTHING BUT USED FINGERS WHENEVER I TURNED AWAY. PINCHED FOOD FROM OTHER PEOPLE'S PLATES. SCREAMED A FEW TIMES
8TH FEB	BREAKFAST. ATE REASONABLY WELL TODAY

(a)

Objective record of behaviour

What to record 1. AMOUNT OF FOOD EATEN (ALL, QUARTER, HALF, THREE-QUARTER, NONE)
2. (√) EACH TIME HE SCREAMS, KICKS, TIPS PLATES OR DRINKS. PUT TICKS IN APPROPRIATE COLUMNS.

When to record SUPPERTIME ONLY

Date	Amount eaten	Screaming	Kicking	Tipping plates/ drinks	Comments
9TH FEB	ALL	√ √		√	
10TH FEB	QUARTER	√√√√√	√√√√	√√√√	AWFUL
11TH FEB	THREE QUARTER	√√√√	√√√√√	√√√	GRABBED FOOD FROM PLATE
12TH FEB	THREE QUARTER	√√	√		USED SPOON WITHOUT REMINDING

(b)

Figure 11.2 (a) Descriptive and (b) specific records of behaviour.

THE IMPORTANCE OF COLLECTING BASELINE INFORMATION

Records are kept in order to evaluate progress. No judgment about the effectiveness of an intervention can be made unless there are measures of the behaviour before a programme starts. This is the concept of a baseline – a measure of the behaviour (frequency or duration) before intervention. Baseline measures allow an objective judgment to be made about whether there are changes in the behaviour following the start of an intervention programme. Thus information needs to be gathered on a continuous basis over time: before, during and after any structured programme of work.

DECIDING UPON THE FREQUENCY OF MEASUREMENT

A serious threat to the value of information occurs if records are kept sporadically and inconsistently. It is important, therefore, to give realistic consideration to how frequently a behaviour can be measured. Can a behaviour be measured every time it occurs or does some form of structured sampling need to take place? Structured sampling of a behaviour is useful because it enables accurate and systematic records to be made when continuous recording is either impractical because of time/staffing constraints or impossible because of the high frequency of the behaviour. If informed judgments about change are to be made, then an accurate record kept daily over 1 hour may be more useful than an inaccurate record kept over a whole day. Planning for the frequency of recording needs to occur before a programme is begun.

SUMMARIZING AND INTERPRETING INFORMATION

The most useful type of visual summaries of information about behavioural change are graphs and charts. There are many approaches to graphing and charting and there is usually no 'best' type of visual summary for a particular score. Even the simplest of scores can be depicted by more than one graphical method. Selection of a specific method of summarizing information may depend on an individual's knowledge of and preference for the various techniques, the time available for preparation of the chart and the particular aspect of the information which needs to be highlighted. It will also depend, to some extent, on the amount of information which needs to be represented.

If organized carefully, graphs and charts can, at a single glance, provide valuable, objective information about changes in behaviour over weeks, months or even years.

1. Graphs and charts can demonstrate trends in behaviour over time – perhaps a gradual upward trend in the performance of a skill or a gradual downward trend in a problematic behaviour (if all is going well!).
2. Graphs and charts can illustrate how a behaviour fluctuates and whether such fluctuations are related systematically to other variables, such as day of the week, occurrence of seizures, menstruation or changes in medication.
3. Graphs and charts can show whether change in one behaviour relates to changes in other behaviours, for example, whether a decrease in headbanging is related to an increase in rocking or in social behaviour.

SUMMARY

Summarizing and transforming behavioural measures into a visual format, such as a graph or chart, is a powerful tool for analysing information. There are a number of specific steps which need to be taken in order to generate accurate and objective records and summaries of progress. The first part of this chapter outlined the general principles and procedures. In the second part, the specific steps which lead to high-quality records and analysis are detailed.

PRODUCING HIGH-QUALITY SUMMARIES OF PROGRESS

Step ⟩ 1 ⟨   Define the behaviour

The prerequisite for any accurate recording system is a definition of the behaviour or outcome of behaviour that is to be measured. Such a definition must be unambiguous and relate to actions that can be observed and agreed upon by all those involved.

Step ⟩ 2 ⟨   Decide what to measure

Frequency, duration and other objective measures

Accuracy and reliability requires that behaviour or its outcome be measured along a predefined scale. The most common way of measuring behaviour objectively is to count its frequency (for example, how often others are kicked, how often a person asks for what he wants). Sometimes it may be more appropriate to measure the duration of a behaviour (for example, how long an activity is worked on, how long a screaming bout lasts). Frequency and duration are the most commonly

Table 11.1 Some objective measures of behaviour

Measure	Examples
Frequency	Hitting, initiating social contact
Duration	Crying, rocking, sitting, working
Latency	Time taken to fall asleep, to respond to request
Distance	Distance walked, distance ball thrown
Weight	Weight of food consumed, of 'wet' laundry
Size	Diameter of wet patch on bed, of bald patch on head

used dimensions for measuring behaviour. There are, however, a number of other objective measures which can be used: these are summarized in Table 11.1. Selecting the most appropriate measure will depend on the behaviour itself and on the aims of intervention.

Rating scales

Sometimes the progress sought cannot be measured along these basic dimensions. Progress in skill learning, for example, may be measured by the amount of help required to perform the task (for example, no help, a prompt from the elbow, a full physical prompt). The tidiness of a room may be measured along a number of dimensions, such as the number of clothes left on the floor, the neatness of the bed, the amount of litter scattered around the room. A person's agitation may be measured along dimensions such as the amount of time the person spends sitting in one place, the number of doors which are slammed, the duration of screaming, the duration and frequency of pacing up and down. One way of measuring these more complex phenomena is to construct a scale of numbers with each point on the scale carefully defined. Meeting the defined criteria thus leads to a 'score' being assigned.

Examples

The amount of help given to perform a skill could be scored in terms of:
1 = a lot of help (a full physical prompt),
2 = a little help (prompt from the elbow),
3 = no help at all.

The tidiness of a room could be scored as:
4 = very tidy (bed made, clothes put away, no litter on the floor),
3 = quite tidy (bed well made, some clothes or litter on the floor),
2 = quite untidy (bed badly made, clothes or litter on the floor),
1 = very untidy (bed unmade, clothes and litter on the floor).

A person's agitation could be scored as:
4 = very agitated (screaming and/or pacing more than 50% of the evening),
3 = quite agitated (screaming and/or pacing between 25% and 50% of the evening),
2 = quite calm (screaming and/or pacing less than 25% of the evening),
1 = very calm (no screaming, no pacing).

The value of such rating scales depends entirely upon how well each point on the scale is defined. Each point needs to be defined in terms of things that can be readily observed and agreed upon. More global ratings (for example, as to how 'good' someone has been) will allow more subjective impressions and therefore disagreements between raters. This in turn makes it hard to interpret the actual meaning of scores given and any change over time.

Step 3 Decide how to monitor change

Continuous recording

The most accurate measure will be obtained from continuous recording, in other words recording each time a behaviour occurs. However, continuous recording is only practicable under certain conditions: namely, if there are sufficient human resources to carry out recording on a continuous basis or if the behaviour is of relatively low frequency.

Sampling

In order to make recording more manageable, behaviour can be sampled. This is the same principle as that which underlies opinion polls and consumer surveys. For present purposes three ways of sampling behaviour will be considered: time-block sampling, momentary-time sampling and interval sampling.

Time-block sampling

This means setting aside a time each day and recording the total frequency/duration of an action within this limited time period. For example, if spitting is a behaviour of concern then a record might be kept of the frequency of spitting in a set half-hour period each day. The following points should be noted.

- Time blocks are likely to vary from 15 minutes to 1 hour in length and there may be one or more blocks a day, depending on the resources available.
- Time blocks selected should be 'typical' so that the behaviour is likely to be observed.
- Time blocks should be fixed in advance so that they occur under similar circumstances each day, i.e. the same time, the same place, during similar activities.
- Time-block sampling is likely to be of greatest use with high-frequency behaviour, when continuous recording is not practicable. Momentary-time sampling and interval sampling (see below) may be organized into a time-block framework.

Momentary-time sampling

Momentary-time sampling is a way of sampling behaviour at specific moments in time during a predetermined period. This means observing the individual very briefly (a few seconds only) at regular, predetermined times. For example, if an individual spins objects at every opportunity, then some estimate of how much time is occupied by spinning would be obtained by observing for 5 seconds every 1 minute and noting whether spinning was occurring at the moment of observation. Momentary-time sampling is particularly useful for actions that occur at a very high frequency or in bouts of extended duration – in other words, for behaviour which occurs almost continuously.

Interval sampling

This provides an estimate of frequency/duration of an action by dividing the observation period up into a series of intervals. The intervals may be anything from a few seconds to several hours in length.

Partial interval sampling involves the observer recording at the end of the interval whether or not the behaviour occurred at all in the previous interval. It does not matter how often it occurred or how long a bout lasted – if the behaviour occurred at all the interval is scored as positive. For example, if a person's social interaction is being recorded, the day could be divided into three intervals: morning, afternoon and evening. An observer would record at the end of each interval whether any initiation was made during the previous interval (Yes or No, Tick or Cross, + or −, 1 or 0).

Total interval sampling is when the action is only scored as present if it has gone on for the whole time during the interval. For example, if sleep is being monitored at the end of every 15 minutes using a total interval sampling approach, then the behaviour is only scored as present if the individual slept during the whole interval. If he was awake for any time during the interval the behaviour is scored as absent.

Interval sampling becomes less accurate as the length of the intervals grows. However, it can be relatively easy to implement, especially partial interval sampling, and has much to contribute to the monitoring of moderate or high-frequency or continuous behaviour.

Figure 11.3 and Figure 11.4 provide examples of some of the methods of monitoring and recording which have been described here. With the range of methods to choose from there is no excuse for a service not to have a system of objective recording that monitors the frequency/duration of specific behaviour over time.

Step ⟩ 4 ⟨　Decide how often to monitor behaviour

Behaviour should be monitored throughout a programme of intervention. Once a decision has been about the monitoring procedure (continuous or sample recording) the next question to be addressed is how frequently to monitor. Again, the more frequently that behaviour is monitored the more sensitive the measure will be to change. Ideally, therefore, behaviour monitoring should occur each day during a programme of change. Practical considerations will determine how feasible this is likely to be. Whatever is decided, it is important that the monitoring should be carried out on a planned basis and not left to chance. The days, times, places and situations when monitoring will occur should be predetermined. It may be daily, one or two days each week or on set days in a month. Whatever approach is favoured it should be organized in advance and not left for carers to remember as necessary or pick what they think is a good time.

With a lot of planning and thought, efficiency can be introduced into any monitoring system, such that the system becomes useful and practical for any service. There can be no excuse for not having a functioning system that generates information as to whether behaviour is getting better, worse or not changing over time.

BLOCK TIME SAMPLING		
What to Record *HAIR PULLING*		
When to Record *THROUGHOUT DAY WHENEVER HE PULLS PEOPLE'S HAIR*		
How to Record *NOTE TIME, PLACE, PERSON*		
Date	**Hair Pulling**	
12TH APRIL	*8.10 A.M. PULLED A'S HAIR IN BATHROOM* *8.30 A.M. PULLED J'S HAIR AT BREAKFAST* *8.54 A.M. PULLED A'S HAIR ON BUS* *9.37 A.M. PULLED D'S HAIR AT DAY CENTRE* *9.40 A.M. PULLED D'S HAIR AGAIN AT DAY CENTRE* *10.56 A.M. PULLED S'S HAIR AT DAY CENTRE* *11.20 A.M. PULLED T'S HAIR WHEN OUT FOR A WALK* *12.30 P.M. PULLED D'S HAIR IN DINING ROOM* *12.37 P.M. PULLED S'S HAIR IN DINING ROOM* *12.50 P.M. PULLED T'S HAIR IN DINING ROOM*	
	TOTAL FREQUENCY	*10*

(a)

INTERVAL SAMPLING		
What to Record *HAIR PULLING*		
When to Record *EVERY HALF-HOUR FOR BEHAVIOUR* *DURING PREVIOUS HALF-HOUR*		
How to Record *(√) IF PULLED HAIR* *(X) IF DIDN'T PULL HAIR*		
Date	Interval	√ / X
12TH APRIL	*7.00 - 7.30 A.M.*	*X*
	7.30 - 8.00 A.M.	*X*
	8.00 - 8.30 A.M.	*√*
	8.30 - 9.00 A.M.	*√*
	9.00 - 9.30 A.M.	*X*
	9.30 - 10.00 A.M.	*√*
	10.00 - 10.30 A.M.	*X*
	10.30 - 11.00 A.M.	*√*
	11.00 - 11.30 A.M.	*√*
	11.30 - 12.00 A.M.	*X*
	12.00 - 12.30 P.M.	*X*
	12.30 - 1.00 P.M.	*√*
	TOTAL INTERVALS IN WHICH *BEHAVIOUR OCCURRED*	*6 (OUT OF* *POSSIBLE 12)*

(b)

MOMENTARY TIME SAMPLING		
What to Record *HAIR PULLING*		
When to Record *LAST 5 SECONDS OF HALF-HOUR* *FOR BEHAVIOUR DURING THESE 5 SECONDS*		
How to Record *(√) IF PULLED HAIR* *(X) IF DIDN'T PULL HAIR*		
Date	Time	√ / X
12TH APRIL	*7.00 A.M.*	*X*
	7.30 A.M.	*X*
	8.00 A.M.	*X*
	8.30 A.M.	*√*
	9.00 A.M.	*X*
	9.30 A.M.	*X*
	10.00 A.M.	*X*
	10.30 A.M.	*X*
	11.00 A.M.	*X*
	11.30 A.M.	*X*
	12.00 P.M.	*X*
	12.30 P.M.	*√*
	1.00 P.M.	*X*
	TOTAL TIME POINTS AT WHICH *BEHAVIOUR OCCURRED*	*2 (OUT OF* *POSSIBLE 13)*

(c)

Figure 11.3 (a) Block-time sampling, (b) interval sampling and (c) momentary-time sampling of a problematic behaviour.

BLOCK TIME SAMPLING			
What to Record *TIME STARTED WORK ACTIVITY AND TIME STOPPED WORK ACTIVITY*			
When to Record *11.00 - 12.00*			
Date	**Time started activity**	**Time stopped activity**	**Total time**
5TH JUNE	*11.00 A.M.*	*11.03 A.M.*	*3*
	11.06 A.M.	*11.11 A.M.*	*5*
	11.12 A.M.	*11.20 A.M.*	*8*
	11.30 A.M.	*11.34 A.M.*	*4*
	11.40 A.M.	*11.50 A.M.*	*10*
	11.51 A.M.	*11.53 A.M.*	*2*
			32 MINUTES

(a)

INTERVAL SAMPLING		
What to Record *IF WORKING AT ALL DURING EACH 5-MINUTE INTERVAL*		
When to Record *11.00 - 12.00 A.M. AT END OF EACH INTERVAL*		
How to Record *(√) IF WORKED* *(X) IF DIDN'T WORK*		
Date	**Time**	**√ / X**
5TH JUNE	*11.00 - 11.05 A.M.*	*√*
	11.00 - 11.10 A.M.	*√*
	11.10 - 11.15 A.M.	*√*
	11.15 - 11.20 A.M.	*√*
	11.20 - 11.25 A.M.	*X*
	11.25- 11.30 A.M.	*X*
	11.30 - 11.35 A.M.	*√*
	11.35 - 11.40 A.M.	*X*
	11.40 - 1145 A.M.	*√*
	11.45 - 11.50 A.M.	*√*
	11.50 - 11.55 A.M.	*√*
	11.55 - 12.00 A.M.	*X*
	TOTAL	*8/12 INTERVALS*

(b)

MOMENTARY TIME SAMPLING		
What to Record *IF WORKING AT MOMENT OF RECORDING*		
When to Record *11.00 - 12.00 A.M. AT TIMES SPECIFIED BELOW*		
How to Record *(√) IF WORKING* *(X) IF NOT WORKING*		
Date	**Time**	**√ / X**
5TH JUNE	*11.00 A.M.*	*√*
	11.05 A.M.	*X*
	11.10 A.M.	*√*
	11.15 A.M.	*√*
	11.20 A.M.	*√*
	11.25 A.M.	*X*
	11.30 A.M.	*√*
	11.35 A.M.	*X*
	11.40 A.M.	*√*
	11.45 A.M.	*√*
	11.50 A.M.	*√*
	11.55 A.M.	*X*
	12.00 A.M.	*X*
	TOTAL TIME POINTS AT WHICH WORKING OBSERVED	*7/12*

(c)

Figure 11.4 (a) Block-time sampling, (b) interval sampling and (c) momentary-time sampling of an on-task behaviour.

Step ⨝ 5 ⨝ Prepare a recording chart

Once decisions have been taken about how behaviour is to be monitored, a recording chart will need to be designed (or selected). Any chart should contain at least the following details.

1. The name of the individual whose behaviour is being monitored.
2. The long- and short-term objectives for the programme of work.
3. A definition of the behaviour/outcome of behaviour to be measured.
4. A statement of how and when the behaviour is to be monitored.
5. The date of each recording.

An example of a simple recording chart is shown in Figure 11.5.

Step ⨝ 6 ⨝ Take a baseline measure

Before embarking on any programme of behavioural change, it is important first to obtain a measure of the current level of that behaviour (using the same measures and procedures which have been decided upon in STEPS 2, 3 and 4). This enables a meaningful comparison of performance before and after a programme has begun and allows a competent judgment to be made about whether a programme should be continued, amended or abandoned. Without such 'before and after' recording a number of judgment errors can be made.

Behaviour may change over time anyway, without specific intervention. For example, if a programme is introduced to decrease spitting at a time when the behaviour is already on the decline then continued decline may be attributed (falsely) to the intervention (Figure 11.6(a)). If a behaviour is very variable and the start of intervention coincides with a low or high period then the programme may be judged wrongly to be effective or to have made things worse, depending on what phase the start of the programme coincides with (Figure 11.6(b)). If a behaviour is getting steadily worse and the programme stabilizes at a certain level, then without a measure of trend before the start of the programme the intervention may be judged to be ineffective (Figure 11.6(c)).

It is difficult to be exact about how many times a behaviour needs to be measured before an intervention programme is started. As a general rule, a baseline should continue until a stable picture of the behaviour and its variability emerges.

• If a behaviour occurs at approximately the same rate each session/ day then keeping baseline records for a week will be sufficient.

BEHAVIOUR RECORDING CHART		
Name TONY		
Long – term Goal TONY WILL STOP THROWING OBJECTS		
Short – term Goal TONY WILL NOT THROW OBJECTS IN THE UNIT AT THE DAY CENTRE		
What to Record (√) EACH TIME TONY THROWS ANY OBJECT ONTO THE FLOOR OR AT ANOTHER PERSON		
When to Record BETWEEN 10.00 A.M. AND 10.30 A.M.		
Date	**Incidents of Throwing (√)**	**Comments**
JUNE 5TH	√√√	A GOOD DAY. MARY ABSENT TODAY
JUNE 6TH	√√√√	
JUNE 7TH	√√√√√√√	ALL THESE DURING MUSIC SESSION

Figure 11.5 Example of a simple behaviour-recording chart.

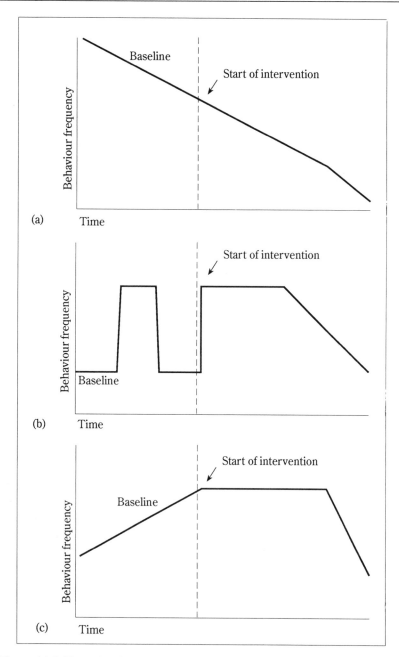

Figure 11.6 The role of baseline information in the interpretation of the effectiveness of interventions.

- If the variability is high then the baseline period will need to continue until it is clear that there is no decreasing trend in the behaviour. This may take 3–4 weeks of observation.
- If there is an increasing trend in a problematic behaviour then this in practice will create pressure to intervene. However, the risk of errors about progress against a rising baseline (Figure 11.6(c)) is not serious.

In general there will be less variability in new skill functioning than in the variability of an established behaviour. Thus measuring the amount of help a learner requires to perform a skill is likely to be a more stable index, so that a baseline of three sessions may be adequate to establish how much can be done independently, before introducing a skill-teaching programme.

Step ⟨ 7 ⟩   Implement intervention and record

Having organized recording and carried out baseline measures, a programme of change can be started with recording continuing on a systematic basis throughout the duration of the programme.

Step ⟨ 8 ⟩   Summarize the data

Use total scores

The simplest way to summarize the information collected is to decide the basic time unit (session, day, week, month) and then add up the total score for each such unit (for example, the total frequency of hitting each day, the total duration of rocking each session, the total distance walked each week, the total number of times that a skill was performed with no help or with some help during a session).

Use average (mean) scores

A number of total scores can be condensed by computing the average for a series of such scores and using this single measure to monitor progress. This may be useful when the number of sessional/daily records is very large. It is essential if records that contribute to a total score are likely to be missed out or lost. For example, if monitoring was set up in terms of weekly totals for incidents of pinching people and on some days records were not kept (for any reason) or a daily data sheet

Table 11.2 Examples of the calculation of an average (mean) score

Total number of hits		Total duration of crying (minutes)	
Monday	= 5	Week 1	= 100
Tuesday	= 9	Week 2	= 145
Wednesday	= 13	Week 3	= 119
Thursday	= 3	Week 4	= 136
Friday	= 6		
Saturday	= 8		
Sunday	= 5		
Total score	= 49	Total score	= 500
Daily average	= 49/7	Weekly average	= 500/4
	= 7		= 125

went missing, then the total for that week could not be compared to the totals for weeks when records were available for every day.

The average (mean) is calculated using the following formula:

$$\frac{\text{Total score}}{\text{Number of units from which total score derived}}.$$

Table 11.2 shows examples of how average (mean) scores can be calculated. Average scores can be useful in reducing the number of data points to be charted and in making comparisons of scores possible when there are gaps in the data collected. In terms of accurately representing what is going on, averages will function best when the amount of variability in the scores is consistent – the variability may be consistently high or it may be consistently low. Averages will be misleading when there are occasional extremely low or extremely high scores in a sequence.

Daily totals of aggressive incidents

Mon.	Tue.	Wed.	Thur.	Fri.	Sat.	Sun.
5	7	4	6	100	5	6

Daily average = 19

The average score of 19 aggressive incidents per day in the above example does not truly represent the frequency of aggression because the unusually high number of incidents on one day has distorted the picture. When there are occasional extreme scores like this it will be better to use total scores as the basis for monitoring.

Step ⟩ 9 ⟨ Prepare a graph or chart

The main aim of presenting information visually is to assess behaviour over time in the simplest, clearest and most comprehensive manner. Visually presented information can also be interesting to see and be very reinforcing to use. The most common forms of visual representation are graphs and charts.

Graphs

Graphs are a very effective means of showing trends or changes in behaviour over a period of time (for example, hours, days or weeks). A simple graph is illustrated in Figure 11.7. Units of time (session, day, week) are represented along the horizontal axis and the total/average scores per unit of time are represented along the vertical axis. The intervals on the vertical axis should be expressed in a convenient unit of round numbers and should cover the entire range of values (scores) likely for the behaviour. A graph is prepared by marking a point for each unit of time at the height corresponding to the score for that unit of time. The series of points thus produced is connected with a straight line.

Histograms

A histogram is an alternative way of illustrating trends or changes in behaviour over time. It is constructed by drawing a series of adjoining columns, with each column representing a time interval. The height of each column represents the total/average score during that time interval. At the base, the column is constructed so that its midpoint is at the midpoint of the time interval. A simple histogram is illustrated in Figure 11.8.

Bar charts

A bar chart is often used to compare information about different categories of behaviour or different situations, for example, hitting versus spitting, playing with toys versus twiddling string, behaviour in unstructured sessions versus behaviour in task-demand sessions. A bar chart is constructed by drawing columns of equal width, separated by a

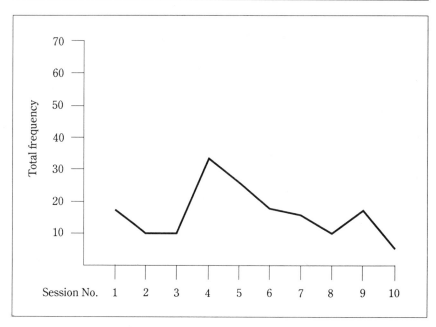

Figure 11.7 Example of a simple graph.

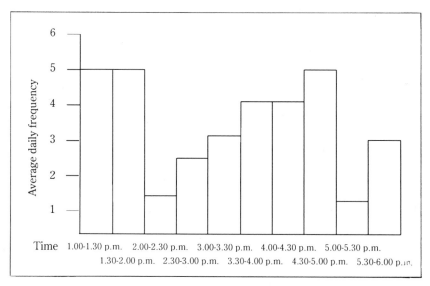

Figure 11.8 Example of a histogram.

space of half that width. The height of the columns is determined by the total or average score for the behaviour/situation. Trends over time are marked as usual on the horizontal axis, moving from left to right. Figure 11.9 illustrates a simple bar chart.

Pie charts

A pie chart is a useful way of representing the proportions of time spent on different behaviour or in various situations, over a given time period. It is not a way of analysing trends over time, although a series of pie charts could be used to show trends. The total number of behaviours or the total number of situations is represented as a circle (pie). Each particular behaviour or situation is represented as a sector of the circle, a slice of the pie. The size of the sector (slice) is determined by the percentage of the time period spent on a particular behaviour or activity. A circle is made up of 360° and the size of each sector is calculated by translating the percentage score into a proportion of 360°. This gives the angle for each sector.

The pie chart in Figure 11.10 illustrates the behaviour of an individual during a work session. It has been constructed from the information in Table 11.3 by using the following steps.

1. Calculating the total time spent in each activity.
2. Dividing each total time by the duration of the session.
3. Multiplying by 360 to obtain the angle of each sector.
4. Drawing a pie chart using a compass and protractor.

Another, less complicated, way of representing this same information is shown in Figure 11.11. This uses a bar to represent the total time of the session and divides it up in proportion to the amount of time spent on each activity. Consecutive days' recordings can be added, as in Figure 11.12(c).

Table 11.3 Calculating the angle of a sector for various behaviours occurring during a 60-minute work session

Work behaviour	Total time (minutes)	Fraction of total session	Angle of sector
On task	15	15/60	15/60 × 360 = 90°
Hand flapping	20	20/60	20/60 × 360 = 120°
Wandering	15	15/60	15/60 × 360 = 90°
Other behaviours	10	10/60	10/60 × 360 = 60°

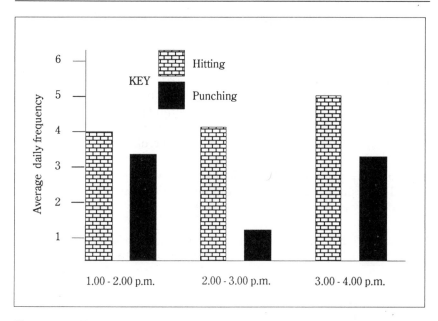

Figure 11.9 Example of a simple bar chart.

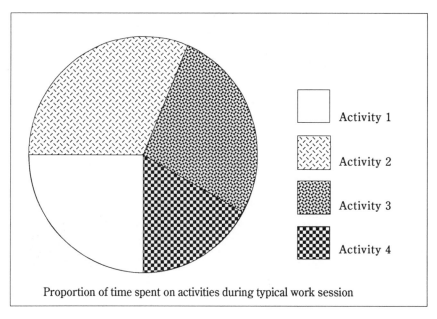

Proportion of time spent on activities during typical work session

Figure 11.10 Example of a pie chart.

Selecting an appropriate visual representation

There is no 'best' way of representing a set of information. The method chosen will depend upon a number of factors, including the purpose for which graphical representation is required, what is to be illustrated, the point to be made, the total amount of information, the variety of information which needs to be shown simultaneously. An example illustrates how the same information can be represented in a variety of ways, none of which is more 'correct' than the others.

Example: A person's activities are observed over a 1-hour unstructured period for 5 days and the time spent on each activity is recorded daily.

Table 11.4 Daily total time (minutes) spent on various activities during a 1-hour unstructured period

Day	Rocking	Walking	Puzzle	Socializing
Monday	35	10	10	5
Tuesday	35	5	15	5
Wednesday	45	5	15	5
Thursday	30	10	15	5
Friday	40	5	15	0
Total	185	35	65	15

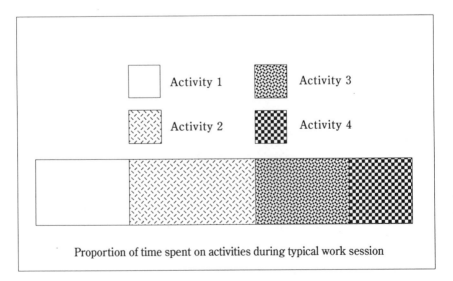

Proportion of time spent on activities during typical work session

Figure 11.11 Example of a horizontal bar chart.

The daily totals are presented in Table 11.4 and Figure 11.12 illustrates some of the ways in which the information collected can be presented in a visual form. Figure 11.12(a) shows the daily variability in each type of behaviour and shows the differences in frequency of each of the four behaviours. Figure 11.12(b) and (c) show exactly the same information but make it easier to judge the relative times allocated to each behaviour. Figure 11.12(d), (e) and (f) focus on the relative times allocated to particular behaviours by using daily averages (weekly totals could also have been used). Variation/trend over time is not represented.

Step $\boxed{10}$ Interpret graphs and charts

In order to interpret a visual representation of information it is important that all relevant information is entered onto the graph or chart. For example, if a specific skill is being encouraged which is functionally equivalent to a problematic behaviour, then putting measures of both behaviours onto the same graph will help to clarify any relationship between them, for example, whether increases in the equivalent skill are paralleled by decreases in the problematic behaviour.

Visual representations which track behaviour over time also make it possible to enter onto the graph or chart events which are considered to be significant. This may demonstrate whether there is any relationship between such events and variation in the behaviour. The most obvious event for present purposes is the start of an intervention: the end of the baseline and the beginning of the intervention should be clearly marked, as should any subsequent changes in the intervention strategy. Other important events such as illness, change of service provision, visits to or from relatives, fits, holidays can also be marked. This will enrich the understanding of the individual's behaviour. Figure 11.13 illustrates how a lot of information can be represented on a basic graph, in a way that facilitates interpretation of that information. The end of the baseline period is clearly entered, as are changes in intervention procedures and other significant events.

MAINTAINING GOOD RECORDING SYSTEMS AND
SUMMARIES OF PROGRESS

If graphs and charts are to be of benefit then they need to be kept up-to-date. Information from recording sheets needs to be summarized and transferred to the chart or graph on (at least) a weekly basis. Observation of a few simple rules will help to ensure that this happens.

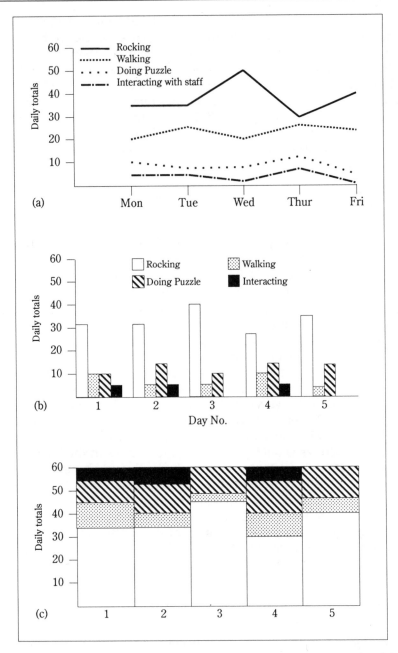

Figure 11.12 Comparison of different ways of representing a single set of data: (a) graph; (b) bar chart; (c) histogram; (d) bar chart; (e) pie chart; (f) horizontal bar chart.

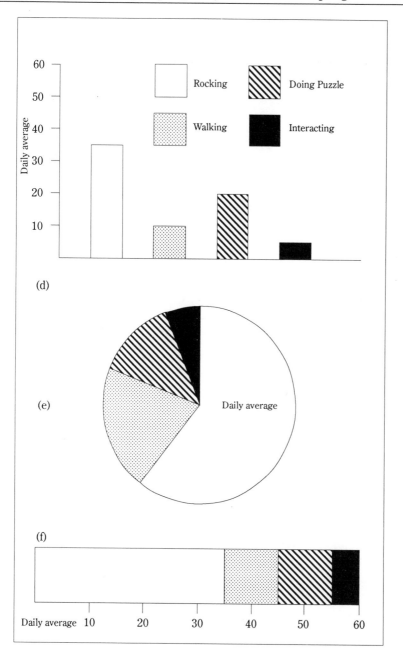

(d)

(e)

(f)

Name: Larry

Behaviour: Screaming, rushing about, pushing, pulling items off walls, shelves, tables.

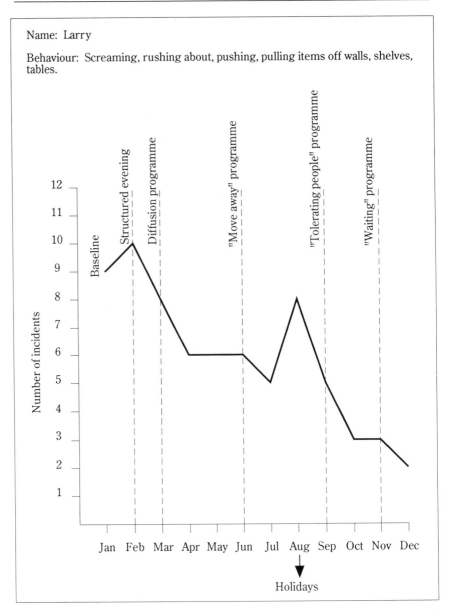

Figure 11.13 Example of the use of a graph to represent different kinds of information.

Appoint a named person to co-ordinate recording

A named person should be identified as responsible for ensuring that recording sheets are always available in the place where they are to be used and that fresh recording sheets are available from the individual's file. That same person should collect completed recording sheets regularly and file them for safe-keeping until they are transferred onto the graph. Alternatively, sessional recordings may be filed after each session in a central place. The named person transfers the information from the recording sheets onto the graph or chart on (at least) a weekly basis. The named person is responsible for ensuring that the graph or chart is available at information-sharing or decision-making meetings.

Without this clear allocation of responsibility it is likely that data sheets will get lost and that graphs and charts will not be kept up-to-date.

Allocate time each week for analysing data

It should never be assumed that time will somehow be found in the course of the day to fill in a chart or graph. Other more pressing activities are sure to take precedence. A specific time should therefore be allocated each week in order to review the information collected, to replenish supplies of recording forms, to bring charts up-to-date and to note important events on the chart.

Ensure that appropriate materials are available

Some service settings will be able to access a computer for the preparation, storage and presentation of graphs and charts. However, in many settings the process will be done by hand and this means that certain basic materials need to be available. These include:

- graph paper
- a ruler
- a pencil and eraser
- a supply of coloured pens.

These materials are notorious for disappearing even in the most carefully managed settings. It is very frustrating sitting down to add a week's recording to a chart where different colours have been used to represent different behaviours only to find that the relevant coloured pens are nowhere to be found. Graphing materials should be stored carefully and separately from general 'office' equipment.

Draw graphs and charts carefully

Graphs and charts need to be filled in accurately – it is a precision task. It is wise therefore to make entries initially in pencil and then to add colour once the accuracy of the entered data has been checked: entries made in ink cannot be erased. When a graph has been built up over weeks and months inaccurate entries will prove very costly in terms of the time required to put them right.

SUMMARY

There are a number of pictorial formats into which behavioural information can be translated to permit visual analysis of a complete set of data at a single glance. Data collection needs to be carefully planned and carried out if such summaries are to be useful. Likewise thought needs to be given to the most appropriate form of graphical presentation. Once the format has been decided, graphs and charts can be easy to prepare and certainly become easier with practice. If the information itself is collected systematically, graphs and charts will show changes and trends that would be difficult to notice by inspecting each recording sheet or from reading extensive written accounts. Graphs and charts are an invaluable aid in making decisions about programme changes and adjustments, but they do more than this – they can demonstrate progress in a powerful way and increase the motivation of carers and service users to persist with their efforts at change.

REVIEWING PROGRESS

SUMMARY OF STEPS

1
Define the behaviour

2
Decide what to measure

3
Decide how to monitor change

4
Decide how often to monitor behaviour

5
Prepare a recording chart

6
Take a baseline measure

7
Implement intervention and record

8
Summarize the data

9
Prepare a graph or chart

10
Interpret graphs and charts

Supporting long-term quality work

12

This book has described a model for understanding and working actively with people who have severe learning and behavioural difficulties. It has described a number of ways of helping such individuals and it has stressed the fact that a range of interventions need to be developed for each individual. Some interventions are intended to have an immediate impact upon the problematic behaviour. Others have a longer-term focus and are intended to decrease the person's longer-term vulnerability to developing new problems, by providing him with the skills and support systems which will enable him to cope better with the pressures of his life. The approach to change and to help, which has been detailed, is based upon a graded approach – one which promotes the use of small steps in the move towards change. Such an approach requires a system of planning, prioritizing and monitoring. It requires sustained effort over a long time-span. The approach, therefore, requires the presence of structures to support such a system. It is this issue which the present chapter addresses.

PROMOTING AND SUPPORTING HIGH-QUALITY PRACTICE – GENERAL PRINCIPLES

The approach described in this book makes it clear that it is the people who live and work with the disabled person who are the major influences upon that person. It is these caregivers, rather than rare and expensive therapists, who have the greatest potential to help. It is their behaviour that will determine the direction of change in the person with learning difficulties.

The behaviour of carers is influenced by exactly the same things as the behaviour of the person for whom they are caring – settings, triggers and results. Successful work is determined by the degree to which the environment offers setting conditions for high-quality work, the provision of triggers to prompt carers to carry out day-to-day tasks, and results which acknowledge and value their efforts and provide feedback on success. In most situations a person with learning difficulties will be in contact with many caregivers, often employed by different agencies. Thus there is also a need to direct and co-ordinate the work of these many different people. A review of the factors involved will help in the understanding of what is needed and 'diagnose' where problems may lie if difficulties in sustaining and generalizing the work are encountered within the organization.

A PHILOSOPHY OF WORK

People with serious behavioural difficulties present a unique challenge to those who care for them. Often they appear actively to reject the care that is offered. They elicit many, often conflicting, emotions from others: pity, anger, despair. This is why people with serious behavioural difficulties are rejected from many service settings.

The sort of painstaking constructive work described in this book requires a very active commitment from carers. It means accepting that it is legitimately a part of their job to work with such a person. Without this acceptance and commitment, sustained constructive work will not be possible. This is true not just for the individual caregiver but for the service agency as a whole. If an agency is to meet the needs of the person with severe behavioural difficulties, it must clearly accept that it is its rightful job to do so. In this book a method has been offered for interpreting severe problem behaviour which will help in this process. Rather than seeing such behaviour as bizarre symptoms of some unknown illness, it has been stressed that it should be seen as expressing powerful emotions or serving important functions, in particular those of communication and stimulation. It is a means whereby an individual seeks to exert some control over a world which is often frightening, incomprehensible and unresponsive. It is important that the agency or agencies involved with the person face these issues and accept 'ownership' of the problem as a first step in working constructively for change.

A TEAM-WORK APPROACH

The system of work described in this book is complex and time consuming. A single caregiver working in isolation is likely to have only limited success and to effect change over a relatively short time period. For long-term broad-based constructive work a team approach is essential. Team work serves a number of purposes.

1. It co-ordinates work within and across agencies. This is clearly essential if the consistency so much stressed in this book as important is to be attained. It is essential if generalization of progress across personnel, places and time is to be attained. Such generalization will not happen automatically.
2. A team approach offers access to a broader range of information, building up a more comprehensive view of the individual.
3. Group problem solving is more likely to be creative, generating more ideas and solutions than could be achieved by a single individual working alone. Such creativity is essential when working with people who have complex needs.
4. A team approach is an important source of commitment. Carrying out therapeutic interventions requires energy, initiative and understanding of the reasoning behind them, and this is enhanced by ensuring participation in decision making about the interventions.
5. A team approach is an important source of social support. Successes need to be celebrated and there needs to be encouragement to keep going when things get difficult. A team approach can offer this kind of support.

Working in teams is not always easy: there are many factors which determine whether or not a group of people work together satisfactorily. Not all of these can be covered here but at the very least the group needs to:

- meet together on a regular basis;
- work together in a spirit of mutual respect;
- have a willingness to work together towards an agreed plan of action.

To work effectively in the ways outlined in this text, a team also needs a very structured approach to planning and decision making. If a team is working in this way with more than one individual, then the need for a highly structured approach becomes all the more important. Such structure can be provided within a system of individual programme planning.

A SYSTEM OF INDIVIDUAL PLANNING

A forum for planning and reviewing progress

A system of individual programme planning provides the structure within which the range of approaches to managing problematic behaviour, which have been described in this book, can be developed and sustained long enough for meaningful change to occur. Such a system involves regular reviewing of individual needs and developing interventions to meet these needs, with such interventions in turn being subject to regular review. This system operates through regular meetings of all team members at which both the goals and the methods of programmes are planned in detail and written out.

Administrative and clerical support

In order to function effectively, a system of individual planning needs to pay attention to clerical and administrative details. A system for information handling is essential. The assessment and monitoring of behaviour and the writing and recording of individual programmes will generate a considerable volume of paper-work. If this information is not to be lost, and if it is to be useful in practice, then an efficient system of storage and retrieval (paper or electronic) needs to be set up. There should be one place to which people can go to find all the necessary information on an individual's achievements and needs, on past and present intervention programmes and analyses of progress.

Quality control

A system of individual planning also needs to incorporate methods of quality control, monitoring whether or not goals are achieved and whether work is being carried out in an efficient manner. If the system is used for just one person, then records of progress, such as those described in other parts of this book, provide the necessary information. If, however, individual programme planning is applied to all the clients within an agency, then further consideration may need to be given to understanding why some programmes succeed and some do not, and to deciding if time devoted to individual planning is being used efficiently. This requires a more general method of system evaluation, which needs to be carried out on a regular, scheduled basis.

STAFF SUPPORT

Working or living with people who have long-term behavioural difficulties and who present those around them with daily challenges can be very stressful. The causes of stress are many.

1. Those working with such individuals are likely to experience a number of powerful emotions which may include fear, anger, anxiety or helplessness. Such emotions may be particularly noticeable during periods when things are not going well for the person with learning and behavioural difficulties. If a person's difficulties persist, despite the efforts of his carers, then it is not uncommon for carers

to experience guilt or to feel incompetent. Emotions can be even stronger when the person's disturbed behaviour is affecting the well-being of others who live and spend their time with that person. Individual carers may not know how to deal constructively and positively with the powerful emotions which are being experienced on a day-to-day basis and may start to adopt unhelpful strategies, affecting their life outside the workplace.

2. Many day and leisure services for people with learning difficulties are unable to support those with severe behavioural difficulties. As a result such individuals may become isolated within their residential settings, with little leisure or constructive activity: carers may share the feelings of isolation and rejection.

3. Carers may have unrealistic expectations of themselves and of the people in their care. As a result they constantly experience failure in their day-to-day work.

4. Carers may lack of some of the key skills for helping a disturbed individual to overcome his distress and the longer-term causes of that disturbance. They may lack the skills and therefore the confidence to protect themselves and others from physical harm which arises from working with aggressive individuals. Thus they may experience fear or anxiety on a daily basis.

5. Working within small and often isolated teams, where there is no opportunity for team members to spend time together away from the person for whom they are caring, there may be little time to provide mutual support for each other. There may be a lack of external professional support networks with whom to share the problems and stresses.

6. At a more immediate level, carers may experience trauma following an assault from the person for whom they are caring (assaults upon carers by clients with severe behavioural disturbances are commonplace). The psychological effects of an assault may persist for some time, resulting in a general increase in anxiety, a loss of confidence, a loss of interest in work, general irritability, etc.

Any of the above stressors can adversely influence the performance of caregivers in the short term and lead to eventual burn-out if not dealt with. Stress can manifest itself through an increase in staff sickness and absenteeism and through a high staff turnover; this in turn will influence the well-being of the person with learning difficulties. Recognition of the stressful nature of working with people who present with severe and ongoing behavioural challenges raises the need for active steps to be taken to prevent stress occurring and, if it does occur, to have structures in place to enable carers to deal with stress in a positive manner.

AN ETHICAL CODE

Acceptability of goals and methods of intervention

An important issue to consider when seeking to change the behaviour of the person with learning and behavioural difficulties is the question of acceptability. A co-ordinated and effective programme of change is not necessarily the right thing. Regularly secluding a person in a room may stop him being aggressive but that does not mean that this is an acceptable intervention. Praising, clapping and saying 'Good boy' may be an effective way of encouraging work skills in an adult with severe difficulties, but this does not mean that such a reinforcer is an appropriate one to use. This is the realm of ethics. The issue of the ethical acceptability of interventions was discussed in Chapter 10 in relation to the use of cost procedures.

Consent

A very central ethical issue is the matter of consent. Good-quality practice is most likely to occur when the individual whose behaviour is the object of change can exert an effective degree of control over those seeking to effect the change. There needs to be a balance of control. This is a very difficult issue for people with severe learning difficulties, whose disabilities may make it very difficult for them to speak for themselves – to give their opinions and consent. Even if they can speak for themselves, they may not be listened to. People with learning difficulties have a devalued status in society which means their opinions are often discounted, especially if they conflict with the opinions of other family members or professional people. People with additional behavioural difficulties are even more vulnerable: their behaviour elicits powerful, often conflicting, emotions in others. These emotions may trigger drastic responses, particularly in times of crisis. It is therefore vital to give the individual an effective voice and to take active steps to protect his human rights.

There are many ways of giving the individual an effective voice to enable him to exert control over those who seek to control him. These methods are not mutually exclusive, and each organization will need to judge which methods are best suited to its own situation. The protection of people's rights cannot, however, be left to chance and the goodwill of staff. High-quality programmes are only possible where there is a balance of control and the possibility of mutual influence.

PROCEDURES FOR SUPPORTING HIGH-QUALITY PRACTICE

A number of specific procedures can be implemented to increase the likelihood of sustaining high-quality work and of protecting the interests of people with learning and behavioural difficulties.

ESTABLISH A SYSTEM OF INDIVIDUAL PROGRAMME PLANNING – A TEAM APPROACH

A system of individual planning requires a number of operational procedures if it is to work effectively.

Accept 'ownership' of the problem

Before engaging in detailed work with the individual, a preliminary meeting should be organized. This should include all those directly involved with the person and the managers of 'front line' staff. The purpose of such a meeting is not to plan therapeutic programmes but to make a public decision about whether the agency or agencies involved are committed to working through the problems (rather than excluding the person). This is why it is essential to have staff managers present. Such a public affirmation of commitment to the individual is essential to establishing the value of that individual and the work that will be undertaken. It may also be a means of 'unlocking' extra resources if these are going to be needed for effective work to be carried out.

Establish the team

A decision needs to be made early on about team membership. All those who work directly with the individual should be full and equal team members. They are the people who have the greatest knowledge of the individual and the greatest influence over his behaviour. This may be quite difficult to arrange and manage, particularly when the family and several agencies are actively involved. Nevertheless, they are the core members of the team and every effort should be made to assemble them into a single working group: their participation will ensure relevant and practical programmes. This participation in decision making is also a means of building commitment to carrying out the interventions. It is a means also of sustaining a long-term focus and a realistic outlook. Managers (who have access to relevant resources, such as staff and equipment), therapists and other specialists with particular expertise should also be involved, and it should be decided whether this will be on a full-time, part-time or consultative basis.

Time-table programme-planning meetings

Meetings devoted exclusively to programme planning should occur on a regular basis, not just in response to crises. Consistency is more important than absolute frequency, but it is probably advisable to meet no less frequently than monthly, i.e. meetings should occur regularly every 1–4 weeks. Length of meetings will depend upon the number of individuals being worked with, but should be determined in advance.

Allocate a co-ordinator for each individual

If the team is working with a number of individuals then its functioning will be improved if a co-ordinator (key worker) is allocated for each individual. The role of the co-ordinator in the team is to gather together all the necessary information and follow up the decisions made to see that they are carried out. There are other ways of fulfilling these functions, but vesting this in a single person who takes a special interest in the individual is probably the most effective.

Set priorities

All of the individuals with whom this book is concerned have multiple needs. If an agency is making plans for more than one individual, it becomes impossible to do everything that is needed for every person, so that some means of prioritizing targets for intervention is needed. Otherwise team members may feel overwhelmed and/or discouraged. Two important guidelines for selecting targets can be offered.

1. In the early stages of programme planning, work should always start with those individuals or interventions which are likely to have the greatest chance of success rather than with those that appear to be the most severe. This may mean not tackling straight away the problems held to be the most critical. It is important to break out from crisis thinking and reacting, as part of the move towards the longer perspective.
2. Always start with positive programmes (such as skill teaching or addressing environmental problems) before beginning any programmes which directly focus on the problematic behaviour.

Identify responsibilities

Any decisions must specify who is to do what by when. This step, coupled to the specification of a review date, will help to ensure that decisions made at meetings are put into practice.

Handle documentation

There should be one file for each person which deals with individual programming work. Such a file should contain all assessment information, all written programmes and all data analysis (such as graphs) and other charts, and should be purely for individual programme planning and separate from any more general record system.

Evaluate individual programmes

Built into the team-work approach and the system of individual planning, with its data collection, is a means whereby rational judgments can be made as to whether interventions are working. Regular meetings and reviews are an essential part of quality control. The evaluation process can also be a source of positive reinforcement for the efforts of carers and a source of positive feedback about the effectiveness of their work.

Evaluate the programme planning system

Review of the whole system of work should take place on a regular basis. In some establishments this may be carried out by a line manager (for example, a head or deputy head teacher, or a manager of a day-centre or residential home). However, many managers are not properly trained for this function, and difficulties arise when multiple agencies are involved.

A second approach is to employ independent external evaluators to 'audit' the system. However, access to such resources is rare, which means that in practice it is often down to those who run the system to try to do it for themselves. One way to do this is to set aside a specific meeting for this purpose. Such a meeting should include all those involved in the system and should occur on a regular, scheduled basis (for example, every 6 or 12 months). Its purpose is not to discuss individual programmes but to review the system of planning as a whole.

1. How well do meetings and the information handling systems work?
2. What proportion of programmes succeed?
3. What support services are needed?
4. What extra skills do staff need?

Following the guidelines for individual planning itself, strengths of the system should be celebrated as well as needs being highlighted Such a meeting may strengthen existing commitment and lead to improvements in both effectiveness and efficiency.

SUPPORT FOR CARERS

The term 'support' is a broad one which encompasses many different areas of activity. The activities share the same general purpose – to help provide carers with the necessary support to enable them to carry out their work with maximum effectiveness. Support can be practical, psychological or technical. Key areas of support are outlined below.

Immediate support following major incidents/assault

Carers who work with people whose behaviour is physically challenging may be exposed daily to the possibility of assault. While some carers will dismiss the psychological impact of such assaults, believing that it is a part of their work to accept such behaviour, for others being the victim of an assault by a person in their care may be profoundly disturbing. Following an assault, a carer may, therefore, require emotional support. Such support is likely to involve the following.

1. Time away from the aggressor and, perhaps, the work setting.
2. An opportunity to express his feelings about the assault and his anger with the person who committed the assault and to do so without feeling guilty or that he is being judged.
3. To review the incident with others to try to understand how the situation arose and whether there may be anything to learn from it.
4. Support in re-establishing a working relationship with the individual concerned. The carer may feel anxious and afraid about facing the person.
5. Individual counselling, in some cases, may be needed for some weeks following the incident, since the effects may linger for some time.

Where carers are exposed to aggressive behaviour from the people for whom they provide care, a structure should be in place within the agency to provide such support as that outlined above as a matter of course to all carers.

Ongoing mutual support from team members

For the most part the care of people with learning difficulties who have additional behavioural and emotional problems is carried out in group settings by a team of carers, frequently working in shifts. The work requires consistency across time and people. It requires a shared understanding of both the problems and the solutions. It requires a sensitivity to the feelings of other carers so that support and help can be offered. It is unavoidable that there will be differing views and opinions, different styles of interacting with the person with learning difficulties. It is also unavoidable that the team will from time to time experience internal difficulties amongst its members, which may impair the quality of their work and increase stress levels.

What is essential is that people working within the team are able to communicate openly and honestly with one another; are able to rely on one another, not just in emergencies but at other times; are also able to maintain consistency and a forward-looking approach. Such work needs to be continued and developed actively throughout the life of the team. If difficulties arise within the team, then additional work may need to be done to resolve these internal difficulties as quickly as possible.

Depending on the problems and skills within the team, such team-building activities may at one level involve informal social events, which enable team members to get to know each other better, to develop greater understanding of one another and to communicate more freely with each other. At another level they may involve the team learning and practising specific skills which it may be lacking, for example, the skills of managing conflicts, of expressing emotions, of providing critical feedback, of running meetings. At yet another level, they may involve the help of an outside consultant who can help the team diagnose its difficulties and plan ways of overcoming these.

Regular supervision

Regular supervision can be a major source of ongoing support for individual carers in a number of areas – to help them develop specific skills, overcome identified difficulties, receive emotional support over the daily hassles involved in their work in addition to the more serious traumas which might be experienced from time to time. Supervision should be provided consistently and regularly.

Feedback on performance

A major source of learning is feedback about performance: both positive and negative feedback is important, so long as it is given sensitively and in a constructive way. It is most effective when given immediately. For this reason, it is important that managers spend time regularly among the care team so that they can observe first-hand the performance of carers and provide them with constructive feedback about their skills.

Presence of manager

Further support can be provided when managers join carers in their direct work from time to time. In this way they demonstrate to carers that their work is valued. Carers feel less isolated.

Professional support services

Working month after month and year after year with the same individuals, posing the same problems, can result in carers feeling that they have exhausted all possible ways forward and feeling stuck for new ideas. This may lead to fixed patterns of interactions which have become so routine that carers are no longer aware of them. External professional support services, such as those provided by psychologists, speech therapists, physiotherapists and psychiatrists, can be a source of support by helping staff look to new ideas and provide feedback on current practices. They are also a much needed link to the outside world which can remove some of the feelings of isolation which staff may experience.

Staff training

The skills needed to work with disturbed and distressed individuals are many and those who work with such a difficult client group must have, in addition to the core skills required of their job, a framework within which to understand difficult and disturbed behaviour, to enable them to assess the difficulties and provide appropriate support. They must share a value system which stresses the importance of respect for the individual and which emphasizes change and development as a key aim of work.

Other important skills are interpersonal skills. Carers need to be able to assert themselves – with other team members, with managers, with professional support services, with the person with learning and behavioural difficulties. Assertiveness skills form the basis of mutually respectful relationships and enable people to express themselves more confidently in ways that do not upset or offend others.

ENSURE GOOD ETHICAL PRACTICES

There are a number of ways of providing the individual with an effective voice to ensure that his rights are protected.

Personal involvement

Decision making about therapeutic intervention programmes should involve the individual as much as possible. Some will be able to participate fully in the decision making and need only the opportunity to do so. Others may need training to develop their participative skills (see below). Even a person whose contribution is difficult to elicit or understand can exert an influence by his physical presence. Simply having the person present when decisions are made will improve the quality of those decisions.

Advocacy

For children, parents or a legal guardian are held to be the legitimate advocate who speaks on their behalf. For adults with learning difficulties, effective advocacy needs specific planning: they may be trained, either individually or with a group of others, to speak for themselves. Self-advocacy training is an important means of increasing control for the individual with learning difficulties. When this is not possible, then a system of independent advocacy will be helpful. Advocates should be 'lay' people, independent of the services and organizations working with the person. They should know the person well and seek to express the view of the person as they understand it.

An ethical committee

Establishing an ethical committee will also help to maintain the quality of work. The role of such a committee is to judge the acceptability of proposed programmes. It may review either all the programmes or only those involving cost procedures. It will work best when it meets regularly, is seen as an important part of the system of work and has access to all information in the individual programme file. Its composition should include senior professional staff but the majority of members should be independent of the organization(s) providing for the individual. There should be representatives from parents' organizations, and membership should include one or more persons with a learning disability.

An ethical code

Drafting an ethical code is an important exercise in raising awareness of ethical issues and in providing detailed guidelines for everyday working practice. Such a code should be developed by the staff themselves, ideally in conjunction with an ethical committee (see above). It will need to cover a number of areas.

1. The processes by which decisions are made.
2. Who speaks for the individual.
3. Who is consulted about programme content.
4. Whose agreement is necessary for a programme to be implemented.
5. How unresolved conflicts should be handled.
6. Specific guidelines about programme standards. For example, it can mandate skill-teaching programmes or setting-level interventions to precede any programmes involving cost or extinction procedures. It can limit the duration of cost procedures by, for example, limiting to a specific time period the length of time for which a person can be ignored following the occurrence of a problematic behaviour.
7. Requirements relevant to good-quality programming. For example, it can mandate that all staff should be trained in ethical issues or setting standards of competence before staff are permitted to design individual programmes.

No code can hope to be comprehensive, but it will prove an invaluable source of guidance and protection for both caregivers and the people for whom care is being provided.

SUMMARY

Working with people who have severe learning disabilities and serious behavioural problems represents a challenge at many levels: it tests professional knowledge and understanding to its limits; it stretches and stresses resources, and increasingly highlights weaknesses in service systems. Yet so much can be achieved.

In this book an approach to understanding and interpreting behavioural difficulties has been offered. This approach has direct and immediate implications for what can be done in practice to help overcome these difficulties. Many techniques have been described, with a system for planning and implementing these techniques on an individual basis. Throughout there has been an emphasis upon a long-term perspective. Complex behavioural difficulties cannot be rapidly eliminated: a more patient, sustained approach is necessary and consideration has been given to organizational factors which will help to implement and sustain constructive work. The very important issue of staff support has also been discussed. It is acknowledged that working with people who have long-term and complex difficulties and who challenge their carers on a daily basis is stressful work and ways must be found and sustained of supporting those who find themselves in the firing line day after day after day. The ethics of intervention are the final critical issues that have been discussed. For people as 'vulnerable' as the individuals with whom this book is concerned, there can never be too much care in the protection of their dignity and rights.

Working with people who have severe learning and behavioural disabilities is a complex enterprise: complex but manageable. Making progress with such people is a long-term enterprise: long-term but achievable. In this book a model has been presented for analysing and intervening with problematic behaviours at several levels. There is no doubt that if people can increase their understanding of the factors that lead to the behavioural problems of people with severe learning difficulties and develop their skills in the management of these, then significant headway can be made with the behavioural challenges of the individuals concerned. There is every reason to be optimistic.

Case studies

13

LARRY

CASE DESCRIPTION

Background

Larry is 20 years old. He has lived in residential care since the age of 12 years because his mother, who lives on her own, was unable to cope with his behavioural difficulties. She is devoted to Larry, visits him regularly and, whenever possible, has him home for a day or a weekend or even a holiday. Larry currently attends a special needs group at his local Social Education Centre.

Physical health

Larry is tall, well-built, strong and active. He is a very healthy young man.

Skills

Larry can ride a two-wheel bicycle but has no road sense and little appreciation of danger in general. For this reason, he only rides his bike in confined and safe places. He can swim and enjoys this activity very much. He also enjoys an occasional run. Larry is quite independent as regards self-help skills. He can dress and undress except for buttons and fasteners. He eats very competently with a knife, fork and spoon. He is clean and dry by day and night, and sees to his own needs in the toilet. He washes himself (except his hair) and brushes his teeth well.

Socially, Larry prefers his own company but he will approach staff if he wants something, pointing or taking/dragging them by the hand.

He will sometimes approach staff for no particular reason; these tend to be staff that he has known for some time and who have a good relationship with him. However, direct approaches to Larry, even by these staff, often lead to him withdrawing – most relationships seem to be on his terms. He does not interact at all with other residents at home or other students at college.

Larry understands some of what is said to him but appears to rely heavily on situational cues. Instructions and requests need to be given in short phrases. He has no speech and is generally silent apart from screaming. He has a small vocabulary of three Makaton signs (drink, biscuit, more), which he will use at mealtimes. At home, Larry will help with domestic tasks, such as bed-making or washing-up, but needs supervision and is not fully competent in any task. He enjoys running small and simple errands for staff. He has a short attention span and this tends to interfere with his performance on all activities.

Likes

Larry enjoys music and knows how to operate the cassette recorder on a music centre. He can also identify which specific cassettes have the music he likes. He enjoys splashing water and he will spend long periods tearing up pieces of paper into tiny pieces: these activities can have a calming effect on him when he is agitated. Larry enjoys being outdoors but has a tendency to run off without warning and is extremely difficult to catch. Larry also enjoys doing jigsaw puzzles and drawing. Above all else, Larry loves food. He particularly likes party food – crisps, sausage-rolls, cocktail sausages, sandwiches, sweets and chocolates, and any kind of fizzy drink. When these foods are left lying around Larry will eat them ravenously. At mealtimes too he has to be watched or he will continue eating until all the available food is consumed. He eats very fast in order to be given more and will continue to ask for more throughout the meal.

Behavioural difficulties

Mealtimes are a particularly anxious time for staff because these are the times that Larry is likely to 'blow': waiting his turn, the noise at the table, the general rush and commotion, being refused more food when he has finished, all get him agitated. His habit of needing to touch things is particularly irritating at mealtimes: every few seconds he will reach out to touch some object on the table. This gets staff cross and they tend to nag him not to do this, which often makes matters worse. As his agitation increases, he starts to sweat, stare at staff and 'bounce' a little in his chair, if seated. He may then go on to screech. If already on his feet, he will start to walk aimlessly up and down, walking in and out of rooms, grabbing hold of staff and unable to settle to anything. If he then gets out of control he becomes quite frightening: he starts a continuous scream and rushes through the building pulling pictures off walls, clearing the contents of shelves and tables onto the floor; he pushes anyone who tries to stop him. If he gets to this stage, he is likely to take up to an hour to calm.

Larry can become agitated and 'blow' at various times in the day. Usually, he becomes agitated on the minibus and arrives home/at college in an agitated state. Hectic days, which involve large-group activities and trips out to busy or exciting places, tend to increase his agitation. Unstructured times of the day when there are a lot of other students/residents milling around making a noise also increase his agitation. Once a certain level of agitation is reached, the slightest provocation, request or demand will set him off. On occasion, these outbursts have resulted in smashed windows, broken furniture and injured staff. Major outbursts can, during bad phases, occur two or three times a week (bad phases have been known to last several months). Bad phases tend to start when changes occur in Larry's routine – summer holidays, Christmas time, birthday parties in the home, staff changes. Once these phases start, Larry is visibly agitated and physically very tense most of the time. Medication has been considered but Larry's mother is resistant to this.

One of Larry's behaviours (screaming) tends to occur regardless of whether he is in a good or bad phase. In all situations (whether he is doing something he enjoys, relaxing or working), Larry will scream if people sit down next to him or stand very close to him, and he will continue to scream until they move away. It is, of course, difficult to move away at all times, for example, when out with Larry, when on the minibus (he is often agitated there and has to have someone sit next to him at all times to stop him attacking everyone around him), at the dinner table, in the sitting-room watching TV, in the bathroom, etc. This behaviour has led to severe problems at college when staff have tried to work with Larry.

ASSESSMENT AND INTERVENTIONS

A sample of a behaviour observation chart which was used to collect information about Larry's screaming was shown in Figure 2.2. The remainder of the assessment information was gathered through discussions with day and residential staff and with Larry's mother. The formulation of Larry's aggressive behaviour (defined as screaming, rushing about, pulling things off walls and shelves, pushing) was presented in Figure 2.5, while Larry's strengths list was shown in

Figure 2.4. The needs list, which was drawn up from the formulation of his behavioural difficulty, is shown in Figure 2.6: this list was used to guide the development of a number of interventions which are shown throughout the text of this book.

Figure 4.2 shows an intervention which was planned to help reduce Larry's agitation during a key time of his day. This was the time after he returned home from his day-centre, when no structured activities were available in the home – a situation which Larry found very difficult to cope with (Figure 2.6, Need 5). The intervention involved a structured time-table between 5 and 7 p.m., which included a regular session of aromatherapy. A pictorial time-table was provided to help Larry understand the sequence of activities. The intervention was also intended to reduce the overall frequency of his outbursts (Figure 2.6, Need 9).

Figure 5.3 shows an intervention which was planned to help Larry to tolerate the physical closeness of people (Figure 2.6, Need 10). The intervention used the principle of graded exposure. This need related to one of the triggers associated with an increase in Larry's agitation. Thus, addressing this problem was also addressing the identified need to have fewer outbursts of agitated aggression (Figure 2.6, Need 9).

Figure 5.2 shows an intervention which was intended to help more directly to avoid aggressive outbursts by working actively to diffuse agitation as it occurred. It was hoped that by using such a consistent method of diffusing Larry's agitation, Larry would eventually learn (incidental teaching) to recognize signs of his increasing agitation himself and develop a strategy which he could use himself (self-management) in these situations (Figure 2.6, Need 1).

Figure 6.4 shows a skill-teaching programme which was developed to meet Larry's identified need of having an appropriate way of asking people to move away (Figure 2.6, Need 11). It used an incidental-teaching procedure to teach Larry to push people gently on the arm instead of screaming (functionally equivalent skill).

Figure 7.2 shows an intervention which was developed to address Larry's difficulty with waiting (Figure 2.6, Need 2), which was another situation that had an adverse influence on Larry's level of agitation. This was yet another intervention intended indirectly to reduce the overall frequency of Larry's outbursts of aggression (Figure 2.6, Need 9). The intervention illustrated in Figure 7.2 was the first step in teaching Larry to be able to wait for increasingly longer periods of time, without becoming agitated. Waiting was defined as a skill which was incompatible with agitation.

Figure 8.4 shows an intervention which was planned to help Larry to learn to remain calm when travelling on transport (Figure 2.6, Need 3). The intervention combined the careful planning of the setting (seating arrangements in the minibus), the opportunity for self-management (method to induce relaxation) and the reinforcement of remaining seated and not screaming while travelling on the bus (DRO).

Two of Larry's other needs were also addressed over time. His need to remain calm during mealtimes (Figure 2.6, Need 4) was addressed by reorganizing the physical environment to make it less stressful for him (setting-level intervention). His need to cope better with holiday periods (Figure 2.6, Need 7) was addressed by providing him with a structured time-table of activities during holidays plus pictorial time-tables to help him know in advance what was going to happen (setting-level intervention).

One need, that of helping Larry to cope with new staff members (Figure 2.6, Need 8), was not addressed directly. However, the availability of written plans, a strengths list and documentation related to the formulation of Larry's difficulties enabled new staff to learn how to work effectively with Larry much more quickly. This, in turn, meant that Larry was able to get used to new staff more quickly. A graph depicting Larry's progress over a 1-year period, following the start of the interventions, is shown in Figure 11.13.

LOUISA

CASE DESCRIPTION

Background

Louisa is 20 years old. She lives in a house with seven other residents. The house is part of a residential community for people with learning difficulties. She moved to the community 4 years ago and has lived in her present unit for two of those years. The unit she was at before was felt by her parents to be unsuitable for her because a number of the residents had profound learning difficulties.

Louisa is the youngest in her farmily and idolized by her parents. A combination of factors brought her into residential care. First, her grandmother moved into the family home when Louisa was 15 years old. She was ill and became completely bedridden over a short time period, and was cared for exclusively by Louisa's mother. Second, Louisa's behaviour was such that her family found her very demanding of their time and difficult to cope with. Since Louisa moved away from her family, they have found life far easier. Louisa's mother is less tired caring for her own mother and finds that she now is able to enjoy Louisa's company far more when she comes home to visit. Louisa was told she was moving away from home in order to attend boarding school. When full-time schooling finished a year ago, Louisa's parents decided she should continue, at least for the time being, to remain in the community in which she was living. They are now beginning to feel that Louisa should remain there permanently.

Staff in her residential unit feel that Louisa is still, at 20, waiting to return home full-time. Her parents have not yet told her that the community is to be her permanent home. Louisa returns home each weekend, Friday through to Sunday. In addition, she returns for extended holidays during summer, Easter and at Christmas. When Louisa is away, her mother telephones her at least twice each week and her father at least once a week.

Personal history

Her parents first noticed that she was slow in her development when Louisa was 2 years old. She was found to have an unusual and rare chromosomal abnormality. She attended a nursery school and a local primary school until the age of 8 years. At primary school she kept herself isolated from the other children and did 'silly things' which, in retrospect, her parents believe occurred because she did not understand what was being asked of her. In her early school years she was already described as stubborn and non-co-operative. She would get reprimanded and punished for her silliness at school. She moved to a school for children with special needs where she remained until 11 years old. Louisa began to 'play up' even more at this school, proving non-co-operative, stubborn, rude and occasionally aggressive. At 11 years, she was moved to a school for children with mild/moderate learning difficulties. Here she remained until she was 15 years old. At this school she was one of the less able pupils and was bullied by the more able children. Her behaviour at home deteriorated. She became aggressive and rude and would 'play up' whenever visitors were around or when she was out shopping or elsewhere in public. 'Playing up' consisted of a number of irritating behaviours, for example, snorting, pulling her pants down, swearing, throwing things around, burping. Her mother felt that she was picking up 'bad habits' at school and removed her from there at 15 years. Louisa remained at home until a place was found for her in the residential community where she now lives. Academically she made very little progress at her last school, having frequent periods at home with headaches and tummy aches.

Development

Developmentally, Louisa shows an uneven pattern. She has excellent self-help skills. She can wash and dress independently (except for the occasional reminder). She keeps her own room tidy and takes care of and pride in her own belongings. She has good dress sense and enjoys picking her own clothes. She can help around the home, vacuuming and laying the table. She will help with the washing-up and cooking (provided there is adequate supervision for this activity).

Louisa talks continually – and loudly. She speak in short sentences and is always asking questions and informing people when she is going home and the activities she will be doing there. Much of her spoken language appears to be repetitive and she uses many 'stock' phrases. Louisa can be quite sociable. She enjoys the company of care staff and will seek them out. When carers whom she likes are unwell she will always show concern for them.

Louisa's excellent skills in some areas mask a number of difficulties which Louisa has in other areas. A recent speech therapy assessment revealed that her understanding of language lags considerably behind her expressive abilities. She understands only very concrete language and can comprehend only two- or three-word sentences. Louisa can count up to two but cannot read or write, although her mother states that she used to enjoy reading as a young child and could write a little. Certainly, she does enjoy looking at picture books and sometimes will scribble with crayons.

Despite enjoying the company of carers, Louisa cannot cope when attention is not exclusively focused on her. She has no friends among her peer group. She tends to be overbearing in her interactions with her peers, always wanting her own way, always trying to take the lead. She finds all group situations extremely difficult. In company, she will become disruptive or aggressive if she is not the centre of attention. Within the home, group discussions or activities cannot take place if Louisa is around, as she will certainly disrupt them.

Louisa has difficulties in other areas too. She has a very poor concept of time and cannot understand beyond the immediate situation. She cannot wait for things to happen once she knows they are on the agenda. Turn-taking is another great area of difficulty. It is at these times that she is likely to engage in some of her anti-social behaviour, which includes swearing, burping, throwing and breaking objects, being rude and hitting out. Being out in public is another difficult time for Louisa. In shops, she will embarrass those with her by her loudness and her anti-social behaviour. This is particularly so when the people with her are busy or engrossed with the task in hand or when the shop is noisy and crowded.

During the last year, Louisa does not appear to have made any progress in her development. In fact, staff say that in many areas she seems to have regressed.

Physical health

Louisa has few problems with her physical health, with the exception of epilepsy. She started to have occasional 'absences' at around the age of 14 years. During the last year she has developed generalized seizures which are becoming steadily worse. She frequently has a bruised face, where she has fallen during a seizure. In addition, some staff have noticed that she will frequently stop in mid-sentence and 'freeze' for a couple of seconds before resuming the conversation. Some days are worse than others but on a bad day such 'absences' can occur every few minutes. Louisa is currently undergoing medical investigations for her fits.

Likes and dislikes

Louisa is at her best when given one-to-one staff time and attention. At such times, provided that the staff member is genuinely interested in her company, Louisa can be charming to be with. She will be helpful and can engage in a two-way conversation, relating the activities she has done (provided that the staff member has some prior knowledge of the activity, to enable him/her to direct the conversation). She enjoys being the centre of attention and 'performing' to a captive audience. She will dance and sing and loves the praise that she gets. She has two or three favourite videos which she will watch over and over. Occasionally she will sit down with a colouring book. At weekends, Louisa's father takes her horse-riding (Louisa enjoys this activity). Before she left school her teacher found that Louisa seemed to enjoy helping out with the profoundly disabled residents who were in wheelchairs. She seemed to feel a sense of responsibility and could be quite gentle with them. However, she finished school a year ago and has not had the opportunity for such activity since then. Sometimes she will take herself to her room and spend time there alone, playing records and looking at her books and ornaments.

Behavioural difficulties

According to Louisa's parents, her behaviour has been much the same for several years but now, at the age of 20 years, this behaviour is no longer acceptable. Much of the anti-social behaviour described above is felt to be done for a reaction: it always succeeds in focusing everyone's attention on herself. Mostly it seems to occur in company. Key times for such behaviour tends to be mealtimes, times when the whole group may be together in the lounge or when care staff are occupied with other residents. She will look around quickly beforehand, then glance around again to see what reaction she has got. She will go through a hierarchy of behaviour – starting with shouting, burping, snorting or breaking wind. If these are ignored, she will throw something or hit out at carers or peers.

At other times this same behaviour may be triggered by a request to engage in a task which she may find difficult. Having said that, most attempts to engage Louisa in any learning activity, both formal or informal, are likely to result in some of this behaviour. When asked to wait or when denied something she wants she may engage in similar behaviour. However, at these times her anger is likely also to develop into a prolonged outburst of temper: she will throw herself to the ground kicking and screaming. The noise can be deafening.

Present management strategies

Louisa's major outbursts (throwing herself on the floor kicking and screaming), which occur approximately once or twice each week, are dealt with by taking Louisa to her bedroom and leaving her there until she has calmed. If she has a major outburst at the day-centre she is sent home. Anti-social behaviour (shouting, snorting, burping, pulling her pants down, breaking wind, throwing) is confronted and Louisa is made to apologize for rude behaviour. If she destroys or breaks things, she is made to clear up the mess. Non-compliance is also confronted: Louisa is not allowed to opt out of activities and, as far as possible, staff make her carry out whatever request has been made. This often results in shouting on both sides. A major outburst may follow. If this happens she is taken to her room. All staff have become very unhappy about using these procedures. They feel that they are very punitive and ineffective. Shouting and confronting simply leads to more shouting and more non-compliance or a prolonged temper outburst. Making an issue of anti-social behaviour usually results in Louisa doing more of it. They feel that each day is one long shouting match with Louisa.

Louisa's escalating behavioural difficulties are causing conflicts between all groups of carers. Her parents feel that the residential unit is being too hard on her. The staff in the residential unit feel that Louisa is confused about where her real home is and feel that they have no authority over Louisa as long as her parents remain in such close contact. Day and residential staff are also in conflict: each has different ideas about how the problems should be tackled and each feel unsupported by the other. Meanwhile, Louisa appears to be becoming increasingly unhappy. She will often become distressed and cry for no reason. She is making little progress in her development and is increasingly losing out on activities both within the home and out in the community.

ASSESSMENT

Assessment of Louisa's difficulties was carried out as follows.

1. Louisa's key workers from the residential unit and from the day-centre completed a skills assessment, using a checklist.
2. A speech therapist saw Louisa for an assessment of her language skills.
3. A referral was made to a neurologist to assess Louisa's epilepsy.
4. A psychologist interviewed Louisa's parents to obtain historical details about Louisa's difficulties.
5. An observation chart was used to record Louisa's anti-social behaviour (defined earlier). It was kept for a period of 3 weeks. The chart was analysed by the manager of the residential unit.

The team (key workers and representatives from the day and residential unit, Louisa's parents, speech therapist, psychologist) met together and a formulation was made of Louisa's difficulties using the S.T.A.R. format, described in Chapter 2: the formulation is shown in Figure 13.1. A strengths list was also drawn up: this is shown in Figure 13.2. Using the formulation of the problem, a list was drawn up of Louisa's needs: the needs list is shown in Figure 13.3.

INTERVENTIONS

1. The team agreed to meet on a monthly basis, as a first step towards working in a co-ordinated way rather than blaming each other for Louisa's difficulties. This also enabled them to review Louisa's progress and to keep a longer-term focus (Figure 13.3, Need 12). Monthly meetings continued for 18 months, then reduced to 3-monthly meetings.
2. The speech therapist conducted a 2-hour workshop at both the day-centre and the residential unit for staff working with Louisa (Louisa's parents attended one of these) to make them aware of Louisa's verbal comprehension limitations and to teach them how to communicate with Louisa at a level she would understand (Figure 13.3, Need 13). This intervention was also intended to ensure that Louisa started to experience some success in aspects of her life (Figure 13.3, Need 8). This workshop continues to be repeated at 9-monthly intervals to ensure that new staff understand how to communicate with Louisa and also to serve as a reminder for existing staff.
3. The neurologist conducted a thorough investigation of Louisa's epilepsy and her medication was adjusted accordingly (Figure 13.3, Need 11). This process took several months and Louisa's medication continues to be under regular review.

A S.T.A.R. ANALYSIS OF PROBLEMATIC BEHAVIOUR THE FORMULATION

Name *LOUISA*

Definition of Behaviour
SNORTING, PULLING PANTS DOWN, BURPING, THROWING, HITTING, SHOUTING, BREAKING WIND, THROWING SELF ON FLOOR, SCREAMING

Appears to achieve the following results

FOCUSING ATTENTION ON HER
STOPPING ATTENTION TO OTHERS
PEOPLE SPENDING TIME WITH HER
GETTING SENT HOME FROM THE DAY CENTRE
OPTING OUT OF DIFFICULT TASKS

Appears to be set off by the following triggers

WAITING
TAKING TURNS
BEING IGNORED
BEING REPRIMANDED
NOISY, CROWDED SHOPS
CARERS BUSY DOING OTHER THINGS
BEING ASKED TO DO A DIFFICULT TASK
BEING DENIED SOMETHING
OTHER PEOPLE GETTING ATTENTION

Seems to occur in the context of the following environmental setting conditions

Physical	Occupational	Social
CROWDED SHOPS	*PRESSURED ACTIVITIES*	*NEGATIVE ATTITUDES OF CARERS*
	MEALTIMES	*TOWARDS HER*
	TIMES WHEN CARERS ARE BUSY	*CONFLICT BETWEEN FAMILY,*
	GROUP SITUATIONS	*RESIDENTIAL HOME AND DAY CENTRE*

Appears to be related to the following personal setting conditions

Physical	Psychological	Cognitive
EPILEPSY	*SADNESS*	*CONFUSION ABOUT WHERE HER HOME IS*
		FEAR OF FAILURE IN ALL SITUATIONS

Appear to be associated with a deficit in the following skill/skill areas

INABILITY TO HOLD HER OWN IN GROUP SITUATIONS
POOR CONCEPT OF TIME
POOR LANGUAGE COMPREHENSION SKILL RELATIVE TO HER OTHER SKILLS

Figure 13.1 Louisa: assessment of her problematic behaviour.

STRENGTHS LIST

Name *LOUISA*

Skills

LOUISA WASHES AND DRESSES INDEPENDENTLY

LOUISA TIDIES HER OWN ROOM WITHOUT REMINDING

LOUISA TAKES GOOD CARE OF HER BELONGINGS

LOUISA HAS GOOD DRESS SENSE

LOUISA HELPS AROUND THE HOME - VACUUMING, LAYING THE TABLE

LOUISA WASHES-UP AND COOKS WITH SUPERVISION

LOUISA SPEAKS IN SHORT SENTENCES

LOUISA CAN ENGAGE IN TWO WAY CONVERSATION

LOUISA SHOWS CONCERN WHEN CARERS ARE UNWELL

LOUISA UNDERSTANDS 2 - 3 WORD SENTENCES

LOUISA CAN COUNT TO 2

Preferences

LOUISA TAKES PRIDE IN HER BELONGINGS

LOUISA LIKE TO BE THE CENTRE OF ATTENTION

LOUISA LIKES DANCING AND SINGING

LOUISA LIKES TO CHOOSE HER OWN CLOTHES

LOUISA ENJOYS PICTURE BOOKS

LOUISA LIKES TO SCRIBBLE WITH CRAYONS OCCASIONALLY

LOUISA LIKES ONE-TO-ONE TIME WITH CARERS

LOUISA HAS TWO OR THREE FAVOURITE VIDEOS

LOUISA ENJOYS HORSE RIDING

LOUISA ENJOYS HELPING WITH MORE DISABLED PEOPLE

Conditions for Positive Behaviour

LOUISA DOES WELL DURING ONE-TO-ONE INTERACTIONS WITH CARERS

LOUISA COPES BETTER IN SMALL GROUPS

Conditions for Learning

LOUISA CONCENTRATES BEST IN A ONE-TO-ONE SITUATION

LOUISA WORKS BEST IN UNCROWDED PLACES

LOUISA CAN ENGAGE IN A TWO-WAY CONVERSATION WHEN ALONE WITH A CARER

LOUISA UNDERSTANDS THINGS WHICH ARE EXPLAINED IN SHORT SENTENCES

Figure 13.2 Louisa: strengths list.

NEEDS LIST

Name *LOUISA*

Description of behaviour

SNORTING, BURPING, SHOUTING, THROWING, HITTING, BREAKING WIND, THROWING SELF ON FLOOR, SCREAMING

1.   *TO LEARN TO TOLERATE OTHER PEOPLE GETTING STAFF'S ATTENTION*

2.   *TO LEARN/USE BETTER WAYS TO GET STAFF'S TIME AND ATTENTION*

3.   *TO LEARN TO FUNCTION WITHIN A GROUP*

4.   *TO LEARN TO WAIT*

5.   *TO LEARN TO TAKE TURNS*

6.   *TO LEARN TO TOLERATE CROWDED SHOPS*

7.   *TO ACCEPT SHE CAN'T HAVE EVERYTHING SHE WANTS*

8.   *TO EXPERIENCE SUCCESS*

9.   *TO HAVE POSITIVE IMPUT FROM STAFF*

10. *TO UNDERSTAND WHERE 'HOME' IS*

11. *TO HAVE HER EPILEPSY REVIEWED*

12. *STAFF TEAMS NEED TO RESOLVE CONFLICTS OVER HER CARE*

13. *STAFF/CARERS NEED TO BE AWARE OF HER LANGUAGE PROBLEMS*

Figure 13.3 Louisa: needs list.

4. Louisa's parents agreed to start referring to Louisa's residential unit as 'home'. They also agreed to start to discuss with Louisa the fact that the residential unit was to be her permanent home but that she would continue to visit them on a regular basis, as long as she wanted (Figure 13.3, Need 10). Discussions were conducted as the opportunity arose. If Louisa asked questions about her living situation or said things which suggested that she was confused about her situation, then they made a point of explaining things to her. After approximately 6 months, once Louisa's parents had discussed the issue with her several times, the residential unit staff began to reinforce this procedure and started to give Louisa explanations about her 'home' situation.

5. A specific programme was set up to help Louisa learn to cope with crowded shops (Figure 13.3, Need 6). The programme was based upon the principles of graded exposure (Chapter 5): this involved taking Louisa shopping, first to very quiet, local shops and then over time (as her behaviour improved in these situations) taking her to shops which were a little larger and a little busier. This process continued over a year until Louisa was better able to cope with large shops. The programme was carried out twice weekly on a one-to-one basis with staff for the first 10 months. As her ability to cope in group situations improved (see below), she began to be involved again in group shopping trips.

6. A combination of approaches was used to help Louisa to cope with group situations. Her difficulties in this area related both to her difficulty in taking turns (Figure 13.3, Need 5), her difficulty in tolerating other people getting the attention of carers (Figure 13.3., Need 1) and her not using appropriate means to attract people's attention – despite having the skills to do so (Figure 13.3, Need 2).

   (a) Louisa was initially withdrawn from all activities which involved large groups at the day-centre. In the residential unit, leisure activities were planned to ensure that Louisa only went out in small groups. This setting-level intervention enabled Louisa to start to experience success in group situations (Figure 13.3, Need 8) because there were fewer people to compete with for staff attention and because this enabled her to practise more appropriate means of gaining staff attention.

   (b) Daily half-hour sessions were set up at the day-centre in which Louisa was involved on a one-to-one basis with staff, learning to take turns in a range of non-pressured interactive games (a precision-teaching approach was used). As she learned to take turns, another student was introduced to the sessions. These sessions enabled Louisa to start to experience success in social situations (Figure 13.3, Need 8) by learning a specific social skill.

(c) In any large-group situation in which Louisa unavoidably found herself, all staff ensured that she was given a lot of their attention. If she started to become too demanding or to use anti-social behaviour, a member of the care team suggested an alternative (physically incompatible) activity to her. This would take her away from the large-group situation. The carer accompanied her to the activity, if she wished (reinforcement of incompatible skill).

7. Staff were instructed that whenever they had to say 'No' to Louisa, they should always accompany the denial by a full explanation. If possible, they should reach a compromise with her.

8. A programme was drawn up to ensure that all those working with Louisa responded in a consistent way to her anti-social behaviour (shouting, burping, snorting, breaking wind, throwing, hitting). All such behaviour was ignored completely (extinction), except in large-group situations where she was encouraged to remove herself from the situation (6(c)). If Louisa managed to remain in any group situation (involving more than three other residents or students) without showing her anti-social behaviour she was given a lot of positive feedback and praise: carers were given informal guidelines of providing positive feedback for each 3 minutes of appropriate behaviour (DRO). This approach addressed a number of Louisa's needs (Figure 13.3, Needs 1, 3, 8, 9). Over time, the 3 minutes was extended to 5 minutes, then to 10 minutes.

9. A specific programme was drawn up to ensure that a consistent approach was taken to Louisa if she threw herself on the floor kicking and screaming. Louisa was quietly told that this behaviour was not very dignified and she was asked if she wanted to go somewhere quiet and explain what had upset her so much. If she got up from the floor, the carer went with her to a quiet place to talk through the problem. If she continued to scream, the carer simply waited quietly, from time to time repeating the offer of going somewhere quiet.

MONITORING

Graphs showing Louisa's progress over a 12-month period are illustrated in Figure 13.4: Figure 13.4(a) is a total frequency count of the times when Louisa would throw herself onto the floor, screaming and shouting; Figure 13.4(b) shows the average monthly frequency of anti-social behaviour (as defined earlier) observed during the first 20 minutes of lunch.

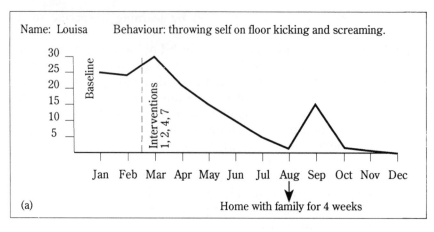

(a)

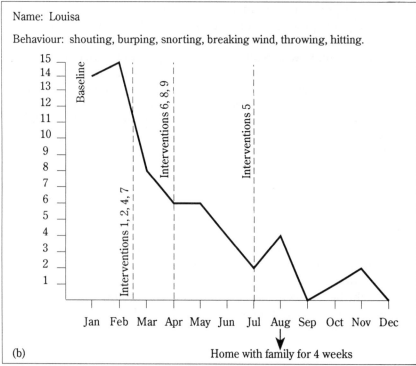

(b)

Figure 13.4 Louisa: progress summary; (a) graph showing total frequency count of the times Louise showed anti-social behaviour; (b) graph showing average monthly frequency of anti-social behaviours observed during the first 20 minutes of lunch.

BILL

CASE DESCRIPTION

Background

Bill was born in 1946, the fourth of five children: there were two older sisters, one older brother and a younger brother who was born when Bill was 2 years old. Bill's father was a truck driver but his mother did not work as far as is known. Early medical records indicate delayed milestones (walking and talking at 2 years) and his elder brother and one of his sisters both attended a school for 'slow learners'. When Bill was 4 years old his mother and younger brother were killed in a house fire. His father gave up work and tried to bring up the children with the help of his elder daughter, then aged 10 years. However, this meant that the daughter often missed school and this brought the father into conflict with the local authorities. In addition, it became clear that Bill was not coping in his local primary school – his progress was very slow and he kept wandering off/running away from school. He was assessed as 'ineducable'.

Eventually, at the age of 7 years, Bill was taken into local authority care, along with his older brother. He was sent to a junior training centre but reports refer to continual absconding and 'behavioural problems' and at the age of 9 years Bill was admitted to a long-stay hospital. He remained there until the age of 30 years, when he was transferred to another hospital, which was nearer to his original family home: he has now lived at this hospital for 16 years. He currently lives on Acacia ward, which is Bill's third residence in the last 2 years. The hospital is scheduled to close in 1 year's time.

Bill talks often of his family, including his mother. He is visited by one of his older sisters about three times a year but he does not see his other sister or brother. Over the years he appears to have had intermittent contact with his father but his father died about 3 years ago. Bill appears to have a long history of behavioural difficulties. His hospital records refer to a range of behavioural difficulties including absconding, throwing and breaking things, hitting people, 'obsessionality' (closing doors and windows) and 'hypochondriasis' (complaints about stomach pains).

Physical health

Bill is 5' 10" and weighs 14 stone. An electroencephalograph (EEG) and gastro-intestinal investigations in the 1970s all proved normal. He has no current problems with his physical health.

Skills

Bill is fully competent at basic self-care tasks, such as feeding, washing and dressing, although he sometimes requires encouragement to maintain good personal hygiene levels. He will help out with tasks around the ward when in a good mood and goes over to a number of the day units within the hospital. However, he rarely stays for long on the units. He likes to chat and have a cup of tea but will rarely engage with the actual tasks on offer (such as basic education, art and craft, woodwork, concrete work). He sometimes takes himself down to the nearby village and will purchase items from the village shop (he has a sweet tooth!). This can lead to difficulties as Bill's understanding of money is limited and he gets upset if he cannot have the item he wants because of inadequate funds. He has thrown and broken things in the shop when upset and every so often is banned from the shop (the people in the village are in general very accommodating to the residents of the hospital).

Bill can express himself in short sentences although he does have a stammer, which makes communication sometimes difficult. He finds it easier to talk with people that he knows well. He talks about his family and incidents in his past life as well as more immediate events. However, his level of true understanding is not certain. His organization of events in time seems hazy – he often talks about long-past events as though they had just happened, he has difficulty in understanding when future events will occur (it does not help to give him too long a warning of a future event as once he is told he expects it to happen right away). He takes a long time to learn the names of new staff members.

Likes

Bill enjoys being with people but more in the sense of being around them. If he becomes the focus of sustained social interactions, which require him to participate actively, he will leave the situation – if unable to do so, he becomes very agitated. He enjoys all outings and is particularly fond of walks and car rides. He loves cups of tea and, as already mentioned, he has a very sweet tooth. He goes to church every Sunday and is fond of music in church. He likes being praised and is always happier in smaller as opposed to larger groups (church services are the exception in this respect). Large groups increase his level of agitation. He has better relationships with some people than with others and he seems to like particularly the company of younger people. It is not known if Bill has currently or has had in the past any sexual relationships. He occasionally masturbates in inappropriate places.

Behavioural and emotional difficulties

Bill is currently diagnosed as suffering from depression and has been treated with trifluoperazine for the last 3 years, since this most recent diagnosis was made. He has in the past been treated with electro-convulsive therapy (ECT) and a variety of medication. His mood and behaviour fluctuate, although the level of synchronization between them has not been clearly established. In a low mood he will neglect his personal hygiene and appearance, will withdraw more socially, will often be seen muttering (? to himself) and will tend to wake early. The variations in mood are relatively transient, lasting a matter of days rather than weeks or months. Bill continues to break things and lash out at people, on average three to four times a month. Sometimes these incidents appear to have no precipitant. At other times they occur when he is asked not to do something (such as closing all the doors and windows on a hot day) or when he is asked to explain why he has done something, even if this is not done by way of criticism. Incidents are much more likely in crowded situations and mealtimes are a particular flashpoint. They are more likely if he is already agitated. The incidents can be quite serious and at least one staff member has gone as far as initiating a complaint to the local police. Bill does show remorse after an incident and will apologize.

It is not clear how much Bill understands about the future. The hospital is due to close over the coming year and Bill will be moving to an alternative residential setting. Staff and many hospital residents are anxious about the future and uncertain about what it holds.

ASSESSMENT

The behaviour which was the subject of the assessment was Bill's hitting of others. The assessment process began with a meeting of care staff who were involved on a regular basis with Bill. A structured discussion was held to gather as much information as possible about settings, triggers and results for Bill's behaviour. Following this discussion, Bill's key worker did some further research about Bill's past life, using hospital records. Checklists were completed by ward staff to find out the things that Bill enjoys. Observations of Bill's hitting were recorded onto prepared charts for a duration of 6 weeks. The charts were analysed by Bill's key worker. The formulation of Bill's behavioural difficulty, using the S.T.A.R. analysis detailed in Chapter 2, is shown in Figure 13.5. Bill's strengths list is shown in Figure 13.6. A statement of Bill's needs, which arise from the formulation, is shown in Figure 13.7.

INTERVENTIONS

1. By involving those who work daily with Bill in the whole assessment process, including the formulation of his problem and generating the statement of needs, a more positive relationship was developed between Bill and staff, who felt that they had a better understanding of the factors involved in his depression and could better understand his agitation (Figure 13.7, Needs 2 and 6). There was an immediate change in attitude towards Bill and this resulted in an immediate reduction in hitting out.

2. With help from the social worker, Bill's key worker undertook to develop a life-story book with Bill. This was intended to help Bill develop a better understand of the major events in his life (Figure 13.7, Need 4). Bill's family was contacted and Bill's brother started to visit Bill on a regular, though infrequent basis. This was felt to be important as possibly providing greater stability to Bill's life (Figure 13.7, Need 1), particularly in the light of his impending move. Information from his brother and family was used to help Bill develop his life-story book. The family provided photographs of the family and important family events.

3. Although the place where Bill would be living when the hospital closed was already determined, it was agreed to design the detailed lifestyle around Bill's needs for privacy and control which arise from his acknowledged difficulty in coping with large groups of people and with comments from people which he often misinterprets. This was expected to go some way to addressing his need to feel happier and more relaxed (Figure 13.7, Need 10). This need will clearly not be met until the move is effected.

4. The speech therapist and an assistant psychologist undertook to start some work to help Bill express his wants and needs more clearly. The long-term goal was for Bill to join an ongoing small self-advocacy group. In the short term it was intended to teach Bill important communication skills (in particular, how to ask people to 'Stop talking' or to say 'I don't understand' when he seemed to experience difficulties with social interactions). A precision-teaching approach was used to teach these functionally equivalent skills (to hitting) as a means of terminating aversive interactions (Figure 13.7, Needs 7 and 8). Ward staff were informed of the content of the sessions and asked to encourage Bill to say 'Be quiet' or 'I don't understand' whenever he seemed to be experiencing difficulties with social interactions.

5. The key worker and Bill developed together a picture time-table (Figure 13.7, Need 5) so that Bill could plan and understand what he would do and when. This intervention was directed at increasing

A S.T.A.R. ANALYSIS OF PROBLEMATIC BEHAVIOUR THE FORMULATION

Name *BILL*

Definition of Behaviour

HITTING OTHERS

Appears to achieve the following results

EXPRESSES HIGH LEVEL OF EMOTION
TERMINATES AVERSIVE SOCIAL INTERACTIONS

Appears to be set off by the following triggers

DENIALS
INTERRUPTIONS
COMMENTS FROM OTHERS PERCEIVED AS CRITICAL

Seems to occur in the context of the following environmental setting conditions

Physical	**Occupational**
NOISY, CROWDED PLACES (ESPECIALLY DINING ROOM)	*UNRESTRICTED TIMES OF DAY (ESPECIALLY ON RETURN FROM DAY CENTRE)* *MAJOR CHANGES IN HIS ROUTINE (HOLIDAYS, STAFF CHANGES)*

Appears to be related to the following personal setting conditions

Cognitive	**Psychological**
UNCERTAINTY ABOUT FUTURE	*SADNESS (FOLLOWING DEATH OF HIS FATHER, UNRESOLVED EARLY TRAUMA AND LOSS)* *AGITATION*

Appear to be associated with a deficit in the following skill/skill areas

DIFFICULTY IN MANAGING HIS ANGER
POOR EXPRESSIVE SKILLS
POOR COMPREHENSION OF TIME
POOR COMPREHENSION OF LANGUAGE

Figure 13.5 Bill: assessment of his problematic behaviour.

STRENGTHS LIST

Name *BILL*

Skills

BILL CAN UNDERSTAND SINGLE REQUESTS AND REMEMBER THEM (FOR EXAMPLE, GOING OFF TO GET SOMETHING REQUESTED)

BILL CAN MANAGE ALL BASIC SELF-CARE SKILLS

BILL CAN BE HELPFUL AROUND THE LIVING ENVIRONMENT

BILL CAN USE A VACUUM CLEANER

BILL CAN IRON HIS CLOTHES

BILL CAN EXPRESS HIMSELF IN SHORT SENTENCES

BILL CAN TALK ABOUT PAST EVENTS AND CURRENT INTERESTS

BILL CAN CLOSE DOORS AND WINDOWS

BILL CAN DISTINGUISH BETWEEN PEOPLE

BILL AVOIDS A LOT OF POTENTIAL FLASHPOINTS BY LEAVING THE SITUATION

Preferences

BILL LIKES SOME FORMS OF SOCIAL INTERACTIONS
BILL LIKES SWEETS
BILL LIKES GOING TO CHURCH
BILL LIKES LISTENING TO CHURCH MUSIC
BILL LIKES PRAISE
BILL LIKES OUTINGS, ESPECIALLY WALKS AND CAR RIDES
BILL LIKES TEA
BILL ENJOYS THE COMPANY OF YOUNGER PEOPLE
BILL LIKES TO TALK ABOUT HIS FAMILY

Conditions for Positive Behaviour

BILL APOLOGIZES AFTER AN OUTBURST
BILL IS MOSTLY TOLERANT OF A VERY UNSATISFACTORY LIVING ENVIRONMENT
NO INCIDENTS HAVE EVER OCCURRED AT CHURCH
NO INCIDENTS HAVE EVER OCCURRED AT ONE OF THE DAY SERVICES THAT BILL CALLS INTO FOR A CUP OF TEA AND A CHAT
NO INCIDENTS HAVE OCCURRED DURING FAMILY VISITS

Conditions for Learning

BILL HAS A BEFRIENDING RELATIONSHIP WITH A VOLUNTEER
BILL HAS GOOD CONCENTRATION SPAN
BILL PREFERS INFORMAL LEARNING SITUATIONS
BILL UNDERSTANDS BETTER WHEN THINGS ARE SAID IN SHORT SENTENCES

Figure 13.6 Bill: strengths list.

NEEDS LIST

Name BILL

Description of behaviour

HITTING OTHERS

1. BILL NEEDS A MORE STABLE LIVING ENVIRONMENT

2. BILL NEEDS A MORE HARMONIOUS LIVING ENVIRONMENT

3. BILL NEEDS AN ENVIRONMENT THAT OFFERS MORE PRIVACY

4. BILL NEEDS A BETTER UNDERSTANDING OF THE EVENTS IN HIS LIFE

5. BILL NEEDS A BETTER UNDERSTANDING OF SEQUENCES OF EVENTS IN TIME

6. BILL NEEDS A BETTER APPRECIATION FROM OTHERS OF HIS LIMITED

   UNDERSTANDING AND HIS PERSONAL FEELINGS

7. BILL NEEDS TO BE BETTER ABLE TO EXPRESS HIMSELF

8. BILL NEEDS TO BE MORE ABLE TO ASSERT HIMSELF

9. BILL NEEDS TO BE MORE ABLE TO CONTROL HIS AROUSAL

10. BILL NEEDS TO FEEL HAPPIER AND MORE RELAXED

11. BILL NEEDS TO HIT OTHERS LESS FREQUENTLY

Figure 13.7 Bill: needs list.

Bill's understanding of time and reducing the triggers (interruptions, denials, criticism) that arise when Bill tries to do things at inappropriate times (Figure 13.7, Need 5). The time-table was prepared on a weekly basis (every Monday morning). A copy was kept on the wall of the office on the ward and Bill carried a second copy with him, in a small plastic wallet.

6. The ward team communicated to everyone involved with Bill the importance of speaking to him in a respectful manner and to explain how easily he misinterpreted comments and jokes made by others. This intervention was aimed at reducing unnecessary triggers (confrontations and criticism) which often set off his inappropriate behaviour. This intervention also helped create a more harmonious living environment for Bill (Figure 13.7, Need 2).

7. The ward team designed and implemented a DRO programme using praise and sweets – the programme involved a token chart with praise and extra confectionery for no incident of hitting during each half-day. The sweets were a 'bonus' and did not interfere with how Bill spent his own money. This intervention was directly aimed at reducing the frequency of Bill's hitting (Figure 13.7, Need 11). The DRO programme was started with reinforcement twice a day. This was reduced to a daily basis, then to every other day (2 days without hitting), then 3 days without hitting and then to weekly. At this point the reinforcer was changed to an additional trip out with a favoured staff member. This was then linked in to the visual time-

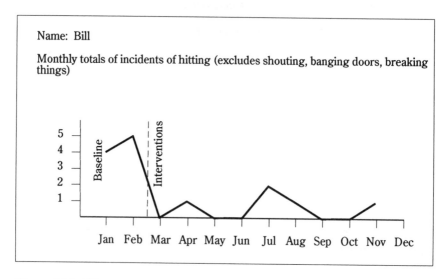

Figure 13.8 Bill: progress summary.

table which Bill was gradually coming to understand and to use spontaneously.

8. The assistant psychologist undertook to teach Bill some basic relaxation skills. Relaxation was considered to be a skill which would enable Bill to feel generally less agitated (Figure 13.7, Need 10) and would be a skill which could be developed by Bill as a good way to relieve tension and reduce high arousal (Figure 13.7, Need 9). The relaxation sessions did not go well: Bill did not enjoy them, became increasingly reluctant to attend and sought to end the sessions quickly (this did provide an opportunity to encourage assertiveness skills). Further thought is now going into whether an alternative approach to relaxation might prove more 'friendly' for Bill.

MONITORING

A tick chart was kept for incidents of hitting out. This was graphed up on a monthly basis (totals). The chart is presented in Figure 13.8.

Further reading

Barrett, R.P. (ed.) (1986) *Severe Behaviour Disorders in the Mentally Handicapped*, Plenum, New York.

Donnellan, A., LaVigna, G., Negri-Shoultz, N. and Sassbender, L. (1988) *Progress without Punishment: Effective Approaches for Learners with Behaviour Problems*, Teacher's College Press, New York.

Evans, I.M. and Meyer, L.H. (1985) *An Educative Approach to Behaviour Problems: a Practical Decision Model for Interventions with Severely Handicapped Learners*, P. Brooks, Baltimore.

Favell, J.E. (1983) The management of aggressive behaviour, in *Autism in Adolescents and Adults*, (eds E. Schopler and G.B. Mesibov), Plenum, New York, pp. 187–222.

McGee, J.J., Menolascino, F., Hobbs, D. and Menousek, P.E. (1987) *Gentle Teaching: A Non-aversive Approach to Helping Persons with Mental Retardation*, Human Sciences Press, New York.

Remington, B. (ed.) (1991) *The Challenge of Severe Mental Handicap. A Behaviour Analytic Approach*, J. Wiley & Son, Chichester.

Repp, A.C. and Singh, N.N. (eds) (1990) *Perspectives on the Use of Nonaversive Interventions for Persons with Developmental Disabilities*, Sycamore, Sycamore.

Waitman, A. and Conboy-Hill, S. (eds) (1992) *Psychotherapy and Mental Handicap*, Sage, London.

Yule, W. and Carr, J. (eds) (1988) *Behaviour Modification for People with Mental Handicaps*, 2nd edn, Chapman & Hall, London.

Index